PRAISE FOR GRANTLEE KIEZA'S BOOKS

'Engagingly written ... one of the most
nuanced portraits to date'
The Australian

'Vivid, detailed and well written'
Daily Telegraph

'A staggering accomplishment that can't be missed by
history buffs and story lovers alike'
Betterreading.com.au

'A free-flowing biography of a great Australian figure'
John Howard

'Clear and accessible ... well-crafted and
extensively documented'
Weekend Australian

'Kieza has added hugely to the depth of knowledge about
our greatest military general in a book that is timely'
Tim Fischer, *Courier-Mail*

'The author writes with the immediacy of a fine
documentary ... an easy, informative read, bringing
historic personalities to life'
Ballarat Courier

Award-winning journalist Grantlee Kieza OAM held senior editorial positions at *The Daily Telegraph*, *The Sunday Telegraph* and *The Courier-Mail* for many years and was awarded the Medal of the Order of Australia for his writing. He is a Walkley Award finalist and the author of nineteen acclaimed books, including the recent bestsellers *Lawson, Banks, Macquarie, Banjo, Mrs Kelly, Monash, Sons of the Southern Cross* and *Bert Hinkler.*

GRANTLEE
KIEZA
The Kelly Hunters

ABC
BOOKS

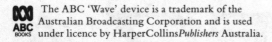 The ABC 'Wave' device is a trademark of the Australian Broadcasting Corporation and is used under licence by HarperCollins*Publishers* Australia.

HarperCollins*Publishers*
Australia • Brazil • Canada • France • Germany • Holland • Hungary
India • Italy • Japan • Mexico • New Zealand • Poland • Spain • Sweden
Switzerland • United Kingdom • United States of America

First published in Australia in 2022
by HarperCollins*Publishers* Australia Pty Limited
Level 13, 201 Elizabeth Street, Sydney NSW 2000
ABN 36 009 913 517
harpercollins.com.au

A catalogue record for this book is available from the National Library of Australia.

ISBN 978 0 7333 4149 6 (paperback)
ISBN 978 1 4607 1339 6 (ebook)

Cover design by Darren Holt, HarperCollins Design Studio
Cover images: Ned Kelly by Nettleton, Charles courtesy State Library of Victoria (H18202); Victorian Police by Madeley, Oswald Thomas, courtesy State Library of Victoria (H96.160/178)
Author photograph by Milen Boubbov
Typeset in Bembo Std by Kelli Lonergan
Printed and bound in Australia by McPherson's Printing Group

For my Irish Colleen, with love and gratitude

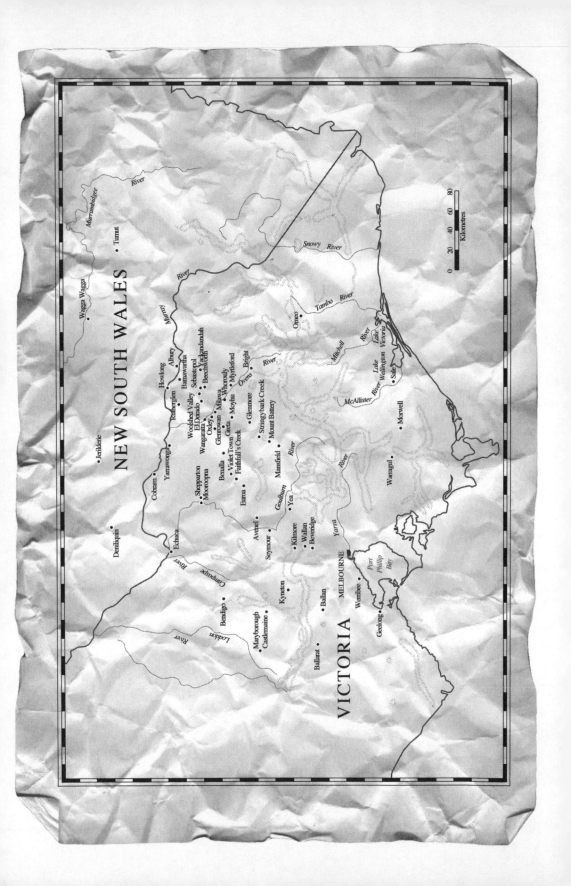

Prologue

FOUR RIDERS CANTERED towards the Murray River with grim faces and hard hearts as the summer sun went down over a land savaged by drought. Ned Kelly,[1] a 24-year-old wanted dead or alive for killing three policemen, cast a long shadow as he waded his horse quietly into the muddy shallows at a point near the town of Cobram, Victoria, and headed towards the opposite riverbank.[2]

It was the late afternoon of Friday, 7 February 1879 and the sunlight glistened on a silvery river that in a dry spell was lower and narrower than it had been for years.[3]

Through his network of sympathisers, Kelly had organised decoys to baffle the manhunters on the tail of his gang, so that, while a few troopers guarded known crossing points along the Murray, a party of heavily armed police had assembled 260 kilometres away at the foot of the Australian Alps near the village of Corryong,[4] expecting the four bushrangers to ride into their trap at any moment.

Kelly had been trouble for the Victorian police since his teenage years, but he and his gang members had sparked unprecedented terror since leaving Sergeant Michael Kennedy[5] and Constables Thomas Lonigan[6] and Michael Scanlan[7] dead in secluded bush beside Stringybark Creek in the Wombat Ranges four months earlier.

EDWARD AND DANIEL KELLY, THE OUTLAWED BUSHRANGERS,

As the Kelly Gang headed towards Jerilderie their likenesses were being circulated around Victoria as they were wanted dead or alive. State Library of Victoria IAN28/11/78/196

Despite the continued efforts of police search parties camping out for days in rugged, dangerous mountain terrain, the Kelly Gang had continued to evade the clutches of the law.

The four outlaws had followed the police shootings with an audacious robbery of the National Bank in the northern Victorian town of Euroa. Their daring, and Kelly's constant protests about police corruption, had won them a degree of sympathy from a fiercely loyal band of supporters, but they had murder on their minds as they headed towards the New South Wales town of Jerilderie, a day's hard riding to the north.

With Kelly was his small and surly teenage brother Dan,[8] and their confederates Joe Byrne[9] and Steve Hart.[10] Together the four wild youngsters had become the most feared criminals in Australia and had sparked the continent's biggest ever manhunt.

Now riding in pairs at a distance so as not to excite suspicion, the gang spurred on their horses into the deeper parts of the river up to their saddle flaps.[11]

They had formulated a plan to rob Jerilderie's Bank of New South Wales, but Kelly had also talked about killing one of the policemen stationed in the town.[12]

On the same day as the gang crossed the Murray into New South Wales, though, another killing spree was being planned almost 3000 kilometres to the north.

Four other men – also well-armed and crack shots[13] – crossed the mouth of the Endeavour River planning to retrieve the possessions of Cooktown's Harbour Master, Captain Albert Sykes, and a local merchant, William James Hartley, who would become the police magistrate of Mackay.

Sykes and Hartley had been badly wounded under a shower of Aboriginal spears after they tried to tow back to Cooktown a valuable cedar log that had washed up on a sandy beach under the long range of hills leading out to Cape Bedford.[14]

The two colonists drove their attackers away with revolver fire before fleeing in their small boat.

On 7 February 1879, the day after the attack, two prominent local journalists, Reginald Spencer Browne, later a World War I general, and William Henry Campbell, later a Queensland parliamentarian, along with two other men, set off in a cutter to take back the possessions of their wounded friends. Each member of the posse had Snider–Enfield rifles and plenty of ammunition.

After negotiating heavy surf like that which had battered James Cook's ship *Endeavour* in the same waters a century before, they found tracks of men and women, and tracing them into the scrub uncovered some of the belongings Sykes and Hartley had left behind in their desperate escape.

Another party of policemen joined the search, 30 kilometres to the north, but they found swampland impenetrable for their horses.

Before long, though, Sub-inspector Stanhope O'Connor,[15] a handsome young Irishman, joined the hunt along with six troopers from Queensland's Native Mounted Police, a unit of Aboriginal recruits under the command of white officers. The Native Police were used as a paramilitary force by Queensland's colonial government to provide protection to settlers on the frontier but also to subdue, chase away and sometimes massacre their own people.[16] Estimates of the number of Indigenous people killed on their raids across a 40-year span range from 20,000 to more than 41,000.[17]

O'Connor was known as 'a terror to evildoers – black and white',[18] and he and his men would leave a trail of devastation and death far greater than that caused by the Kelly Gang.

The brutal, ruthless efficiency of O'Connor and his trackers would make them the most feared of all the Kelly hunters in the biggest and most expensive police operation Australia had seen.

Chapter 1

FROM A YOUNG AGE, Ned Kelly knew about the brutality of the Native Police and the tracking skills of Aboriginal hunters. He was born at Beveridge, north of Melbourne, in December 1854 at the time of the Eureka Stockade rebellion when soldiers and police attacked a group of protesting miners at Ballarat, resulting in more than two dozen deaths from bullets, bayonets and swords.

Much of the angst among the miners had been caused by the savagery of the Victorian government, which used the Native Police to administer frontier justice against white men as well as black. The Aboriginal troopers were such a dreaded presence during the brutal mining licence hunts on the goldfields that the journalist Alfred Clarke called them a 'Satanic Battalion of Black Guards' for the beatings they doled out to impoverished diggers without money for mining permits.[1]

While early jailers had used Aboriginal men to track escaped convicts, and the vexatious Sydney wool baron John Macarthur had employed uniformed Dharawal and Gandangara men as his personal bodyguard,[2] the Native Police officially came into force in 1837, establishing a camp on what is now the Melbourne Cricket Ground carpark.

By the early 1850s, they were based along Merri Creek,[3] downstream from Wallan, where Kelly's Irish father, a former convict named John 'Red' Kelly,[4] was working as a fence splitter and bush carpenter while raising a hard-up family with his wife, Ellen,[5] the Irish-born daughter of a free settler. Ellen was 18 and six months' pregnant when she became Mrs Kelly on 18 November 1850.

Edward 'Ned' Kelly, their third child and first son, was weaned on horror stories of what he later called Ireland's 'Saxon yoke': tales of merciless British rule and its heavy hand during the potato famine that wiped out a large part of the Irish population. Kelly's father told him of Irish convicts who later 'were flogged to death and bravely died in servile chains, but true to the Shamrock and a credit to Paddy's land'.[6]

The colonial governments in Australia could be just as harsh, and when Kelly was a small boy every colonist knew about the terror caused by the Native Police.

ON 3 FEBRUARY 1860, just outside Queensland's riverside hamlet of Maryborough, Lieutenant John O'Connell Bligh[7] led a hunt by the Native Mounted Police for a group of Aboriginal men who had irked local settlers.

Bligh's foul-tempered grandfather had sparked the mutiny on the *Bounty* in the previous century when he was a naval captain, and now the young police lieutenant brought the same callous streak to his command in this newly formed Australian colony. Bligh had been chasing the group of Indigenous men for days after one of them, nicknamed 'Darkey' by the settlers, had escaped from police custody in chains from a steamer on the Mary River. The lieutenant ordered his men to chase their targets out of the bush and onto Maryborough's dusty streets. Some of the local Aboriginal people had recently been poisoned by gifts of flour laced with arsenic,[8] but Maryborough's townsfolk still complained of the black menace that made white women afraid in their beds and made bullock drivers travel with the whip in one hand and a gun in the other.

As Darkey and his supporters fled into Maryborough with the Native Mounted Police and their horses herding them like cattle, the white settlers ignored their pitiful cries for help. The terrified quarry scampered in all directions, pleading for their lives and making for places where they thought friendly whites would offer protection.[9] Darkey realised that the only help he would get was from the bush where he was born, and he sprinted towards towering eucalypts. One of the Native Mounted Policemen raised his rifle and killed him with a bullet in his back.[10]

Bligh and his men were not finished. Some of the escapees dived into the Mary River near the public wharf, and the police commandeered boats to finish the hunt.

With white men, women and children watching from the riverbank, Bligh stood in the bow of his vessel ordering it to be rowed in circles around and around an exhausted and petrified man known as 'Young Snatchem'.[11] Forty or fifty shots were fired around 'Snatchem' to add to his torment, five or six by Bligh himself, before the lieutenant finished him off.

The Native Police also captured a grey-haired old man who was blind in one eye, and who had the reputation of being 'a constant and popular visitor to the town'. He was triumphantly marched through Maryborough in handcuffs and, like some of the other men arrested that day, was never seen again.

While the carnage was being wrought, there were some muttered protests from the Maryborough folk of 'shame' and 'oh, the poor blacks', but at a public meeting a week later 400 of the settlers declared that Bligh was 'deserving of all praise, not only for his gallant conduct in pursuing the well-known tribe of depredators, but for the manner in which he punished them'.[12]

Although one Brisbane newspaper asked, 'What honour can there be in occasionally slaughtering the naked, unarmed, flying savage?',[13] Maryborough presented Bligh with a ceremonial sword, 'profusely embellished with embossed flowers and scroll work' and inscribed with the words 'for his services in suppressing the outrages of the blacks'.[14]

One critic said a butcher's knife would have been a more fitting gift.[15]

WHEN NED KELLY WAS eight years old, his struggling parents uprooted their six surviving children, packed their few sticks of furniture and household goods onto a cart, and set off on a week's trek from Beveridge to what would be even tougher times in Avenel, about 100 kilometres further north.

In this peaceful hamlet of yellow, sun-bleached grass fields, Esau Shelton's Royal Mail Hotel was used as watering stop for Cobb & Co coaches. Travellers seeking refreshment there could also buy handwoven baskets from Aboriginal women and listen to stories of how Aboriginal men could track anything, anywhere in the bush. Ned Kelly heard, again and again, that there was no escape for a man if an Aboriginal tracker was on his tail. Those stories were hammered home when Kelly was not quite nine years of age and the Native Police were leading New South Wales detectives to the central Queensland hideout of Australia's most wanted man, Frank Gardiner, whose string of armed hold-ups included Australia's largest ever gold heist at the Eugowra Rocks, near Forbes. Not far away from the scene of that audacious crime, Gardiner's confederate 'Bold' Ben Hall died with thirty bullets in his back in 1865 after police and Aboriginal trackers brought him down.

The Kellys, a big, hungry family with lively children in hand-me-down clothes and holey shoes, became tenant farmers in Avenel. Kelly made his first pocket money by hiding local horses until a reward was posted, bringing at least one valuable Avenel stallion back to Esau Shelton, and telling the dubious publican that he just saw it 'up in the bush'.[16] He redeemed himself in the family's eyes, though, leaping into the flooded waters of Avenel's Hughes Creek to save the life of Shelton's six-year-old son Dick.[17] As a token of their thanks, the Shelton family presented Kelly with a bravery award that he would treasure for the rest of his short life: a sash made of green silk with a gold bullion fringe at each end.[18]

IN MAY 1865, when Kelly's mother was six months pregnant with her eighth child, and the rest of her brood were famished, Red Kelly slaughtered a wayward calf that wandered onto his land. He was fined £25, but unable to pay, he spent four months in the Avenel lock-up, where he fell apart physically and mentally. He died in Avenel two days after Christmas 1866 and Ned Kelly's growing grudge against the law became a festering psychological wound that grew more toxic every time he had dealings with the police.

Broke and bitter at her husband's treatment, Ellen Kelly, now a 34-year-old widow with seven children all under the age of 13, packed up her brood and their meagre belongings and trekked another 120 kilometres north to the remote hamlet of Greta, where two of her married sisters were living. As Kelly led the way out of Avenel, a description of him under the headline 'Charged with Horse Stealing' was being circulated around Australia courtesy of the *Victoria Police Gazette*.[19] The charges weren't pursued, but with no money and little education, the burly 12-year-old was soon immersed in a world of crime, encouraged by a bunch of wild uncles who were mad, bad and dangerous.

During a drinking spree Ned's uncle James Kelly, just out of prison after serving three years for cattle stealing, set fire to Mrs Kelly's temporary home in Greta, with three families sleeping inside. All of them escaped the flames, though the shanty was destroyed. The imperious judge Sir Redmond Barry[20] sentenced Uncle James to death, but it was commuted to ten years' hard labour.[21]

With her home turned to cinders, Mrs Kelly took in sewing and washing and moved her children to an isolated shack on 88 partly cleared acres (35.6 hectares) beside the Eleven Mile Creek, outside Greta. She leased the land under the government's selection policy, and rented out a room to travellers, becoming a 'sly-grogger', selling alcohol without a licence for a shilling per glass. Before long police claimed her shack was a 'groggery and a gambling hell',[22] and that the family lived by 'immorality and dishonesty'.[23] It was claimed that the older Kelly children robbed travellers during card games and took their horses, only 'finding' them when rewards were offered.[24]

By his early teens Ned Kelly was involved in far more serious crimes, and police regarded him as 'an incorrigible thief'.[25] He became known as 'The Juvenile Bushranger',[26] helping the eccentric middle-aged highwayman Harry Power[27] during stagecoach robberies in northern Victoria. At 14 he was shot at for the first time after Dr John Rowe, a founding member of the Melbourne Medical School and University of Melbourne, saw him and Power lurking near his Mount Battery property outside Mansfield. An Aboriginal tracker named Wellington was brought in to lead a posse but rain washed away the bushrangers' tracks in that wild mountain country and Wellington couldn't find them again despite spending ten days in the 'worst and most difficult part of the country'.[28]

Before Kelly's fifteenth birthday, a Chinese hawker with the unfortunate name of Ah Fook accused Kelly of assaulting and robbing him outside Mrs Kelly's farm on 14 October 1869. Irish-born Sergeant James Whelan[29] and Constable David McEnerney[30] resolved to arrest the youngster the next day. Whelan, a pale, bearded man, was one of the earliest and most determined of the Kelly hunters. He had once interrogated the teenage Kelly in court over some sheep stolen by Kelly's brother-in-law and thought he was a villainous young liar.

Whelan was said to be a modest, unassuming man at home but a bloodhound at work.

A former member of the Royal Irish Constabulary, Whelan had been in Victoria since 1856 and once worked alongside the ill-fated explorer and policeman Robert O'Hara Burke. On 15 October 1869, Kelly's mother saw Whelan and McEnerney approaching her shack from 800 metres and went inside to warn her son. Whelan then saw Kelly bolt out of the front door and race for the hills 'as fast as his heels could assist him'.[31]

Mrs Kelly released two savage dogs that attacked Whelan's horse[32] but press reports said, 'Whelan, who was well mounted, and dressed in civilian's clothes, immediately gave chase, and although the fugitive was fully three quarters of a mile in advance and selected a flight through thickly-timbered bush, the sergeant ultimately rode him down and took him into custody'.[33]

Kelly managed to beat the charges but only with some inventive testimony from family and friends.[34]

Whelan resolved to sniff out whatever he could on Kelly's illegal activities. He kept notes on the Juvenile Bushranger's

Sergeant James Whelan first arrested Ned Kelly when the 'Juvenile Bushranger' was just 14 and he was at the Gang's demise 11 years later. He became 'a perfect encyclopaedia of all useful knowledge' about the Kelly family and their illegal activities.

comings and goings and those of Kelly's associates, so much so that he became 'a perfect encyclopaedia of all useful knowledge' about the Kelly family. Whelan's 'diligence, his fidelity, his wisdom in counsel'[35] was said to have made him a dangerous enemy.

Whelan arrested Kelly again the following year, breaking Mrs Kelly's door down at dawn on Wednesday, 4 May 1870,[36] along with Superintendent William Nicolas[37] and Mounted Constables Patrick Mullane[38] and William Arthur.[39]

This time Kelly was facing a long prison sentence for helping Harry Power in the commission of armed robbery.

Though Kelly was not much more than a boy, his involvement in crime had already made him so notorious that he was interviewed in nearby Benalla by two of Victoria's leading police officers,

Charles Hope Nicolson[40] and Frank Hare,[41] who were both trying to outdo each other in the hunt for Power and thus win the favour of Police Commissioner Frederick Charles Standish,[42] whose powerful position and love of the high life made him many enemies within government and his own force. Critics claimed Standish arranged prostitutes to service his friends, including Queen Victoria's son Prince Alfred on a visit to Australia.[43] It was also claimed that he once encouraged women to strip at a dinner party so he could pose their curvaceous white bodies on black velvet chairs.[44] He earned what in 2022 terms would be a seven-figure salary, but it is said that he once lost half his annual wage at the gambling table in a single night,[45] that he was more at 'home in club land than at police headquarters',[46] and that he was 'too much a man of pleasure to devote himself seriously to the work of his office'.[47]

Harry Power's string of robberies embarrassed Standish and at the Benalla Police Station Ned Kelly was dwarfed by Superintendents Hare and Nicolson.

Big and bombastic Frank Hare, born in South Africa, was the son of a British army officer. With a long beard and a carefully coiffed mane, he was a 6-foot 3-inch (190-centimetre), 20-stone (130-kilogram) action man. Charles Nicolson was a dour Scot, born in the Orkney Islands. He had a hairy face and receding hairline, and was courageous and tough but plagued by ill health that made him ill-tempered and heavy handed.

He once instructed his bumbling inspector Alexander Brooke Smith[48] that, when dealing with the Kelly family and their sympathisers 'without oppressing the people, or worrying them in any way, [police] should endeavour, whenever [settlers] commit any paltry crime, to bring them to justice, and send them to Pentridge even on a paltry sentence … that is a very good way of taking the flashness out of them'.[49]

In an interview room at the Benalla Police Station, Ned Kelly presented a dismal, frightened figure for the two veteran lawmen.

Hare couldn't hide his contempt for this 'flash, ill-looking young blackguard',[50] but the watchful Nicolson won Kelly's trust. He thought the teenager showed potential, and he had what he called 'a serious talk with the lad', urging him to contemplate an offer to exchange the bad company of Greta for work as a shearer in New South Wales. Nicolson would later lament that, while Kelly 'seemed somewhat eager to go', his old ways and family loyalty dragged him back, and that 'the opportunity to save him from the career of crime upon which he subsequently entered was thus unhappily lost'.[51]

KELLY SPENT WEEKS IN custody and, such was his importance in establishing the whereabouts of Power, the 15-year-old was taken more than 200 kilometres south along the railway line to Melbourne for an interview with Standish himself at the police depot at Richmond.[52] Then, at the bluestone police and court complex in Kyneton, Kelly was photographed for the first time, sitting in a wooden chair; his long, dark, thick hair brushed back, his thin lips pressed into a grimace, his coat buttoned against the cold austerity of incarceration. His rebel gaze looked beyond the camera and revealed a lazy left eye.

A month and a day after Kelly's arrest an Aboriginal tracker nicknamed Donald helped a party of policemen find Harry Power at his remote mountain hideout.

Power's alarm system, a screeching peacock, had been driven undercover by driving rain as the lawmen approached the bushranger's camp over a huge precipice above the King Valley.

Superintendent Nicolson rushed Power, dodged the barrels of his shotgun and grabbed his wrists before he could pull the trigger or grab the pistol lying by his side. Frank Hare and Sergeant William Montfort snared the bushranger by the legs and ankles, and as he tried to wrestle free Montfort handcuffed him.

Kelly managed to escape jail for his role in Power's robberies amid rumours that the 'cub' had betrayed the 'old fox'[53] even though it was Kelly's uncle Jack Lloyd who received a £500 reward for leading police to the old highwayman.

After his next court appearance, Kelly, still just 15, started a four and a half month lag in Beechworth Gaol on 11 November 1870 for assault on a travelling merchant and using foul language

Charles Hope Nicolson beats Frank Hare for the prize of arresting Ned Kelly's boss, the bushranger Harry Power. State Library of Victoria, IAN18/06/70/105

to his wife. On behalf of a friend, a hawker and former Van Diemen's Land convict named Ben Gould,[54] Kelly had forwarded to her an obscene letter accompanied by a set of calves' testicles.

The Kellys would claim constant harassment by the police[55] and the claims seemed valid when Kelly was arrested again on 20 April 1871 just three weeks after leaving prison. Now 16, he was riding what he thought was a friend's horse through Greta when a 100-kilogram bear of a policeman named Edward Hall,[56] with a reputation for extreme violence, dragged Kelly from his mount and beat him so badly with the butt of his pistol that the youngster's forehead became 'a mass of raw and bleeding flesh'.[57] Hall tried to shoot the teenager at point-blank range, but his revolver misfired. In Beechworth Courthouse, Ned received three years' jail for receiving a stolen horse – twice the sentence of 'Wild' Wright,[58] the young man who actually stole it.[59]

Breaking rocks in the Beechworth Gaol quarry made Kelly stronger, harder and more ferocious. Every time he looked in a mirror and saw the ugly scars on his forehead and scalp, his grudge against the police was reinforced. He served his sentence at Beechworth, then Melbourne's Pentridge Prison, and then on the prison ship *Sacramento*, anchored in Hobson's Bay off Williamstown.

While he was imprisoned, Kelly's older sister Annie died in childbirth after being abandoned by her lover, a married police constable named Ernest Flood.[60] Kelly's rage festered even more when he heard that his brother Jim, a small 13-year-old boy, was given an astonishingly severe five-year sentence in Beechworth for driving two heifers and two steers that turned out to have been pilfered by a cousin.

Kelly finally left jail on 2 February 1874 and headed back to Greta with £2 10s 11p in his pocket and permanent chips on both shoulders.

Charles Nettleton,[61] the official photographer for Pentridge, had taken a confronting mugshot of the prisoner.

Ned stood 6 feet (183 centimetres) tall and weighed around 12 and a half stone (79 kilograms). The prison photograph showed he had short-cropped hair and stubble, hazel eyes and heavy eyebrows that met in the middle.

He also had scars across his forehead and a glare that would unnerve the devil.

When the photograph was eventually circulated around Australia, it caused alarm and fear wherever it was shown.[62]

Chapter 2

NED KELLY'S CRIMINALITY escalated off the scale after he left prison in 1874, despite him showing great promise as an industrious member of the community once released. He had started working as a tree feller in the wooded hills around Moyhu, near his mother's house, and earned a reputation as a diligent, hard toiler,[1] making at least £2 10s a week,[2] roughly double a labourer's wage. He would later be employed in a sawmill at Killawarra, near Wangaratta, where workmates would say he was 'an excellent axeman'[3] who 'made a bold attempt at reformation'.[4] At other times he worked as a farmhand and horse breaker, as a fencer at Bailey's vineyard at Taminick, near Glenrowan, as a builder's labourer at nearby Chesney Vale and Winton Swamp, and as a woodcutter in Gippsland. He and young Steve Hart also joined the moveable workforce as travelling shearers and spent time at the Gannawarra[5] sheep run on the Murray between Echuca and Swan Hill. Kelly's reputation for reliability earned him a position of trust at a sawmill near Greta, where he was made the overseer of a team cutting sleepers for the Wangaratta–Beechworth railway line. But the fog of criminality was always swirling around Kelly, his clan and his collection of loutish mates known as the Greta Mob, who dressed loudly, with bright-coloured sashes, their hats tilted and tipped over one eye and their chin straps under their noses.

On 8 August 1874, Kelly had gained a measure of revenge over Wild Wright, the man who had loaned him the stolen horse, beating the usually ferocious bully to a pulp in a 20-round bareknuckle boxing bout at the back of the Imperial Hotel in Beechworth. Wright was now family, married to Kelly's cousin Bridget Lloyd, but Kelly did not hold back with his punches.

It only made Kelly's reputation fiercer and, despite regular police surveillance, by August 1877 he was the leader of what became known as the 'most perfect horse-stealing organization that ever existed in Australia',[6] complete with 'ample paddock space'[7] for his stolen property. Kelly boasted that he had stolen 280 horses[8] and 'cattle innumerable',[9] and was not fussy where they came from either, sometimes taking large mobs, once 15 plough horses, from battling farmers in a single spree.[10]

Even Bill Frost, a local boundary rider who had fathered a child with Kelly's mother, had two horses go missing.[11]

Horses were taken on either side of the Murray and their brands changed.

Kelly's accomplices included Joe Byrne, Aaron Sherritt[12] and Wild Wright, Kelly's neighbour Brickey Williamson[13] and Kelly's new stepfather George King, a mysterious young American who on the 1874 marriage licence with Ellen Kelly listed his place of birth as California, *South* America, though he couldn't remember the name of the town.[14]

Because horse stealing became so rampant around Greta, 21-year-old Constable Alexander Fitzpatrick[15] was despatched from Melbourne's Richmond Depot to Benalla on 1 August 1877.[16] He had an illegitimate child back in Melbourne and a very high opinion of himself as a good-looking lady-killer and horseman. By his estimation he could 'ride like a centaur',[17] a legacy of his time as a boundary rider south of Ballarat at Meredith, where he fathered a child with his girlfriend Jessie McKay before taking off, the maintenance payments docked from his wages as a farewell gift. By the time he reached Benalla, Fitzpatrick had a new girlfriend named Anna Savage but some of the locals believed that 14-year-old Kate Kelly[18] caught his eye, too. He befriended many of the local larrikins on his beat, especially Ned Kelly, the charismatic local hard man with a soft

Irish lilt flavouring his speech. Kelly would later claim Fitzpatrick swore that they were 'intimate friends'.[19]

Before too long, though, Kelly was saying of his 'intimate friend': 'I have heard from a Trooper that he never knew Fitzpatrick to be one night sober and that he sold his sister to a Chinaman … he looks a young strapping fellow, rather genteel, more fit to be a starcher to a Laundress than policeman. The deceit and cowardice is too plain to be seen in the puny cabbage hearted looking face.'[20]

Fitzpatrick was involved in the arrest of Kelly for trying to ride his horse across a footpath while drunk in Benalla on 17 September 1877. Sergeant Whelan, who had previously chased the 15-year-old Kelly through the bush, decided he needed back-up to escort the prisoner from the lock-up to the Benalla Courthouse. Whelan was joined by Fitzpatrick, veteran watch-house keeper Constable Patrick Day[21] and the rugged Mounted Constable Thomas Lonigan,[22] a 32-year-old Irishman who had been cracking heads since he joined the force six years earlier. Kelly managed to break free from their clutches and bolted around the corner and into the little store of Benalla bootmaker Robert King where the four officers trapped him.

Fitzpatrick grabbed Kelly by the foot[23] and then tried to choke him but Kelly sent him flying with a punch, remarking later that Fitzpatrick was 'very subject to fainting'.[24]

Lonigan was made of tougher stuff, though, and grabbed Kelly by the testicles, squeezing with all the power he could muster from his thick sinewy forearms. Kelly roared in agony and said later that Lonigan's savagery caused him severe pain for more than a year afterwards.[25] Onlookers claimed that the anguished Kelly told his tormentor: 'If ever I shoot a man, Lonigan, you will be the first.'[26]

Kelly's penchant for violence and his hatred for the police had turned a minor incident into a catastrophe. He was fined just 1 shilling for being drunk and disorderly but £2 for assaulting police in the execution of their duty, £2 for resisting arrest, and 5 shillings for damaging Fitzpatrick's clothing.[27]

THREE THOUSAND KILOMETRES away in North Queensland, Stanhope O'Connor was sporting a pith helmet, an impressive handlebar moustache and a burning desire to make a name for himself in this wild frontier. As the second son of a colonel,[28] he had arrived in Melbourne in 1869 as a first-class passenger from England,[29] but the badlands of North Queensland were a world away from such cossetted refinement.

O'Connor was a young man of means, a well-educated Irish gentleman whose cousin was New South Wales Governor Hercules Robinson.[30] But it seems the spirit of adventure and the constant threat of danger enticed him to Australia's wild north[31] and he was sworn in as a sub-inspector of Queensland's Native Mounted Police on New Year's Day 1873.[32]

He was originally stationed at the Conway Barracks near Bowen,[33] but the discovery of gold along the Palmer River turned the wilds west of Cooktown into a war zone.

In October 1873, a Queensland government party including 90 prospectors had set off from Cooktown for the Palmer River to proclaim the goldfields. It seemed that the purpose of the Aboriginal troopers with them was to exterminate as many of their own people as they could.[34] In what became known as the Battle of the Normanby, a large number of Aboriginal people who had not interfered with the group in any way were hunted and shot down near a large lagoon.[35] More were killed at the Kennedy River.[36]

It was said, though, that the Aboriginal people of the Palmer put up a better fight against the white invasion than anywhere else in Australia,[37] creating fear among the settlers. Reports circulated that the 'wild blacks' not only ate horses but also the humans that they speared.[38]

There was only ever going to be one winner, however, when long-range rifles were pitted against spears and boomerangs.

A prospector on the Palmer recalled with a touch of satisfaction that in 1876 he heard one dawn break to the sound of 'volley after volley of rifles' against a 'mob of wild blacks'.

'They must have been a hundred strong,' he said. 'There were two large fires … where the trackers had burnt the dead bodies.'[39]

Stanhope O'Connor with some of his Native Mounted Police trackers. State Library of Queensland, 9044693

Stanhope O'Connor first sailed down the Endeavour River into Cooktown from Bowen on Boxing Day 1875 aboard the steamer *Western*. With him were 24 Aboriginal troopers and 40 horses. As a sub-inspector (second class) he was posted to Boralga, the Native Police Camp on the Lower Laura River, 150 kilometres and a week's ride inland from Cooktown along a narrow track through rugged, dangerous territory.[40] The Aboriginal policemen with him had signed five-year contracts at £3 a month, half the average pay of white troopers. They had also been given demeaning pet names, such as 'Hero' and 'Sambo' as though they were horses or dogs. Their attachment to land was part of their very being and they understood disturbances caused by footprints better than any white man. The troopers were usually recruited from areas distant from their postings so that any family or tribal loyalties would not dull their aim when they had to kill other Aboriginal people.

A century earlier James Cook and the wealthy English botanist Joseph Banks had spent seven weeks camped beside the Endeavour River and had engaged in the first known reconciliation ceremony between Australia's First Peoples and white visitors.

They had also given the local Guugu Yimithirr people a tour of the ship that was taking the British explorers around the world.

But now O'Connor was under orders to let the Indigenous population of North Queensland know exactly who ruled their land.

The Laura camp, a collection of huts surrounded by ironwood trees and near a lagoon that was home to water birds, fish, crocodiles, stray cattle and feral pigs,[41] became the base for Queensland's frontier war in Cape York Peninsula for 20 years. One of O'Connor's specific instructions was to offer protection to prospectors and carriers at a 'dreaded' ambush point known as Hell's Gate that was atop an escarpment.[42]

On the day after his arrival at Laura, Indigenous tribesmen attacked O'Connor's camp but the police rifles won the day and O'Connor said the attackers 'suffered for their temerity'.[43]

'I found the country in a very bad state, as the blacks were daring and warlike,' O'Connor explained. 'The Hell's Gate and Battle Camp tribes were the worst ... I saw at once my only plan was to put a stop to these murders with a strong hand, and ... [I explained] to the blacks that any murder committed by them would be punished by me, but that I would also protect them from outrage by the whites.'[44]

O'Connor faced a constant battle stopping deserters,[45] the nature of the 'dispersals' they administered often being unconscionable for his men − 'dispersals' being a euphemism for chasing the Aboriginal people off their ancestral land and, in many cases, slaughtering them.

As a way of enticing his troopers to stay, O'Connor offered cash prizes out of his own pocket to the best rifle shots and some of his troopers developed into expert marksmen.[46]

Two years into his Laura posting, O'Connor wrote to his superiors in Cooktown about the impressive appearance, prosperity and courage of local Aboriginal people, telling them, 'The Blacks are very numerous and plucky. As a race they are tall and well-made and fat − they have only the woomera-spear as a weapon of defence or offence, but these they can throw nearly 200 yards.'[47]

Their spears were nowhere near as effective, though, as the police rifles.

William Corfield,[48] who became the Queensland Legislative Assembly member for the Gregory electorate, was working as a carrier out of Cooktown when he complained to O'Connor that two of his horses had been speared and butchered by local tribesmen.

Corfield took O'Connor and six trackers to where the horses were killed and, though rain had apparently obliterated all traces of those responsible, two of the trackers rode ahead while the others drove their packhorses behind.

O'Connor called out to his best man, Corporal Sambo, 'Where track?'

The corporal pointed to a blade of spinifex.

Corfield dismounted, and barely visible on the grass was a tiny speck of blood from the horsemeat that had dropped on the root and not been washed off by the rain.

The posse later came to where there had been a great feast on the bank of the Kennedy River and Corfield found the shoes, tail and mane of his favourite horse.

The troopers followed the river for three days before they saw a column of smoke about a mile ahead. By moonlight at 2 a.m. five of the troopers stripped naked, their only dress consisting of a cap in hand and a cartridge belt round the waist, as they waded into the water, carrying their rifles above their heads, to approach a small sand island. Just before daylight Corfield, O'Connor and Sambo heard shots a mile down the river.

When O'Connor and Corfield arrived at what had been the Aboriginal camp they found most of their prey had fled. But they burnt everything left behind by the Indigenous group, including what Corfield said were 'several dilly-bags containing the dead bodies of infants, which they carried about with them. The stench of burning human flesh was sickening.'

Corfield accompanied one of the troopers down the river, where the soil at the roots of a large gum tree had been hollowed out by the water. Beneath it resembled a huge cave. Suddenly the trooper fired two shots into the cave. Corfield said, 'What are you firing at?' and the trooper replied, 'Two fella sit down there.' He then hauled out two bodies for burning.[49]

The *Cooktown Courier* was disappointed that O'Connor and his men had not killed more Indigenous people.

'Of course, when writing on this subject, we leave all question of morality or Christianity on one side, they have nothing to do with the treatment of blacks in this country,' it said, 'we are simply now discussing the best manner of protecting the lives and property of the whites. If we put aside the plan of extermination as impracticable, why not adopt some other settled plan. Let the shooting of the blacks be carried out systematically as punishment for outrages.'[50]

IN THE LAST DAYS OF 1877, Ned Kelly ploughed some of the money from his horse stealing back into building a new cottage for his mother near Greta's Eleven Mile Creek. Together with Joe Byrne, Kelly's brother-in-law Bill Skilling[51] and their neighbour Brickey Williamson, Kelly fashioned ironbark slabs for the outer walls, bark sheets for the interior and a roof of stringybark, with jockey poles and riders for the roof. There was a stone fireplace, three bedrooms and store-bought windows.

It became a local legend around Greta that after Kelly's stepfather George King hit Kelly's mother across the face with a whip,[52] Kelly gave him a taste of his own medicine, beating the young American black and blue.[53] There was speculation that Kelly then took George for a ride into the secret caverns of the nearby ranges and only Kelly came back.[54]

While King vanished from police notice, Kelly loomed larger than ever as a person of interest and on 15 March 1878,[55] in Chiltern, a warrant was issued for his arrest over the theft of 11 horses from the family of wealthy grazier James Whitty, a long-time Kelly enemy.

Sergeant James Lynch, who had spent almost a quarter of a century in the police force, took out a warrant for the arrest of Dan Kelly and his cousin Jack Lloyd for horse stealing on 5 April 1878.[56]

History would not be kind to Constable Fitzpatrick, but in April 1878 he was regarded as a reliable policeman and given temporary charge of the Greta station despite the area becoming a hotbed of crime, with the Kelly boys at the centre of it. One newspaper described Greta as a town terrorised by 'a regular gang of ruffians, who from their infancy were brought up as rogues and vagabonds, and who have been constantly in trouble'.[57]

Fitzpatrick's promotion was approved by 43-year-old Inspector Alexander Brooke Smith, a surgeon's son from Kent, who had joined the Victorian police as a 17-year-old cadet and almost immediately won acclaim for his courage on the Bendigo goldfields when he arrested the fiery agitator 'Captain' Edward Brown,[58] an Irishman who claimed he had once ridden with the Texas Rangers and lived among the Comanches.

Fitzpatrick read in the *Police Gazette* about warrants for Dan Kelly and Lloyd, and told Sergeant Whelan that he would arrest Dan at his mother's new home if he were there and take him to the Greta lock-up.[59] Fitzpatrick didn't have a warrant, but under the law he didn't need one,[60] and in fact could be disciplined if he did not arrest a suspect.[61]

Whelan told him to be careful because the Kellys were dangerous and likely to 'put up a fight',[62] but Fitzpatrick believed Ned Kelly was miles away and thought he could handle Dan alone. Unlike his big, burly brother, the 16-year-old Dan was short and only slightly built.

Fitzpatrick had arrested Dan and his cousins Jack and Tom Lloyd a year earlier to face charges of robbery and indecent assault. The three youngsters had fled to the bush but Brooke Smith told Ned Kelly it would be better for all three if they surrendered. Kelly had refused to hand them over to the inspector he regarded a fool, but instead talked the wild teenagers into allowing Fitzpatrick to arrest them at Benalla.[63] They were sentenced to three months in Beechworth Gaol for damaging property. Tom Lloyd was given another four months for common assault, though he beat a charge of intent to commit a rape.[64]

At about 2.30 p.m. on 15 April 1878, Fitzpatrick rode out of Benalla on his dappled bay, with a Webley revolver in his holster. Witnesses saw him stop on the two-hour journey for just one drink of brandy and lemonade,[65] making a lie of claims by Kelly supporters later that he was rolling drunk when he arrived at the Kelly shack late in the afternoon.

Fitzpatrick claimed he arrived at the Kellys, scanned the surrounds for Dan, dismounted and called out to Mrs Kelly that he'd like a word. Just two days earlier, the 46-year-old grandmother had endured a difficult labour, delivering her 12th child, Alice King. Mrs Kelly shared her sons' hatred for the police. Her middle boy, Jim, first jailed at 13, was now serving a three-year sentence in Sydney's Darlinghurst Gaol after brutally beating a policeman who was trying to arrest him at Kiandra in the Snowy Mountains on a horse-stealing charge.

But Mrs Kelly knew it was better to have the local lawmen as friends rather than enemies, so she invited Fitzpatrick to sit at her kitchen table in a dark room warmed by the glow of a fireplace. Baby Alice was asleep, but four of Mrs Kelly's other children were about the house.

Fitzpatrick waited an hour or so until Dan arrived home and, in his version, told the 16-year-old that he had to take him into the Greta lock-up, though he would let Dan eat the supper his mother had made. Dan had dark hair and a dark complexion, with small dark piercing eyes. Some said he looked Chinese. He also had a vicious temper and a burning desire for attention, partly because he was always wearing his brother's hand-me-down clothes and living in his shadow.

Fitzpatrick claimed that Dan agreed to go quietly but suddenly the ominous figure of Ned Kelly appeared at the house, rushed in through the doorway and fired a shot that missed from a small low-powered .31 calibre 1849 model Colt.

In Fitzpatrick's version, Mrs Kelly grabbed a shovel from the fireplace and smashed the policeman over the helmet, leaving a big dent in the side and caving it in completely over his eyes.[66]

Little Dan Kelly in his hand-me-down clothes was already a hardened criminal by his mid-teens. Victoria Police Museum

Simultaneously, Ned fired a second shot, which lodged in the policeman's left wrist as Dan snatched Fitzpatrick's revolver and pointed it at him.[67]

Fitzpatrick said Bill Skilling, also carrying a revolver, came to Ned's side at the door just as the second shot was fired, though it's possible Fitzpatrick was mistaken and the man with the gun was really Joe Byrne.[68] Skilling was a farmer married to Kelly's sister Maggie[69] and lived nearby.

Taking advantage of the commotion, Fitzpatrick said he spun around and grabbed Kelly's pistol only for it to fire a third time with the bullet passing through the sleeve of the policeman's jumper. He noticed Brickey Williamson also arriving with a gun.

According to Fitzpatrick's tale, he became dizzy from the wound to his wrist and fainted.[70] When he came to, Kelly's attitude had changed dramatically as he realised that he was now in more strife than at any time in his life. Hoping to avoid repercussions, Mrs Kelly bandaged Fitzpatrick's wound, Kelly gave him back his empty revolver and Dan gave him back his handcuffs. Kelly told the policeman to make up a story that two strangers had wounded him – that Fitzpatrick would be well rewarded if he told the right story and that he would get badly hurt if he didn't.[71]

Chapter 3

CONSTABLE FITZPATRICK arrived back at Benalla Police Station in a highly distressed state at 2 a.m. Sergeant Whelan took the young policeman's statement, which he would later say did not 'prevaricate in the least' over the next few years of scrutiny and cross-examination.[1] In fact, Fitzpatrick's version would hardly deviate in the 33 years between 15 April 1878 and when he was interviewed for newspapers in 1911.[2]

Ned would later claim that not only was Fitzpatrick drunk when he got to the house, but also that he wasn't shot at all but injured his wrist himself to frame the Kellys. At different times Ned would say he was 15 miles[3] from Greta when Fitzpatrick was injured, then 200 miles, and even 400 miles,[4] though Kelly's cousin Joe Ryan had a receipt for a horse Kelly sold him in Greta, dated on the same afternoon as the shooting.[5] Kelly would at one point say that Fitzpatrick's revolver 'accidentally exploded' while he was 'attempting to take liberties with Kate Kelly, the result being that the ball lodged in Fitzpatrick's wrist',[6] but at another time said any suggestion Fitzpatrick had tried to molest Kate was 'a foolish story'.[7]

Knowing that the police would soon come in numbers to arrest them, though, Ned and Joe Byrne planned to ride through the Victorian high country and cross the Murray to their horse-stealing haunts in New South Wales. Dan Kelly rode on to hide at a gold-mining camp he and Ned had established outside Mansfield, not far from a narrow stream called Stringybark Creek.

As soon as the Benalla Telegraph Office opened at 8 a.m. on 16 April, Sergeant Whelan rushed through the front door, telling the clerk to tap out the most urgent messages to Standish and Victoria's police detectives that Ned Kelly had tried to murder Fitzpatrick and that Dan Kelly, Ellen Kelly, Skilling and Brickey Williamson had aided and abetted him.

An hour later at the Wangaratta Police Station, 40 kilometres north of Benalla, Sergeant Arthur Steele[8] bristled with the scent of the hunt. Like Whelan, the pugnacious 40-year-old, with a hawkish nose, walrus moustache and eagle eye for law-breakers, had been chasing the Kellys for years.

Steele was born at Tours, France, the son of an Irishman who was a captain in the 6th Inniskilling Dragoons. At the age of 12 he was sent to the Military Academy in Dublin in preparation for service with the British Army in the Crimean War.

He was in Gibraltar on his way to the front in 1856 when news came that peace had been declared. Back in Ireland he met a brother of Robert O'Hara Burke, then in charge of police at Beechworth, and Steele decided to try his luck in Victoria, which was said to be awash with gold. He joined the Victorian police in 1856, first as an armed escort for gold transports, then as a senior constable in charge at Omeo and then at Yackandandah, near Beechworth, where he arrested two murderers.

Commissioner Standish appointed Steele to Wangaratta in November 1876, and he immediately began trying to smash Kelly's horse-stealing racket.

When Steele received the telegram about Kelly shooting Fitzpatrick, he donned his trademark tweed hat and together with Detective Joseph Brown, who had been investigating Kelly's horse thefts, rode off to Greta to bring in the accused.[9]

The policemen took up a vantage point on a hill opposite Mrs Kelly's house and waited until the late afternoon, wary that Ned would likely kill to defend his mother. Steele received reinforcement with the arrival of Irish-born Senior Constable Anthony Strahan,[10] a 16-year veteran of the force.

At 9 p.m. Steele, Strahan and Brown rode down to the little

house, which was in darkness except for a fire inside. Ned Kelly would later say that the police burst in 'with revolvers' and threatened to blow his mother's brains out if she moved.[11] Steele said the arrest was much more restrained, though – that he gave Mrs Kelly time to say goodbye to her three-day-old baby, her psychotic jailbird brother 'Mad' Jimmy Quinn[12] and the other children before finally handcuffing her at 1 a.m. and taking her on horseback to the Greta lock-up.

At first light, Mrs Kelly, Brickey Williamson and Bill Skilling were loaded onto a dray like cattle for market and driven into Benalla for further questioning and arraignment.[13]

Mrs Kelly was confined in Beechworth Gaol awaiting trial but reunited with baby Alice as they shared a cold stone cell overlooking the unmarked graves of executed prisoners.[14]

In the aftermath of being wounded, Fitzpatrick sought out to make a confidante of Joe Byrne's best mate Aaron Sherritt, a cocky young tearaway said to be 'as flash as Lucifer, dressed up to Kill!'[15] Sherritt promised to take him to the Kelly boys and told Fitzpatrick that Ned and Dan were camped near Beechworth, working on ways to get Mrs Kelly out of jail, and that Ned wanted to rekindle his friendship with the constable.

Fitzpatrick informed his senior officer Detective Douglas Kennedy[16] that Sherritt could lead them to the Kellys 'in a very short time'.[17] Kennedy, no relation to Michael Kennedy, was a wise old copper, though, having joined the force way back in 1856, and his service included the arrest of the bushranger Andrew Scott aka Captain Moonlite[18] in 1872 after Scott had robbed the Mount Egerton bank 100 kilometres north-west of Melbourne. Kennedy vetoed Fitzpatrick's plan, believing it was either a trap or false information designed to throw the police off the scent. Sherritt was adamant that he wouldn't assist any of the other police, and certainly not Detective Michael 'Mick' Ward[19] or Patrick Mullane.

Those two officers had arrested Sherritt and Byrne for cattle stealing near Beechworth in 1876, resulting in six-month jail terms, and they were resolute Kelly hunters.

Before arriving in 'Kelly Country', French- born Sergeant Arthur Steele had trained at the Military Academy in Dublin in preparation for service with the British Army in the Crimean War. State Library of Victoria H96.160/162

'As flash as Lucifer'. Joe Byrne's childhood friend Aaron Sherritt played a dangerous game giving useless information about the gang to the police. Here he wears a low-crowned hat with chinstrap under the nose – the sign of the Greta Mob. Burke Museum, Beechworth

Mullane had assisted Sergeant Whelan in the arrest of the teenage Kelly eight years earlier, and he and Constable Flood had also arrested Kelly's uncle Mad Jimmy Quinn, after he beat and cruelly disfigured one of his own sisters and a local farmer he had quarrelled with.[20]

Ever since Mrs Kelly's arrest, Detective Ward had been doing his best to hunt down her runaway sons and he became the main co-ordinator for spies and informants in the Kelly hunt. A native of Galway, Ireland, Ward was a dapper, well-built man with an elaborate waxed moustache, which was good for twirling, and a neat chin beard. He wore round, rimless spectacles over eyes that were always on the lookout for law-breakers. He had joined the Victorian police in October 1869 and was almost immediately sent to north-eastern Victoria to help in the search for Harry

Power. While stationed in Wangaratta and Beechworth, Ward became well acquainted with the crimes of the Kellys, Quinns and Lloyds.[21]

Ten days after Fitzpatrick's wounding, Ward, Strahan and two constables headed out from Benalla to Mrs Kelly's shack hoping to uncover her sons, who they suspected were hiding nearby. Instead they met a fearful storm on a black night before finding a dray, minus its horse but with two bags of flour and other articles, in the middle of the road. They searched the nearby bush and found Kelly's younger sisters Maggie Skilling and Kate Kelly sitting on a log, most likely in the process of dropping supplies for their brothers. The girls' light clothing was soaked through. They told the police, whom they knew all too well, that they were 'benighted, and could not find their way home' because it was so dark. Ward had a flask of whisky and gave some to Kate, and he left the other two officers to guide the girls to safety. He and Strahan, meanwhile, rode to a vantage point outside the Kelly home, taking positions in the bush hoping to see Kelly or Dan emerge from hiding for a report on how Mrs Kelly fared at court.[22]

The lawmen waited in vain through that dark and stormy night, but despite the disappointment Ward soon heard that the Kellys were mining gold in a secluded part of the densely forested Wombat Ranges outside Mansfield. He sent his first report from police informants on 7 May 1878 to Inspector Frederick Secretan, the head of Victoria Police's Detective Branch in Melbourne, saying that at least one and perhaps both of the fugitives were at 'the old diggings place' at 'Bullocky Gully or at the head of Ryans Creek'.[23] Ward then went on a three-day search about 10 kilometres from Stringybark Creek, along with Strahan, Constables Mooney and Hayes,[24] and Charles Whitty, one of Ned Kelly's boyhood chums. But Ned, Dan and Joe Byrne were higher up in the mountains and went undetected.[25]

On 29 April, the Victorian government offered a £100 reward for information leading to Ned Kelly's capture[26] and Kelly's rage boiled when he heard that the police were treating his young sisters 'very ill', dragging them out of bed at night and using them as human shields.[27] His sisters claimed that police would march them into darkened rooms in the house in case Kelly was hiding there so that the children would be shot first in a crossfire.

WHILE THE KELLYS WERE HIDING OUT, Superintendent John Sadleir[28] was made the senior lawman in Victoria's North Eastern Police District, moving from Mansfield to new headquarters at Benalla in July 1878. Like Kelly's father, Sadleir was a Tipperary man, but he had taken a different route through life. His ancestors had been close friends with William Shakespeare,[29] and he was regarded as 'an efficient and exemplary officer of police, with a high sense of duty'.[30]

Sadleir had arrived in Australia in 1852 on the maiden voyage of the mighty steamship *Great Britain*, at a time when thousands of migrants were arriving on Australian shores each week. He could remember the days of the Native Police laying down the law with a heavy thump on the goldfields. He had first seen the almost supernatural powers of Aboriginal trackers during a posting to the grazing lands of Hamilton, in Victoria's western districts, in 1859.

He said they could succeed in bush searches where white men were 'hopelessly at a loss', and told how an Aboriginal man from the Coleraine area, a man known as 'Paunchy' to the white settlers, had killed one of the Black Swamp men at a large gathering before a corroboree outside Hamilton. Local police could find no trace of any remains, even though they examined the ashes of every fire at the Indigenous camps. Then police brought in an Aboriginal tracker.

'He took up various positions to leeward,' Sadleir recalled, 'where he stood for a time, still as a statue. Then he would make a short sudden run towards the camp, when after a few repetitions of these short runs [he] pointed to some blow-flies resting on the ground where there had been one of the numerous fires. There, covered by a few inches of soil and ashes, was found the body of the murdered black.'[31]

For the time being, though, Sadleir and his men relied on more conventional policing methods in the hunt for the Kellys.

On 10 August, Sadleir wrote to an officer he regarded as a man of 'remarkable merit' — Sergeant Michael Kennedy — who was based in Mansfield. Sadleir proposed sending two constables who knew Kelly personally to Mansfield in order to search with Kennedy from that end. Sadleir also wanted another unit to join forces with police in Greta with both teams searching simultaneously up and down the King River and its surrounds. On 16 August, Kennedy wrote back to tell Sadleir that 'the offender Kelly could be routed from his hiding place if the arrangements proposed by the Superintendent were properly carried out'.[32]

The distance from Mansfield to the King River is so great and the country so impenetrable that a party of men from here would, in my opinion, require to establish a

John Sadleir was a Tipperary Man who had served in the Victorian Police force since arriving in Melbourne in the Gold Rush days of 1852. Victoria Police Museum

Detective Michael Ward exploited Sherritt's close ties to the gang with fatal consequences.

kind of depot at some distance beyond the Wombat – say, Stringybark Creek. I feel sure that by efficiently carrying out this plan Kelly would soon be disturbed, if not captured. I believe Kelly has secreted himself in some isolated part of that country lying between Wombat and King River. I am not aware if Mounted Constable Michael Scanlan, [Police number] 2118, of Mooroopna, is personally acquainted with Kelly, but I am sure there is no man who could render more service in the proposed expedition than he could, as he knows every part of that country lying between here and the King River.[33]

Kennedy had been involved in the prosecution of Wild Wright in 1874 for horse stealing[34] but the arrest was made by Scanlan, an Irish-born bachelor who had been in Victoria for 11 years and had been a mounted constable for nine, after a brief stint running a store in Beaufort, west of Melbourne. Scanlan's police record has been blighted four times by drink but he received a commendation for bringing in Wild Wright. Kennedy and Scanlan also shared a reward from local squatters for the arrest and conviction after Wright was given a three-year sentence.[35]

Kennedy's scouting mission into the Wombat Ranges was delayed by other pressing matters.

On Tuesday, 17 September 1878, the sergeant leapt into action with his offsider Constable Thomas McIntyre, whom he regarded as 'a zealous, conscientious man',[36] as they led a search party of local farmers and station hands after a 13-year-old boy named Alexander Campbell became lost in the bush. The search was co-ordinated by Sub-inspector Henry Pewtress,[37] a man Superintendent Sadleir regarded as 'a thoroughly good officer unacquainted, however, with bush work'.[38] Kennedy and McIntyre scoured the ranges and gullies for miles. They stopped the search at nightfall with plans to resume at dawn, though young Alexander wandered home a few hours later unscathed, albeit cold and wet and feeling sick after eating a raw pigeon.[39]

Kennedy, a 35-year-old Irishman, was physically impressive at 5 feet 10 inches (178 centimetres) and 13 stone (83 kilograms),[40] with a calm temperament. He had arrived in Australia with his father, Hugh, and mother, Roseanna, impoverished flax growers from Castlepollard, and in his youth had laboured on the land alongside them[41] before a short stint with the Dublin Metropolitan Police.

He was appointed a foot constable in Melbourne on 19 August 1864 and given the number 2009. Although there were some cruel and crooked men in the force, Kennedy gained a reputation as a fair and honest cop. He became a mounted constable a year into his service, and at Dry Creek, an alluvial goldfield near Mansfield, Kennedy married 19-year-old Bridget Mary Tobin, a Catholic girl from Tipperary who came to Australia as a baby.[42] He fell in love with the raven-haired girl as soon as they met and before long they were inseparable.[43]

Kennedy developed a powerful personality and became known for talking wrongdoers around rather than beating them over the head. He soon had postings to Doon and Broken Creek and the only criticism on his record was that he once failed to handcuff two Chinese prisoners when they were being taken to Mansfield, and only because he believed it would be quicker to get them there if their hands weren't bound. He began to make good money from rewards offered for the arrest of cattle thieves, collecting £100, or about six months' additional pay, from the Albury District Association for the Suppression of Cattle Stealing, for the conviction of William Donnelly, who stole eight head of cattle belonging to Alexander Kirkham Finlay of Bethanga, the biggest cattle run in the Beechworth area.

Included in his reward was a certificate of appreciation, and a £50 gold pocket watch made in London, with his initials MK[44] engraved on the case.

By the time Sergeant Kennedy became a Kelly hunter, he and Bridget had five children and another on the way, but they grieved for their infant son John Thomas who had died in 1877.

Policing in Victoria was a dangerous, poorly paid occupation, largely undertaken by young Irishmen. Native-born Australians mostly avoided it. The *Census of Victoria, 1871,* recorded that 45 per cent of Victoria's population had been born in the colony, yet by 1874 there were just 35 native-born constables in a force of 1060. At a time when Irish settlers represented only 14 per cent of the population, the ranks of the Victorian police were 82 per cent Irish, of which 46 per cent were ex-members of the Royal Irish Constabulary, a group often seen as Britain's occupation force oppressing the poor on behalf of rich landlords.[45]

With little training and a base salary of just six shillings and sixpence a day, a police constable had to buy his own uniform at a cost of £12, more than a month's salary. Policemen worked a seven-day week and were granted only twelve days leave a year. A typical working day for a constable was 5 a.m. to 5 p.m. while night duty was 9 p.m. to 5 a.m. 14 days straight before rotating back to day shift. The pursuit of rewards from squatters for arresting cattle thieves was an economic necessity.

At the same time as Michael Kennedy was making preparations to search for the Kellys, Detective Ward was scouring north-eastern Victoria in disguise, as a butcher, swagman and splitter, sometimes on horseback, sometimes on foot, sometimes with a secret service man in tow, eavesdropping on conversations and quizzing strangers about any tough-looking young strangers staying in the area.[46]

Ward had received information on 29 August 1878 that Kelly had been seen about three weeks earlier between the villages of Woolshed and Sebastopol by a Woolshed blacksmith. He was said to be riding, and carried a gun under his arm and had a revolver strapped on his saddle. Ward surmised that Kelly was most likely making for the home of Joe Byrne's mother at Sebastopol. He warned police not to even hint at the identity of the informant under any circumstances as Kelly or his supporters would kill the man's cattle.[47]

Ward had set off in pursuit on 9 September 1878, carrying a small pocket Webley revolver, believing that, while Kelly and his companions might fight him, he 'never had the remotest idea they would shoot'.[48]

MRS KELLY'S CASE WAS FINALLY heard in October 1878 by Redmond Barry, who nearly ten years earlier had sentenced her brother-in-law to death for arson.

While the Kellys thought they had great sympathy in north-eastern Victoria, newspapers suggested that Ned fired at the policeman inside his mother's house because in the dark, and in the rush of violent excitement, he mistook the lawman for his sworn enemy Constable Ernest Flood.[49]

Almost six months after the incident, Judge Barry handed Mrs Kelly a sentence of three years with hard labour on 9 October 1878, while Skilling and Williamson received six years each.[50]

In his hideout near Beechworth, Ned pronounced his own verdict against the police and later barked:

> … the Police got credit and praise in the papers for arresting the Mother of 12 children, one an infant on her breast; and those two quiet hardworking innocent men who would not know the difference in a revolver and a saucepan handle and kept them six months awaiting trial and then convicted them on the evidence of the meanest article that ever the sun shone on.[51]

Commissioner Standish formed a low opinion of Fitzpatrick and considered the sentence on Mrs Kelly unduly harsh, claiming 'it formed one of the many causes which assisted to bring about the Kelly outrages'.[52] Mrs Kelly agreed. Brickey Williamson was in the yard with her at Beechworth and Kelly's mother said her boys would take the news of her heavy sentence badly.

She feared that their tempers would explode and 'that there would be murder now'.[53]

Ned Kelly joined his brother in the mountain hideout near Stringybark Creek, and talked about roasting Sergeant Steele alive.[54]

The Kelly boys had been on the run for six months, all the time well aware that they would one day face a showdown with police.

They hatched a plan for the release of their mother and baby half-sister, using their uncle Pat Quinn as an intermediary to approach Alfred Wyatt, the deliciously eccentric Benalla police magistrate. Wyatt was a local curiosity, riding a horse to the various courts on his circuit wearing a velveteen suit, goggles and a huge towering 'pyramid of a hat' with long white tails streaming from it.[55] Wyatt said that Mrs Kelly's sentence was 'a very severe one'[56] and he listened intently when Quinn proposed that the Kelly boys would surrender 'if the old woman [was] let out'.[57] But the police were not prepared to make a deal with a convicted felon now accused of shooting a policeman.

IN BEECHWORTH GAOL, Brickey Williamson was constantly telling police they had the wrong man – that it was Joe Byrne who had been with Kelly when Fitzpatrick was shot and not him.[58] He told Inspector Reginald Green that the Kellys usually carried rations for about a month and were likely to get more supplies from their sister Maggie Skilling.[59] He claimed that Maggie planted food and ammunition for them in a large log in a scrubby range. Tom Lloyd, Ned's cousin and closest mate, was likely to join them, he said, and they might be planning a robbery. Brickey warned the inspector that hunting them through the ranges would be dangerous for police because the Kellys occupied vantage points from where they could roll down large rocks on anyone in pursuit.

He said Joe Byrne had joined the Kelly brothers; that he had been staying regularly at Mrs Kelly's home for a year before the Fitzpatrick incident. Brickey described Byrne as being 'about 25 years, 5 feet 10 inches [178 centimetres] high, stout build, thin features, fair whiskers, small very fair moustache, blue eyes, small hands, thick legs'. He looked very much like George King, Mrs Kelly's missing husband.

Byrne had a vicious temper. Once, when he was yarding horses, one of Byrne's sisters let some of them out and he belted her across the face with a bridle, severely injuring her. Byrne's mother, Margret,[60] a native of Galway, was widowed in 1870, and as she tried to raise eight children and 14 cows Byrne was of little help, stealing cattle and horses and racing through the local towns, dressed to the nines looking for girls and fights. Ned Kelly said Byrne was a great mate, as 'straight and true as steel', but Brickey told Inspector Green Byrne was 'a dangerous man ... a man who would fire on any one that would attempt to arrest him'.

The three youngsters had four revolvers and one old rifle between them, Brickey said, 'but the rifle' was 'not much use'.[61]

Kelly later claimed that after his mother's conviction he intended to make money at his mountain hideout from a gold-sluicing operation that he'd worked at over the last couple of years and by distilling whisky so he could 'procure a new trial' for her.[62]

At Bullock Creek, Ned, Dan and Joe Byrne were soon joined by Steve Hart, a bush jockey and horse thief looking for some wild adventure. Hart was a similar size to Dan Kelly who he had met in Beechworth Gaol. Hart came from Three Mile Creek near Wangaratta, where he briefly attended the local Catholic school. He had 'a slight girlish figure' but dark features, a low forehead and what one newspaper described as a 'cruel, sensual mouth'.[63] Like Dan, he had a foul temper and vindictive streak but he was also a local hero among the larrikins of Wangaratta for his feats of daring, including jumping the railway gates at level crossings.

Hart was not long out of Beechworth Gaol after receiving a few weeks' remission from his 12-month lag for unlawfully using horses and other similar charges.[64] It was Sergeant Arthur Steele who nabbed him, and Hart's sister Rachel[65] reckoned Steele always had it in for her brother because he once tied the tail of Steele's horse to a fence one night, humiliating the no-nonsense lawman when he tried to ride off.[66]

After Hart's release on 4 June 1878,[67] Steele remarked that the young tearaway went back to Wangaratta promising he would work, 'but when he had been at his father's place it appears he threw down the axe they were grubbing with, and said, "A short life and a merry one," and he got his horse and rode away.'[68] As he saddled his chestnut, Hart told his older brother Dick that he planned to go shearing again in New South Wales but the Harts had not heard from him since. Hart had learned of the Fitzpatrick business in jail and was keen to catch up with his friends. Life on the run, stealing horses and leading the police on wild chases seemed much more exciting to him than the hard toil of his father's farm or the shearing shed.

ON 15 OCTOBER, SIX DAYS after Mrs Kelly was sentenced, Detective Ward received information that Dan Kelly was on the Fifteen Mile Creek, working with a man there and that Ned Kelly was 'going about armed', though the informer thought it was just with the low-powered pocket revolver that wounded Fitzpatrick.[69]

Six days later, Sadleir reported that Kennedy and three other officers would leave Mansfield on 25 October, 'commencing the search for offenders Kelly from the Wombat end'.[70] While Kennedy's men were to travel north, another party would start from Greta and head south with Senior Constables Strahan and Edward Shoebridge[71] and Constables Hugh Thom[72] and Cornelius Ryan.[73] The plan was to trap the Kellys somewhere in the middle. Sergeant Steele was supposed to lead the Greta force but was subpoenaed to appear before the Equity Court. Due to a clerical error, the police records also included the name of an additional man in the party, Constable Baird, who did not ride with them.

Kelly's spies incorrectly told him that there would be 13 police in three parties, led respectively by Kennedy, Strahan and Steele.[74] Constable Strahan, they said, had been boasting that he would not ask Kelly to stand; that he would shoot him first 'like a dog'.[75] Strahan's boasts were later cited by other police as a chief cause of the 'mischief' that followed.[76] Ned also heard that around Violet Town Lonigan had 'blowed [that] if Ned Kelly was to be shot he was the man that would shoot him'.[77]

The Kellys had turned an old mining hut at their mountain hideaway into a fortress, made of logs 'fully two-feet-thick in diameter'[78] and 'quite bullet proof'.[79] The door was reinforced with a sheet of iron, cut a quarter of an inch (half a centimetre) thick from a ship's water tank. The Kellys' cousin Tom Lloyd provided them with regular supplies. All round the hut, for a radius of about 90 metres, the white gums and peppermint trees were chopped down and heaped into piles, giving the occupants a clear shot at unwelcome strangers. Strewn around the ground were seven or eight cattle carcasses with bullet holes in the centre of their heads, along with gunpowder flasks and boxes of percussion caps to fire the bullets. In every direction there were trees marked by bullets fired into them at ranges varying from 20 to 400 metres.[80] The lead bullets were gouged out and melted down to be used again for more target practice. On one small tree a circle of charcoal 15 centimetres in diameter had been traced, and into this revolver bullets had been fired, one striking the black dot meant to represent the bullseye. Much of the shooting was done with the pocket Colt that Kelly fired into Fitzpatrick, though he carefully weighed the powder to make sure these bullets had more force. Kelly also had an ancient muzzle-loading Enfield that fired a heavy .577 calibre bullet, though the gun looked more likely to blow up in his face. He most likely had it since his days riding with Harry Power and it appeared more like a long pistol than a rifle, the butt having been sawn down to just 13 centimetres, and the barrel – held in place at an angle with string and wax – chopped in half to about 36 centimetres. Kelly reckoned it could 'shoot round the corner' and said he was prepared 'to back it against any firearm in the country'. He claimed he could hit a kangaroo with every shot at 100 yards.[81]

A canopy of trees muffled the noise of gunshots and it was easy for the Kellys to conceal themselves in country that consisted of deep gullies, long grass and scrub, 'with immense fallen trees and almost perpendicular hills'.[82]

Sergeant Kennedy had told Superintendent Sadleir that he, together with Michael Scanlan and Constable Thomas McIntyre[83] – all Irishmen – 'would be quite sufficient to undertake the working of that country' in pursuit of the Kellys without any more assistance.[84] Sadleir, though, was worried that none of the three could definitely recognise Kelly, so he selected another Irishman, Thomas Lonigan, to accompany them. Lonigan knew Ned well – intimately, in fact; and as Ned Kelly blasted away in target practice near Stringybark Creek, he still felt the acute pain from the time Lonigan had him by the balls.

Chapter 4

SERGEANT MICHAEL KENNEDY was understandably worried about going into dense bushland to hunt the dangerous Kelly brothers. Leading a search party through a dark forest for a lost child was one thing, tackling armed men who had been in jail and had no intention of going back was another.

Victorian police were seriously underpaid and underequipped.

The colony had seen ten different governments in the previous ten years and the latest premier, English-born Graham Berry,[1] had a plan to destroy the power of the wealthy landowners in the colony's Upper House.

As a result the house had refused to grant Berry supply to run the government, and he responded on 'Black Wednesday', 8 January 1878, with a cost-cutting campaign to sack County Court judges and police magistrates. John Sadleir said the police force was only spared because of a sex scandal involving 'a high officer of the State' who 'was found late at night under ambiguous circumstances on the private premises of a gentleman'.[2]

Kennedy knew that his team of four Irish-born policemen – armed only with Webley revolvers that were not effective at long range – would be severely underpowered against men with rifles, even though he thought he only had Ned and Dan to deal with, and that they would probably mount 'no more than a show of resistance'.[3]

So it was that on Thursday, 24 October 1878, when a gold escort carrying £20,000 worth of the precious metal from Wood's Point[4] arrived at Mansfield on its way to Benalla, Kennedy saw his opportunity to boost his firepower.

Senior Constable John Kelly[5] – a County Limerick Irishman and no relation to Ned and Dan – was based at Wood's Point and he rode the coach as head of security. As a senior constable he earned sixpence a day more[6] than his offsider, Constable Horwood, who was equipped with an American-made Spencer repeating rifle, used by the Union Army in the American Civil War. It was a mini-cannon firing a fat bullet that, in .52 calibre, was a little thicker than a centimetre in diameter. In the right hands, the Spencer could fire seven bullets in seven seconds, but the lever action and cocking system were complicated. Kennedy and Scanlan knew how to use the rifle from their days riding on gold escorts,[7] though McIntyre said in the 16 months that he had known his sergeant, he could not recall him ever firing a shot.[8]

John Kelly had been in the force 16 years and was not keen on giving Kennedy a weapon he regarded as vital for the perilous gold run. The 41-year-old told the sergeant, 'It's the only rifle between us, and it would be bloody dangerous on these roads without it.' Kennedy had a persuasive personality, though, and before long Kelly said, 'Well, go get a second revolver and give it to Horwood and you can have the rifle.'[9]

Kennedy managed to round up another weapon, too: a double-barrel, breech-loading shotgun that he borrowed from the Reverend Samuel Sandiford,[10] Mansfield's Anglican clergyman.

Sadleir insisted that Kennedy leave his striking white horse behind, because it was far too conspicuous for officers travelling in plain clothes. He arranged for Kennedy to bring a saddle to Benalla with him on a coach and to then ride back on 'another quiet, handy horse'.[11]

Kennedy suspected that Ned Kelly would be a tough opponent, and he kept a prison photograph of him on the mantelpiece of the police barracks room, the dark eyebrows framing the frightening

Senior-Constable John Kelly loaned Michael Kennedy his Spencer repeating rifle in case there was trouble with the Kelly brothers. State Library of Victoria, IAN17/07/80/121

stare. The sergeant told every officer, 'I don't like the look of that fellow.'[12] He put the haunting photograph into his pocket for the trek into the mountains.

Kennedy and his men prepared to move off on Friday, 25 October, with the plan to meet the police unit from Greta at Hedi Station on the King River. The night had been frosty and that morning, with the sun still not risen, Kennedy gathered his wife and their five children around him inside their house next to the police station. He kissed each of the children goodbye – Mary, Roseanna, Kate, Laurence and baby James. He embraced his wife of ten years. Bridget still hadn't recovered emotionally from the death of their son John Thomas a year earlier. The Kelly brothers had declared they would not be taken alive, and Bridget, pregnant again, despaired at the prospect of losing her husband. Being a country policeman meant long hours for low pay and constant danger. But someone had to do it.

Outside the house, Constables Lonigan, Scanlan and McIntyre waited in the dark with their horses. Scanlan had come all the way from Mooroopna, 110 kilometres away, fearing it could be his last mission. Before leaving home and his beloved retriever two days earlier, Scanlan had told his mate Joe, a wardsman at Mooroopna Hospital, 'Look after my dog in case I don't come back.'[13]

McIntyre, from County Down, had worked alongside Kennedy in Mansfield for the last few months. Like his father, the 32-year-old had served in the Irish Constabulary back home and he had a spotless record since joining the Victorian police in 1869, following a stint as a schoolteacher in New South Wales. McIntyre believed Ned and Dan Kelly were criminals because of their 'hereditary and environment' and said that the fact Ned had been so successful as a horse thief for so long indicated that, far from persecuting him as the Kellys had claimed, the Victorian police had given the young law-breaker too much leeway for too long. In McIntyre's mind, Kelly only had himself to blame for his mother's imprisonment.[14]

Lonigan had said goodbye to his pregnant wife, Maria,[15] and their four children at Violet Town the previous day.[16] He had married Maria back in his native County Mayo, but he had made a life for his family in the Australian bush and a share of the £100 reward money for arresting the Kellys[17] would be more than welcome in his struggling household. Taciturn,[18] with a propensity for violence and a face that only a family could love, Lonigan had a soft underbelly. After he farewelled his small children the previous day they had started to weep. He was so affected by their tears that after riding for a couple of miles the renowned walloper wheeled his horse around and galloped home as quickly as he could to kiss his wife and children one last time.[19]

Lonigan did not tell Maria or the children, but he had always been worried about Ned Kelly. He told friends that he was afraid he wouldn't come back from the mountains alive, but that he was 'resolved to go' wherever he was ordered.[20]

Kennedy and his team, all well-built and bearded, left Mansfield at daylight[21] dressed as gold prospectors. They were all on horseback and leading a packhorse that carried supplies for eight days and a white tent 3 metres by 2.4 borrowed from Scottish-born Mansfield contractor Archibald McKenzie.[22] They had the Spencer with 21 rounds of ammunition, the vicar's shotgun with 36 cartridges and their four Webley revolvers, with each man carrying 18 rounds of the fat .442 slugs.[23] Years later it would be claimed that the policemen carried special straps to tether the bodies of Ned and Dan to horses, and that Kennedy, a diligent, empathetic family man and pillar of his community, had led some sort of government-sanctioned execution squad,[24] yet no one ever mentioned body straps at the time, nor did Ned Kelly ever raise the issue in his defence.

The spring morning air was bracing,[25] and McIntyre felt that it was 'good to be alive'[26] as they pressed on 40 kilometres north, up through the Wombat Ranges. Along the way McIntyre and Lonigan saw a deadly tiger snake sunning itself on a rock and they raced to kill it. McIntyre broke its back with a stick and with a nervous laugh remarked, 'first blood Lonigan'. At about 2 p.m. the four arrived at Stringybark Creek and pitched their tent in the north-east section of a patch of clear ground about an acre (4000 square metres) in size, near a burned-out hut. The surrounding area had been denuded of trees by gold miners before they abandoned the region. The site was about 70 metres from the narrow creek, which in dry weather was more like a shallow ditch. All around the camp, in soft, swampy soil, were thick rushes.

McIntyre was given the job of camp cook. Kennedy tossed him the Spencer rifle and asked him to shoot a kangaroo for dinner. McIntyre had carried a Spencer many times guarding gold escorts but had never fired one, and since the kangaroos appeared to be hiding he missed out again.[27]

Ned Kelly quickly learned that the police horses hobbled in the yard at Mansfield Station were now gone. One of Kelly's friends, Henry Perkins, was rumoured to have acted as a double agent, telling Kennedy about the gang's hideout[28] and then telling Kelly that the police were on their way.

The day the police reached Stringybark Creek, Kelly came upon their tracks between Toombullup and 'the bogs'.[29] Later that evening, between Emu Swamp and Bullock Creek, he saw another set of tracks only about a mile away from his own hut and shooting range. Kelly rode on to tell Dan, Byrne and Hart of the danger on their doorstep. The four spent a sleepless night, afraid to light a fire.

It was just as uncomfortable for Kennedy and his nervous men in their tent, lying upon an oilcloth over the cold, lumpy ground. McIntyre frequently rose during the night to warm himself by the fire, and at first light boiled a billy for tea and then rounded up the police horses after his mare broke her hobbles.[30]

By this stage Ned and Dan Kelly had crept from their camp to hide in the undergrowth and watch the police movements, the grey mist rising above the mottled grey-green of the mountain foliage, the smell of eucalypts in the air.

Ned and Dan then retreated to the Bullock Creek hut and told the others that the police carried long firearms. Ned said his doom was sealed if they could not overcome those lawmen before another police detail arrived.

'If they came on us at our camp,' Kelly wrote later, 'they would shoot us down like dogs at our work as we had only two guns.'[31]

McIntyre would later claim that Kelly was lying, and that all four of the young men were armed.

STANHOPE O'CONNOR HAD a dangerous job leading his contingent of Aboriginal troopers west of Cooktown. It paid well – £180 in wages, £25 a year in a travelling allowance and an annual ration allowance of £100, with free quarters and servant or orderly at his command.[32] Yet O'Connor managed to rack up huge debts and was declared bankrupt,[33] though he soldiered on, an adventurer at heart, waiting for his next big opportunity.

Two years into his posting O'Connor had gone on a five-week patrol with six troopers into the Coen country about 160 kilometres north of his barracks. He said that after some 'considerable trouble and danger' he managed to make peace with 'several large mobs of blacks', hunting and fishing with them by day and at night 'feeding, playing, and dancing'. They told him that a white man 'always shot at a blackfellow when he had a chance'.

'We left them grieving much at our departure and promising that they would never harm a white man,' O'Connor wrote.[34] At least that was his story.

One Brisbane newspaper writer claimed that, after a number of animals were speared around Cooktown, O'Connor, and his 'native troopers ... went in pursuit, the result being, I imagine,' the journalist thought, 'far more satisfactory to the European portion of our population than it was to the original holders of the soil'.[35]

AFTER A BREAKFAST OF salted meat and bread on Saturday, 26 October, Sergeant Michael Kennedy decided that he and Scanlan would scout out the surrounding area while McIntyre put ferns and long grass into their tent to make it more comfortable.

McIntyre baked some soda bread while Lonigan tended to the horses and read a pamphlet of *Argus* articles called 'The Vagabond Papers' in which Harry Power was interviewed and described the teenage Kelly as a coward and a traitor who had betrayed him. At Bullock Creek, Kelly and his men dressed in the colours of the Greta Mob, with red sashes around their waist. They put the chin straps of their low, flat hats under their noses.

At about noon, McIntyre was still busy baking his bread when Lonigan, lying down and reading about the young and unpredictable Ned Kelly, called out that he heard a strange noise down the creek. McIntyre hadn't heard anything but, suspecting it might be a kangaroo or wombat for his cooking pot, grabbed the vicar's shotgun and went to investigate.

He found magnificent lorikeets, rosellas and sulphur–crested cockatoos and shot two birds for dinner.

At 5 p.m., with the sun starting to sink, McIntyre began to build a large bonfire at the intersection of two fallen logs. He wanted to guide Kennedy and Scanlan home in case they were out after dark in the forest. McIntyre asked Lonigan to give him a hand carting wood.

From a thicket of tall speargrass, four sets of fierce eyes watched their every move.[36] Ned Kelly would later claim that he thought he was watching the policemen Flood and Strahan but there was nothing wrong with his eyesight or trigger finger, as subsequent events demonstrated. He cradled the old sawn-off .577 carbine.

Suddenly McIntyre picked up a shotgun and there was a rustle in the speargrass as the four observers ducked their heads.[37] McIntyre didn't notice. He wandered off to bring in a horse and then hobbled it near the tent.

'We could have shot those men without speaking,' Kelly claimed later, 'but not wishing to take life, we waited.' McIntyre laid the gun against the stump and Lonigan sat on the log.[38] He had been strangely silent, troubled and lost in thought all day, and he gazed intently into the fire.[39] McIntyre was boiling the billy, with his face to the blaze and his back to the speargrass, when he heard four voices crying out: 'Bail up, hold up your hands!' At first, he thought it was Kennedy and Scanlan playing a trick, but as he turned, he saw four young men all advancing in a line from the thick grass, a few yards apart. They all had guns.

McIntyre immediately recognised the biggest one on the right as Kelly from the photo Kennedy had, and he threw his arms out horizontally. Lonigan, though, made a run for cover behind a log and reached for the clasp on his holster.

He had taken only a few steps when Ned and his mates unloaded. Lonigan exclaimed, 'Christ I am shot,' and then Ned pumped a .577 slug bullet down the wonky barrel of his old carbine and straight through Lonigan's right eyeball. Lonigan fell flat, his legs and arms extended, his head thrown back and his chest heaving.

McIntyre was so stunned he dropped his hands, and Kelly charged at him. Kelly tossed the carbine into his left hand, then reached behind his back, pulled out a revolver with his right and roared: 'Keep your hands up. Keep them up.'[40]

McIntyre did as he was told.

All the time Lonigan was struggling on the grass, 'plunging on the ground very heavily' but after thirty seconds or so he ceased to breathe.[41]

McIntyre shut his eyes and said softly, 'Oh God, my time has come.'[42] Standing there in his shirtsleeves and a black oilskin cap,[43] he trembled as Kelly and the others pointed their weapons at his chest.

McIntyre's recall of what happened in those chaotic, mad moments would be shaken by his trauma, but it would remain consistent over time.

Dan, the youngest of the gang at just 17, was nervously excited by the whole business and was giggling, almost hysterically.[44] McIntyre thought there was something 'grotesque' about the youngster's appearance; that he was a strange, sinister character, used to wearing hand-me-downs from his brother that were always too big for him, and developing a huge chip on his shoulder.[45] Kelly told McIntyre to lift his hands high above his head and then he frisked him, patting him all over the body and checking his boots to make sure he wasn't hiding a small revolver. Then he jumped over the log to Lonigan's corpse and took his Webley. 'Dear, oh, dear! What made that bugger run?' Ned had just realised the enormity of his crime and his downcast expression made McIntyre think that 'he may not have contemplated murder in the first instance, relying on taking us separately and unprepared'. Firearms in the hands of desperate young hot heads rarely ended well, though, and this killing made Kelly and his companions murderers. McIntyre now feared there would be a massacre to cover up the crime.

When Kelly realised it was Lonigan he had shot he told McIntyre he was glad because 'that bugger gave me a hiding once in Benalla'. He still felt no remorse weeks later, writing, 'I did not begrudge [Lonigan] what bit of lead he got as he was the flashest and meanest man that I had any account against.'[46]

Dan Kelly produced a pair of handcuffs from the police tent and prepared to slap them on McIntyre, but the policeman appealed to Ned, who relented while tapping the butt of his rifle and remarking that his gun was the only set of handcuffs he needed.

Dan accepted the order from his big brother 'very sullenly' and with gutter language. He gave McIntyre such a hateful look that the policeman knew who his executioner would be if it came to that.[47]

McIntyre tried not to look at Lonigan's lifeless, bloodied face lying nearby, but he couldn't help glancing at his comrade as the sun began to set behind the trees all around them.

Kelly and his men feasted on the policemen's ham and McIntyre's freshly baked bread. They made McIntyre drink the policemen's tea first, though, in case it was poisoned.

As night approached, Kelly armed himself with two rifles and a revolver and told his men to take their places as he hid behind a log. Hart remained in the policemen's tent, and Byrne and Dan Kelly secreted themselves in speargrass about 1.5 metres high. Kelly told McIntyre to stand near him and he asked him about the other police on their way back.

McIntyre said Kennedy was a good man with a large family and that Scanlan was good-natured and inoffensive. Kelly said he would not kill them if they surrendered and that he could already have shot McIntyre if he had wanted to. He would have no qualms, he said, about shooting and roasting Fitzpatrick, Flood, Strahan or Steele.

Kelly asked him how Kennedy and Scanlan were armed. 'Very meagrely.'

'What do you mean? Have they got revolvers?'

'Yes.'

'Have they got a rifle?'

McIntyre hesitated.

'Tell the truth, you bugger,' Kelly snarled, 'or I swear I will put a hole through you.'

'Yes, they have a rifle.'

'A breech-loader?'[48]

'Yes.'

'You did come to shoot me! I think you planned to riddle me with bullets?'

'No, to arrest you. We are not sent out to shoot people, we are just sent out to do a certain duty.'

'You know I am no coward. Those people lagged at Beechworth the other day [Ellen, Skilling and Brickey] had no more revolvers in their hands than you have at present. In fact, they were not there at all – these are the men.' Ned nodded towards his mates.

McIntyre didn't believe Ned for a minute but he was not about to argue – not with Lonigan lying dead only a few yards away.

'You cannot blame us for what Fitzpatrick has done to you,' McIntyre said.

'No, but I swore after letting him go that I would never let another go, and if I let you go now you will have to leave the police force.'

McIntyre would say anything to save his skin.

'I will. I will leave the police force. My health has been bad anyway, and I have been thinking of going home for some time.'

'Good, see that you do,' Ned snarled.

'If I got these other two men to surrender, what will you do with us?'

'Well, you had better get them to surrender, because if they don't surrender, or they get away, we will shoot you. But we don't want their lives; we only want their horses and firearms.'

Ned had his revolver in his waistband and two rifles resting against the log. McIntyre eyed them, thinking to himself that if Kennedy and Scanlan showed up he might be able to take advantage of the surprise and take one of the rifles with 'a sudden spring'.

Hart was watching McIntyre from the tent, though, and sensed his thinking.

'Ned, look out,' he cried, 'or that bugger will be on top of you.'

Kelly seemed unconcerned. 'If you try anything,' he said, 'you will soon find your match, for you know there are not three men in the police force a match for me.'

McIntyre believed that Kelly for all his big talk was a 'lazy blackguard' who would rather steal than put his muscularity to work for good wages.[49]

But he kept his opinion to himself.

'How many of you bastards are out here looking for us?'

'There was another party to leave Greta.'

'With who?'

'I don't know, but they were under the command of Sergeant Steele.'

Suddenly, Kelly heard horses approaching from the north.

Sergeant Kennedy's gold watch told him it was approaching 6 p.m. as he and Scanlan made their way through the dense forest back towards what they expected would be McIntyre's warm supper.

Kelly whispered to McIntyre to sit on the log and do exactly as he said – *exactly* – or he would be killed.

Kennedy was about 45 metres away, riding towards the camp on the 'quiet, handy horse' Superintendent Sadleir had given him, with Scanlan 10 metres behind.

When Kennedy was within 6 metres of McIntyre, the constable stammered: 'Ssss ser-ser-ser-geant, you had better surrender; you are surrounded.'

Then Kelly bellowed out: 'Bail up.'

Kennedy thought it was McIntyre and Lonigan playing a gag, and as Scanlan started to dismount, the Spencer rifle strapped over his shoulder, Kennedy playfully moved his hand towards the revolver in his side holster.

But a shudder roared through him as Kelly fired a warning shot over the sergeant's head and his three accomplices roared: 'Bail up, throw up your hands.'

Scanlan, about 25 metres from Kelly, tried to unsling the Spencer, but the shooting frightened his horse and it reared. Three or four shots were fired at the same time. Scanlan was hit under the right arm and fell off his horse and landed on his knees. He struggled up but fell again as blood stained his coat.

Kennedy ducked down, using his horse's neck as a shield, and rolled off, getting a shot from his Webley that winged Dan in the shoulder.

But the sergeant dropped his revolver in the commotion. His riderless horse reared with the noise of gunfire and McIntyre, suspecting Kennedy had been killed,[50] leapt onto the mare's back, held on for dear life and, without his spurs,[51] booted her flanks into a gallop. Shots rang out behind him as Dan Kelly cried, 'Shoot the bugger, shoot the bugger.'[52]

Kennedy fumbled to regain his revolver and started firing back. He ducked behind trees, trying to escape in the direction of Kelly's fortress on Bullock Creek. Ned grabbed the Spencer from Scanlan's now-lifeless hand, but he didn't know how to work the lever action and tossed it aside to hunt Kennedy with the vicar's shotgun. Kennedy broke open his Webley and reloaded it with six more bullets, but his pursuers were close behind and they had rifles with much greater range.

Kelly would later tell Henry Perkins about the killings and Perkins relayed the information to the editor of the *Mansfield Guardian*, George Wilson Hall.[53]

According to Kelly, Kennedy kept firing while his four attackers sheltered behind trees. He took cool and deliberate aim as he fired five more shots. One of his bullets passed through Kelly's whiskers, and another through his sleeve. Then Kennedy started running again with the Kelly brothers on his heels.

Kennedy ran for about half a mile. He then hid behind a tree and fired the sixth and final bullet in the Webley. As Kelly saw him levelling the revolver at his head, he dropped to his knees just as the bullet whizzed over him,[54] and he then shot Kennedy in his right side.[55] The sergeant fell, wounded and helpless, at the foot of the tree.

Kelly said that they interrogated the dying man for two hours about how many other police were coming for them, how they were armed, and whether Kennedy had come to kill him.

All Kennedy wanted to talk about was Bridget and his children. He told Kelly that he had five little ones and that Bridget would soon be having another baby.

Kelly told Dan to get some water from the creek for Kennedy's parched lips and he later said that Kennedy, knowing he was dying, scratched some lines of affection for his wife on three slips of paper he had in his pocket. He asked Kelly to give the letter to Bridget, but Kelly never did.[56]

Kelly knew that McIntyre would likely soon sound an alarm and that out here Kennedy would soon be at the mercy of ants, flies and dingoes.[57]

No one thought about getting help for Kennedy. Instead, Kelly put the muzzle of the vicar's shotgun to within a few inches of Kennedy's chest.

'Let me alone, for God's sake,' Kennedy mumbled, 'let me live, if I can, for the sake of my poor wife and family; surely you have shed enough blood already.'[58]

As Sergeant Kennedy fretted about how his wife and children would survive without him, Ned Kelly blew a huge hole in his chest.

Chapter 5

STEVE HART AND JOE BYRNE had tried to catch the frantic, desperate Thomas McIntyre, the only eyewitness to the murders, but he escaped on Kennedy's mare into the dense bush. Riding furiously as night fell, McIntyre crashed through trees in the darkness, fearing the killers were still close behind. Branches leapt at him from all angles like fierce enemies until one caught him full force across the chest, and he was thrown from Kennedy's horse 'with great violence', leaving him bloodied and bruised.[1] He suspected that the mare had been wounded, so took off her saddle and bridle, hid them in some long ferns and chased the horse into the scrub, hoping her tracks would confuse the killers.[2]

With his heart racing, McIntyre hid in the hollow of a tree and then in a wombat hole, squeezing in feet-first. He took out his notebook and by the meagre moonlight scrawled:

> Ned Kelly and others stuck us up to-day when we were disarmed. Lonigan and Scanlan shot. I am hiding in a wombat hole till dark. The Lord have mercy on me. Scanlan tried to get his gun out.[3]

He hid the notebook inside his shirt, reasoning that if Kelly or the others shot him, his body would not be searched, and those who eventually found him would discover the truth about the killers.[4] Finally, still under the cover of darkness, McIntyre emerged from the hole and, navigating by the stars on a 'beautiful bright clear night', began a slow trudge towards the Benalla Road, climbing over rocks and logs, getting his boots soaked crossing streams and chafing his feet so badly that he eventually continued his escape in his socks.

At sunrise the next day, 27 October, McIntyre was stopped dead by a noise coming from some long grass. He saw figures rustling through foliage almost as tall as him. Bruised, bloody and exhausted, he feared his pursuers had finally caught him, and tensed his body for their bullets. He almost fainted with joy at seeing it was a mob of kangaroos, poking their heads out of the tall grass.

After a few more hours of painful plodding McIntyre arrived at Ewen Tolmie's Dueran sheep run at about noon, only to spy two horses tethered there that looked like the ones Scanlan and Lonigan had been riding. Fearing that the Kellys may have bailed up the place, McIntyre retreated back into the bush and kept stumbling and staggering for three more hours until, ragged, scratched and hatless, with one boot on his foot and one under his arm, he flopped down at the farm of John McColl, a couple of miles from Mansfield. An elderly neighbour, Matthew Byrne, unaware of his distant cousin Joe's involvement in the murders, had his son hitch up a buggy and take McIntyre straight to the home of his boss, Sub-inspector Pewtress, who was in bed, sick with influenza. As Pewtress's hazel eyes squinted at the startling, bedraggled figure before him, McIntyre could barely get out the words: 'They are all killed, Sir. Everyone shot by the Kellys except myself.'[5]

WHILE BRIDGET KENNEDY had been fretting about how her husband and the other policemen were getting on chasing the wanted men up in the frosty air of the mountains, Ned and Dan Kelly were looting Kennedy's mangled corpse and turning out his pockets. Kelly took the sergeant's prized gold watch as well as a small sum of money and the prison photograph of himself glaring at the camera. He missed a pocketknife, though, that had slipped through a hole in Kennedy's waistcoat pocket and lodged in the lining.[6]

Struck by a pang of remorse, Kelly put Kennedy's cloak over him and said he left the body 'as honourable as I could'.[7] Back at the police camp on Stringybark Creek, Hart and Byrne took £13 from the corpses of Scanlan and Lonigan[8] and Byrne tore the rings off their fingers and put them on his own.[9] They did not worry about covering those corpses, but instead left them in the open with their pockets turned out and at the mercy of the weather and scavenging animals. Then the gang took all the police provisions, rounded up the lawmen's horses and set fire to the police tent.

The four returned to the miner's hut on Bullock Creek, but just as they were about to flee 'in their wild fright',[10] Tom Lloyd arrived with his regular supply of store-bought provisions and about £12 from the sale of gold the Kelly boys had mined. Kelly told Lloyd that he had no choice but to kill the policemen, and justified his actions, saying it was the officers' fault, because after all 'it is only foolishness to disobey an outlaw'.[11]

Tom Lloyd kept watch while the gang had a tortured sleep.[12] Superintendent Sadleir later remarked:

These four young criminals must have had a bad time while they tarried for the night at this hut. It was all very well that they should have prepared its defences against possible attack by the police, and have talked bravely of selling their lives dearly if need be, but it was a different thing altogether now to find themselves actual murderers with the gallows awaiting them. The two Kellys were of a very brutal nature. With their two companions the case was different. We know now that they had not started out that afternoon deliberately to take life, and that the shock of finding themselves involved in so dreadful a crime was very great.[13]

Before dawn, the four young cop-killers saddled up and Ned set fire to the hut. Like everything else at Stringybark Creek,

Ned's plans went horribly wrong, though, and rain extinguished the flames.

The desperate gang then rode through the thick mountain forests towards Greta, accompanied by Tom, and driving the three police horses and their packhorse as well as two spare mounts in the downpour. Kelly told his companions that he would take all the blame for the killings. He had landed the other three in the mess with him, and he knew they would all hang if caught, just as his mother was doing a long lag in jail because of the attention his horse stealing brought to her little house.

SUB-INSPECTOR PEWTRESS was unused to bush work, but the grey-haired, soft-eyed 51-year-old was a policeman from his boot-heels up to the top of his wiry frame. He had been a sergeant in England when recruited in 1852 as part of the 'London Fifty' – a body of British policemen brought to Melbourne to form a Victorian constabulary after so many local officers had deserted for the goldfields.[14]

With McIntyre's startling news, Pewtress forgot that he was ill and clambered out of bed. He made immediate arrangements to recover the bodies of Scanlan and Lonigan, and hopefully find Kennedy still alive. As the news of the killings quickly spread, though, Mansfield was gripped with fear.[15] The townsfolk whipped themselves into 'a high pitch of horror and excitement' and the wildest stories soon circulated that Kelly and his 'cutthroats', now with nothing to lose, were coming out of the bush 'to rob and burn the town'.[16]

There was no difficulty in finding hardy volunteers ready to confront the killers and venture out to the scene of the tragedy. McIntyre had dictated his first report of the killings by 5.40 p.m., but Pewtress couldn't get a telegram through to Benalla 60 kilometres north, so he sent the short and stocky Irishman Constable Thomas Meehan[17] on horseback with the news. Meehan gave McIntyre his revolver, the only gun left at the police station, because McIntyre was terrified that Dan Kelly would hunt him down and burn him alive.[18] A five-year veteran of the force with a thick sandy moustache, Meehan was feeling more than edgy, too. Nervously, he rode about 16 kilometres up the Benalla Road to Barjarg Station but saw 'two suspicious looking men on the road'[19] near the Broken River, and in uniform and without a gun he feared the same fate as Kennedy and the others. He couldn't hide the look of terror on his round, pockmarked face.[20] Saying to himself, 'I must do something; I must use my head as I have no firearms', he elected to confuse the ominous strangers by removing his boots to minimise tracks and chasing his horse away, hoping the strangers would follow it and not him.

Meehan set off through the dense scrub on foot and wandered all night in a cold sweat. By the time he limped into Benalla almost 24 hours later,[21] the telegraph operators had already sent news of the slaughter around Australia.

COMMISSIONER STANDISH took charge as soon as Pewtress's telegram about the atrocities reached Melbourne at about 10 p.m. on Sunday night, 27 October. The commissioner informed Premier Graham Berry and was effectively given a blank cheque to hunt down the killers. Some Spencer repeating rifles that were in store were collected, and reinforcements were readied for dispatch. Assistant Commissioner Charles Hope Nicolson was selected to take charge of the pursuit.[22]

At about midnight, an officer from the Victorian detective branch left its Melbourne headquarters and walked to the nearby Polo Hotel, where Senior Constable John Kelly was sleeping. Three days earlier Kelly had reluctantly handed over his Spencer rifle to Kennedy before heading to Melbourne on a week's leave. The detective banged on Kelly's door and shouted through the wooden barrier, 'Kennedy, Scanlan, and Lonigan are shot.'[23]

The veteran officer sat bolt upright on his bed as he tried to digest the sickening news. He then cancelled his leave and immediately went down to catch a pre-dawn train north that would also carry Standish, Nicolson and some other Kelly hunters including Anthony Strahan and Alf Falkiner.

Victoria had just changed its police uniform, dispensing with a military look that included sashes and black leather cylindrical shako hats to a new design, modelled on that of the British Metropolitan Police, complete with navy blue trousers, capes and leather bobby helmets.

But every officer knew that in Kelly Country a uniform was now a target, so the men dressed as farmers and prospectors.

Over the next few weeks, the Victorian government would approve the purchase of nearly 300 new guns – revolvers, rifles and shotguns – and would transfer 140 men for the hunt, most of them from Irish backgrounds like the Kellys, almost tripling the force in north-eastern Victoria.[24]

SUPERINTENDENT SADLEIR was reviewing the police station at Dookie, 40 kilometres west of Benalla, on the morning of 28 October, when the news of the murders finally reached him. He raced back to Benalla to find Superintendent Nicolson just arrived from Melbourne.

Sadleir leapt on his horse to ride to Mansfield, 60 kilometres away, and each man Sadleir met along the narrow bush road was 'astonished' that he was riding through such dangerous country alone.

The superintendent had spent 44 years in the Victorian police force and faced many grim, heartbreaking days dealing with murders, rapes, robberies, fatal accidents and occasionally corruption within his own ranks. Yet no day was more harrowing than the one when he paced nervously to the front door of Bridget Kennedy's Mansfield home to break bad news.[25]

Only the Kellys knew for sure whether Kennedy was dead or alive, and Sadleir came to Bridget's door to 'offer such condolence' as he could in her 'dread uncertainty'. 'Her grief was piteous to witness,' Sadleir wrote, 'and one dared not venture to buoy her up with the hope of her husband's safety.'[26]

THERE WAS NO TIME FOR Thomas McIntyre to recover from his ordeal. At Mansfield, he vomited as the effects of trauma hit home and, praying that history would not brand him a coward for leaving Kennedy behind,[27] he was soon lifted back into the saddle to lead a search party of a dozen men including Pewtress, Dr Samuel Reynolds, Constable William Moore and new recruits 22-year-old Constable Tom Kirkham[28] and 23-year-old Constable Jim Allwood[29] from Warrnambool. Allwood had only been in the force three months after first serving as an artilleryman working the cannons that guarded the entrance to Melbourne at Queenscliff on Port Phillip. There would have been more in the search party, but the men only had two borrowed rifles between them for a perilous journey to potentially face armed killers on the loose. Kirkham's brother George was a Crimean War hero but Tom liked the theatre and dance as much as adventure, and rather than chasing armed killers he would much rather have been home with his beautiful ballerina wife Ada, a lithe 21-year-old he had married a year earlier in South Melbourne.

McIntyre was so ill that he could only tolerate riding at walking pace as they made their way through terrain that was heavily forested, sparsely settled and cut up by valleys and creeks, with the banks clothed in almost impenetrable scrub.[30] In the dark the men made it to a sawmill owned by a selector named Ted Monk.[31] He and his wife were in bed and were stunned by the news of the murder, as they had known Scanlan well. Without the slightest hesitation or fear of reprisals out in the wilderness, Monk supplied packhorses and led the police through a rainy night to Stringybark Creek, all the way supposing that Ned Kelly and his gang were secretly watching their every move.[32] There was hardly any sound except for the rain on the leaves, an occasional mournful cry of a mopoke or the crashing of a wallaby through the undergrowth.[33] The searchers were afraid to light a large fire in case it drew an attack, but in the cold, wet and dark they used the bare light of matches to find the rotting corpses of Lonigan and Scanlan at about 2 a.m.

Dr Reynolds never forgot the horror of seeing the two dead faces in that ghostly half-light. He ordered that the slain officers be wrapped in hessian. The corpses resembled Egyptian mummies as they were then fastened with stirrup leathers on either side of Monk's packhorse, Tommy.[34] There was no trace of Kennedy, but near the ashes of the tent McIntyre found Kennedy's blood-stained notebook with a few pages missing.[35]

Three days after they set out on their dangerous mission, Lonigan and Scanlan finally came home to Mansfield on Monday, 28 October, passing Bridget Kennedy's home before their bodies were placed in the morgue at 1 p.m.[36] Tom Kirkham would face his own personal horror in a few weeks.

WHILE THE POLICE WERE bringing back their dead, Ned Kelly and his men were making their escape. With Tom Lloyd riding ahead to make sure the coast was clear, they covered 50 kilometres in heavy rain[37] until they reached Greta, where Kelly's kin supplied them with hot breakfasts and a change of clothes. They called in at the Lloyds, and the Lloyds' in-laws, the Tanners – 'members of the criminal class' according to Assistant Commissioner Nicolson, but 'too cunning to place themselves within reach of the law'.[38]

Tom Lloyd stayed in Greta, but the four mounted killers and their six spare horses reached the Pioneer Bridge on the swollen Ovens River near Everton at about 3 a.m. on Monday,[39] not long after the bodies of Lonigan and Scanlan were found. Joe Byrne woke up the manager of the Pioneer Hotel to buy a bottle of brandy to treat the bullet wound in Dan Kelly's shoulder, while the others waited anxiously outside.[40] They had decided they wouldn't rob ordinary folk but would pay for their provisions, even if their cash had been stolen from the bodies of the dead policemen. Soon newspapers would hint that Ned Kelly intended to rob banks at Milawa and Oxley, not far from Greta, to provide for his sisters after his death, 'which he knows is not far off'.[41]

The distinctive horseshoes of the police mounts left tell-tale tracks in the mud as the gang rode on through the rain, crossing the first of nine bridges that spanned the Ovens and its swollen channels. The current of the floodwaters was strong enough to knock horses off their feet.[42]

To reach Everton they had to make a round trip of 25 kilometres to cross at Taylor's Gap, where they were spotted in the distance[43] by Constable Hugh Bracken,[44] a 38-year-old Irishman. Bracken had joined the Victorian police not long after arriving in Australia on the *Champion of Seas* in 1861. He raised the alarm by telegram but, by the time 14 officers under Sergeant Steele arrived to investigate days later, the gang were long gone.

The four horsemen finally arrived at Everton at 6 a.m. and they bought tins of sardines and oats from the general store of a Geordie named Edward Coulson.[45] He later told police that they crossed the railway bridge and rode off towards Eldorado. Police suspected the Kellys were heading to see the Byrne family,[46] unaware that Joe was riding with them. In fact, the four made for Sheepstation Creek, near Beechworth, and a morning rendezvous with Byrne's mate Aaron Sherritt. Ned and his gang slept in a remote cave while Sherritt stood guard.

THE DAY AFTER THE BODIES of Scanlan and Lonigan were returned to Mansfield, loudmouth Wild Wright and his mute brother, Robert, 'the Dummy' rode into town. Wright began telling everyone that Ned Kelly was a better man than all of them put together. He said he was riding out to join him. He warned one or two people to stay in the township unless they wanted to get shot as well. He said he believed Kennedy was still alive but that Kelly would torture him, and he was only sorry for Scanlan.[47]

The Wrights were accosting townsfolk in the streets on Tuesday as Pewtress organised another search party to find Kennedy. The sub-inspector ordered McIntyre to arrest 'Wild'. After the horrors he had just experienced, McIntyre was in no mood for a physical altercation with a powerful and belligerent knucklehead. He drew his revolver, stuck it in the wild man's face and told him through gritted teeth, 'I have come to arrest you, Wright. I have seen my mates shot and if you don't walk quietly over to the lock-up I will shoot you.' Wild turned pale and became meek as a lamb. Without saying a word, he held out his hands, palms together, to be handcuffed. But when they were walking across the street Wild muttered: 'McIntyre, when I heard one of the police had escaped, I was glad it was you, I'm damn sorry for it now. You have escaped once, you won't next time.'[48] McIntyre resisted the temptation to blow his brains out.

The newspapers had a field day over Meehan's caution on his ride to Benalla, saying he had stood 'in tremulous terror in a swamp in stockinged feet'.[49] Pewtress later took the humiliated constable aside and told him quietly: 'Meehan, I will never forget you as long as you are in my district for making such a fool of yourself as you did that night when you went out.'[50] Sadleir was more blunt, telling the shamefaced constable it might have been better for him in the long run had he been shot, though Meehan later remarked that 'of course I differed with him in that'.[51]

DR REYNOLDS WAS ONE of those rare men with no sense of taste or of smell[52] and that handicap was actually a blessing when dealing with the decaying corpses of Lonigan and Scanlan as he began the autopsies at 10 a.m. on Tuesday, 29 October. He noted that Lonigan was about 5 feet 9 inches (175 centimetres) and powerfully built. He found four wounds: 'one through the left arm, one on the left thigh, one on the right temple, and one on the inner side of the right eyeball'. 'The one on the thigh travelled round the thigh under the skin, and I extracted [the bullet],' he wrote. 'The wound on the temple I might describe as a graze. I did not find the bullet which caused the wound through the eyeball; it entered the eyeball and must have caused death in a few seconds.'[53]

Reynolds's findings made a lie of the gang's subsequent claims that Lonigan had drawn his pistol and was aiming at Ned Kelly when the bushranger fired the shot through his head to defend himself. The bullet had entered on an oblique angle, suggesting Lonigan was actually trying to duck for cover when he was killed.

Dr Reynolds then found wounds on Scanlan's right hip, the top edge of the sternum, the right shoulder and the right side.[54]

With decomposition having already set in, the funerals were hastily arranged. Maria Lonigan arrived from Violet Town in great distress, with newspapers reporting that 'the family have been left almost helpless'.[55] Her four young children were said to be 'very badly off'.[56]

Michael Scanlan had no family in Australia and no one to collect his things. Another Irishman, Father John Lawrence Scanlon[57] from Benalla, performed the funeral services. He was asked whether he was related to the dead policeman and said no, but that given the young man's courage he would have been proud to call him a kinsman.[58]

Bridget Kennedy and her five children continued to finger their rosary beads and pray for Michael's safe return, hoping that he had somehow escaped and was now making his way home through the bush. There was also speculation in the press that the Kellys had gone to the King River 'and taken Kennedy with them' as a hostage.[59]

Eleven volunteers and six constables started out on another search on the same day as the autopsies. They searched until dark without success and returned to Mansfield at midnight. Another search party with 16 volunteers and five constables then left for Monk's hut on the afternoon of Wednesday, 30 October. They stopped there for the night. Then at 8 a.m. the next day, Henry Sparrow, an overseer from the Mount Battery Station, found what was left of the sergeant in the midst of some ferns.

Sparrow slowly lifted the cloak from the body and the rotting remnants made him recoil. Four and a half days out in warm weather and heavy rain had taken a terrible toll. Half of Kennedy's face was missing.[60] One of his ears has been hacked away, though Dr Reynolds later said the damage was probably done by a quoll. There was a huge hole in his chest, the obvious result of a gun blast at close range.

Aaron Sherritt and others told police that Dan Kelly, a man Sadleir described as a 'ferocious little savage', had actually fired the fatal blow;[61] that Dan had wanted to kill Kennedy straight away, and several times the sergeant had pushed aside Dan's gun as its muzzle was laid against his chest. Although the autopsy findings didn't support Sadleir's theory, he believed that Ned Kelly 'insisted

Police recreate the discovery of Kennedy's body at Stringybark Creek. Ned Kelly had covered it with the sergeant's cloak. State Library of Victoria, H2634

on each of his companions discharging their weapons into the dead bodies ... thus fully implicating' all of them.[62]

Sadleir was now faced with breaking the news to Bridget of her husband's death. The Kellys may not have set out to commit cold-blooded murder, but the marriage of firearms and hot heads rarely ended well. They had killed three good policemen and left their families and friends devastated.

Bridget Kennedy and Maria Lonigan soon suffered miscarriages.

Chapter 6

O N THE DAY THAT searchers found what was left of Michael Kennedy, Sergeant James Lynch reported that Ned Kelly and his companions had been sighted on the Victorian side of the Murray between Howlong and Albury.

With Aaron Sherritt scouting ahead, the four desperate young men had left the Sherritt house at Sheepstation Creek, their every move spotlighted by flashes of lightning that lit up the leaden sky.

Riding through the storm, driving the six spare horses ahead of them, the Kelly Gang waded through the flooded channels and drenched plains, and then tried to swim their animals across the mighty Murray, which was now roaring at full blast.

A farmer named George Munger told police he was detained by four armed men and robbed of provisions on the banks of a lagoon on the Victorian side of the river.[1] He claimed they kept him prisoner for three hours.

Another farmer named Gideon Margery[2] told Detective Douglas Kennedy that he saw four men on the flat, 'one of them winged' – or wounded. Margery gave them some bread, cheese and two bottles of wine and they lit a fire in a hollowed-out log while the rain cleared. Margery refused to tell the police any more except that the men were carrying guns that looked like police weapons[3] and that 'one of them had a face like a Chinaman'.[4] The biggest of the bunch told him he was 'Kelly the bushranger' and that he 'intended calling on a man named Whitty, at Moyhu, about some horse-stealing case'.[5] Police suspected that this was a red herring to throw them off Kelly's tail. Two of Margery's sons said a wounded man lay on the grass the whole time the party stayed talking to their father.[6]

At Bungowannah, on the New South Wales side of the Murray, the four were said to have bailed up a man named Neil Christian,[7] taking provisions from him before daylight near the home of Gustav and William Baumgarten, who had been jailed for their role in Kelly's horse-stealing caper.

Kelly threatened to shoot Christian if he gave the police any information but Christian told the lawmen one of the robbers was wounded and could not sit upright.

On the same day, Parliament in Melbourne quickly passed the *Felons Apprehension Act*,[8] reintroducing the rarely used provision of outlawry that had been used to bring down Ben Hall in New South Wales 13 years earlier.

Ned and Dan and the two still 'unknown persons' riding with them were given until 12 November to surrender at the Mansfield Courthouse. If they didn't walk in with their hands up, it would become lawful for anyone to shoot them dead.[9]

Victoria's Premier Graham Berry announced an £800 reward for information leading to the arrest of the four offenders[10] and McIntyre's description of them was sent by telegram around the colony and to New South Wales:

1st. Edward Kelly, 23 years of age, looks older, sallow complexion, dark-brown hair, full beard and moustache of a dirty dark red colour, moustache cut square across the mouth, hazel eyes with a greenish tint; wore dark tweed clothes, red silk sash, dark low hat.
2nd. Daniel Kelly, 17 years of age, looks older, 5 feet 5 or 6 inches [165 or 168 centimetres] high, very dark hair and complexion, small dark piercing eyes. Beard not grown.
3rd. Name unknown [Joe Byrne], 21 years of age, 5 feet 9 inches [175 centimetres] high, very fair complexion, fair

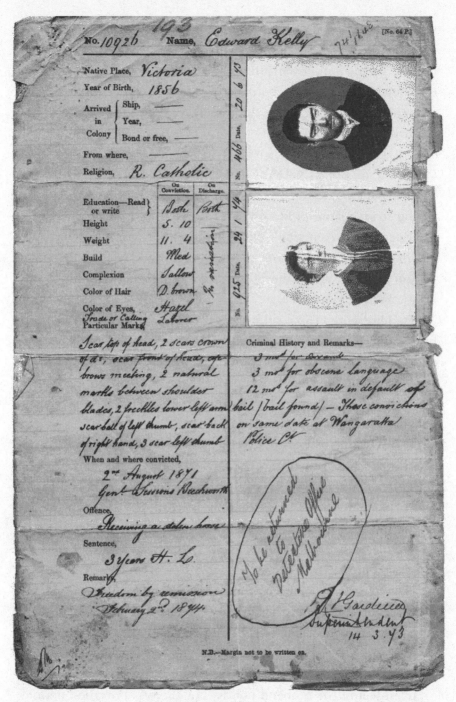

Ned Kelly's prison record including a confronting photograph of him were circulated around Victoria and New South Wales following the killing of three policemen. By the time he was outlawed Kelly was much taller and heavier than the information collated when he 16. His birth year is also mis-reported as 1856, instead of 1854.

Public Record Office of Victoria

moustache and long beard on chin, very fine, like first growth, respectable-looking.

4th. Name unknown [Steve Hart], 19 or 20 years of age, 5 feet 8 inches [173 centimetres] high, fairish complexion, rather stout, straggling hairs over face, slightly hooked nose, sinister expression.[11]

IT HAD BEEN SIX DAYS since Michael Kennedy had kissed his pregnant wife and five children and ridden off to a cruel death trying to arrest the most notorious horse thief in Victoria. On 31 October 1878, Kennedy's eldest child, nine-year-old Mary, was out in the street at the front of her home beside Mansfield's police station waiting with some of her siblings and their friends for any news about her dad.

Two horsemen came riding towards her ahead of a cart. On the back of it, Kennedy's mutilated body was covered with blankets and gum-tree boughs as camouflage. Before the children could see what the policemen were towing, one of them jumped off his horse and told the youngsters to run inside. Kennedy's boots were sticking out from underneath a blanket.[12]

Mary Kennedy ran to tell Bridget as the morbid procession continued to the hospital.

Superintendent Sadleir trudged dejectedly towards Bridget's front door. He didn't have to speak a word; the look on his face said it all.

Numb with pain, Bridget asked if she could see her husband one last time.

Having been sickened by the sight of Kennedy's corpse, Sadleir pleaded with her to stay home.

Melbourne's *Herald* newspaper reported:

Great difficulty was experienced in keeping Mrs Kennedy from seeing her husband's body, but she was prevailed upon not to, as it was thought better that she should not do so, as it was in an advanced stage of decomposition, and the sight would have been awful. It was considered advisable to let the bereaved widow simply remember the father of her children as she had been accustomed to see him, and as she saw him depart on his fatal mission last week.[13]

ON THE FOLLOWING MORNING, Friday, 1 November 1878, Dr Reynolds began delving into Kennedy's remains.

His report noted: 'There is a large wound in [the] centre of the sternum which I believe was caused by a charge of shot fired at very close range which passed completely through the body and out at the back. He also received other wounds one being in the right arm and one in the body under the arm.'[14]

A funeral was quickly organised for that afternoon at 2 p.m. Even in a state of trauma Bridget insisted that Michael be buried alongside their little boy John Thomas and near the fresh graves of Lonigan and Scanlan in Mansfield Cemetery. The Anglican Bishop of Melbourne, James Moorhouse,[15] had to talk her out of visiting the morgue for a final goodbye.

In a letter to friends in England, the bishop said that it would have been 'wicked' for Bridget in her fragile state of health to experience the shock of seeing what had been done to Kennedy because it would 'print such a fearful spectacle on her mind'.[16]

Despite her grief, Bridget held herself with dignity in the rain at the graveside[17] to mirror the courage Michael showed in the last hours of his life. Father Scanlon performed the ceremony again but asked Bishop Moorhouse, carrying a wreath from his wife, Mary, to walk with him at the front of the funeral procession. Scanlon called upon all 'right-minded people' to help the police and maintain the authority of the law.[18]

Vicar Sandiford, who lent Michael his shotgun only for it to become his murder weapon, didn't know what to say. About 200 people came to pay their respects. All business in town shut down as a mark of respect[19] to a well-loved man who McIntyre said would have risen high in the Victorian police because of his strong personality 'and force of character'.[20]

Bishop Moorhouse wrote that the people in north-eastern Victoria were living in absolute terror and that with nerves tense everywhere there was a real fear that innocent horsemen could be shot on sight if suspected of being the Kellys. He said he pitied the killers, 'crouching among the trees like wild beasts, afraid to sleep, afraid to speak, only awaiting their execution',[21] but that 'the horror of the deed' required vigilance by the police in 'hunting down all such criminals'.

After burying the sergeant, Father Scanlon travelled by night along a wild road that was nothing more than a rough bush track. He held the reins in one hand and a revolver in the other.[22]

KENNEDY, SCANLAN AND LONIGAN had been shown just how violent death could be for a Victorian policeman. Senior Constable John Kelly knew how tough life could be for one, too. After joining the force in 1862, the County Limerick man had been stationed for nine years at Ararat and Beaufort, then spent time as a detective in Dandenong and Oakleigh before he was put in charge of the gold escort from Wood's Point.

He had been involved in two murder investigations at Mornington and had arrested William Hastings, who was hanged[23] at Melbourne Gaol for the murder of his wife near Mount Eliza.

Forty-year-old Senior Constable Frank James,[24] a man who John Sadleir said was like Michael Kennedy in possessing 'remarkable merit',[25] was brought down from Beechworth to lead a five-man search party from Benalla that included John Kelly and Thomas Meehan.

On their first night out hunting the Kellys they were riding to Moyhu, but with thunder and lightning as their lullaby they decided to camp beside Boggy Creek.

It rained all night but they had no tents and, while the other men made do with a small blue blanket each, John Kelly had only the wet clothes on his back.[26]

The next night they found a little more comfort at Hedi police station and then started up the King River the following morning. Near the Bungamara cattle station, they met the Kellys' uncle Jack Quinn and two other men who said they were looking for livestock. The police stayed at Bungamara that night, and the following day met Sergeant Steele and some constables who had been exploring further up the King.

Steele received a telegram from Sadleir, ordering him to return at once to Benalla after reports that the outlaws had bailed up George Munger on the Murray flats. John Kelly and his team also returned to Benalla that night. On the road, they met Wild Wright, his mute brother and one of the Kelly's female cousins, all riding on horseback. The Wright boys had just been released from the Mansfield lock-up. This time Wild gave the police no lip.[27]

ON THE DAY OF KENNEDY'S FUNERAL, Ned Kelly rode up from the lagoons made by all the rain, onto the property of William Baumgarten. Ned was the last person that Baumgarten's wife, Margaret, wanted to see as her husband was doing four years over Kelly's horse-stealing racket. Blaming Ned for her family's troubles, she told him and his mates to get back on their horses and push off.

Despite having nothing to lose, Kelly accepted Mrs Baumgarten's fury with good grace and, instead of enjoying warm beds, the four miserable, bedraggled bushrangers camped 200 yards from the Baumgarten house from 1 p.m. until sunset.

Only a few minutes[28] after Mrs Baumgarten watched the wanted men drive their horses across more of the Murray's overflow, she was giving directions to a party of police led by Detective Kennedy and veteran officer Henry Harkin,[29] a 44-year-old sergeant.

Harkin had fathered four children and buried two of them, and as he chased along the watery path after the Kellys he was determined to see the killers brought to justice. With the Victorian government now upping the reward to £2000,[30] there was even more incentive for the gang's capture.

The Kellys were trapped by floodwaters in the front and by raging backwaters behind[31] as Detective Kennedy and his policemen closed in. The gang abandoned the horses and waded up to their necks into the fast-flowing brown water. They concealed themselves in thick reeds as the police searched for a way to ride across in pursuit, before the bushrangers doubled back to find another route.

'Their weapons under water, and ... benumbed with cold,' Superintendent Sadleir noted, 'the gang could have offered no resistance whatever had it been the fortune of the police to see them, but they did not. Immediately the police were out of sight the Kellys got out of the water, picked up their horses, which were hidden in the scrub, and took a different direction from that taken by the police.'[32]

When they finally felt safe enough, the sodden gang lit a fire to dry themselves, their weapons and ammunition,[33] then headed to the Bungowannah wharf to risk a punt ride to New South Wales, listening the whole time for sounds of sploshing police horses behind them. Their frantic escape became more panicked when they found that the pull of the water had dragged the punt under and the river was now unapproachable.[34] They decided to head back to safer ground, riding 50 kilometres south to Aaron Sherritt at Sheepstation Creek, both 'men and horses pretty well worn out'.[35]

With water, water everywhere the Kellys headed back through Everton to again tackle the Ovens River, five days after their first abortive attempt.

IN PENTRIDGE PRISON, Brickey Williamson was still shaking his head at the mess the Kellys had dumped him in, and telling the police everything they wanted to know about the gang, hoping it would lead to early release.

Sitting there in his drab prison garb, looking at the rusty iron bars and wondering if he would ever see home again, he told Inspector Frederick Winch[36] that he might be able to pump Kelly's mother for information that would lead to the capture of the killers.[37]

The 51-year-old Winch had first come across Kelly when he was chasing Harry Power. As a close friend of Commissioner Standish, Winch was also fighting corruption claims that he had allowed Melbourne's grog shanties and whorehouses to thrive,[38] and was desperate to save face by making inroads into the police murders. Winch believed that Brickey had 'great power over Mrs Kelly' and suspected that he, and not the missing George King, was really the father of baby Alice who she was now nursing in Melbourne's Pentridge Prison after being transferred there.[39]

Ned and his gang were moving fast, and already had a scheme to rob a bank. And then another. One of Kelly's horse-stealing confederates, Big Mick Woodyard, was also giving up as much information about the gang as he could. He told Winch he was certain that 'beside the Kellys, is a man named Burns [Byrne]. He was with them at the time the horses were stolen. He took to the bush with them and they were then under arms.' Big Mick said Byrne had 'bullet eyes' and had been knocking about the Beechworth district for some time with the Sherritts, who had a small selection.[40]

He thought the fourth gang member could be one of the Stricklands, a family from Moyhu, who were friends of the Kellys and he suspected they might all ride to Howlong to kill a man named Andrew Petersen, who was a witness against them in the horse-stealing case.

'I know all their associates, their habits and their haunts and should be [able] to give every assistance in my power to trace them,' Big Mick told the police. 'If I were free I would willingly go with the police. I am willing to risk anything to take these men and believe I could do it … I was dragged into this trouble by the Kellys and the Quinns.'[41]

As he had hoped, Mick earned early release for 'police purposes', to act as a spy.[42]

A SPECIAL FORCE OF 22 POLICE was sent to Wangaratta, and even though the town was on high alert, watching for armed men on the run, Steve Hart knew of a culvert that could provide an escape route.[43] At 4 a.m. on Sunday, 3 November, 'just at grey in the morning',[44] the four young men came through the Wangaratta streets, driving their horses at full gallop, under the noses of the sleeping policemen.[45] Mrs Mary Delaney, who lived on the north-western fringe of Wangaratta between the railway station and the One Mile Creek bridge, heard the noise of 'galloping and chains rattling, coming towards the house'.[46] She had her own horses running out on the flat and feared the noise was that of horse thieves approaching. She was right.

She told police she 'saw four young men riding four horses, two horses with two packs on each horse in front, and four other horses'. The horses, four of them bareback, seemed exhausted.[47] Two of Mary's sons saw Hart, the well-known local larrikin and daredevil, coaxing his mount into the creek underneath the railway bridge by the back of the hospital.[48] Hart worked his way across a narrow underwater ledge.[49] The three other riders drove the loose horses ahead of them into the water before they all scrambled up the bank on the other side. Ahead were the Warby Ranges and, 40 kilometres away at Lake Rowan,[50] tea and sympathy from Kelly's aunt Ann – his father's sister – and her family, the Ryans.

The gang kept driving the horses hard the whole way and Scanlan's hollow-backed[51] horse finally broke down with bleeding feet[52] after having covered 320 kilometres of hard running in just over a week. The bay gelding was unsaddled and set free, the Kelly Gang showing it far more mercy than they did to Scanlan.

THOMAS McINTYRE, black and blue all over after his fall from the horse and suffering terribly from his physical and emotional ordeal, was moved from Mansfield to the police hospital at the Richmond Depot in Melbourne. His nerves were 'still considerably shaken'[53] and he went into post-traumatic shock.[54]

McIntyre told Standish that more than anything he wanted to catch the brutes who murdered his mates. Standish, though, wanted the shattered wreck of a constable to stay as far away from the hunt as possible. He was the only eyewitness to the first two killings and the commissioner wanted him protected 'until all danger of his being assassinated' was over.[55]

McIntyre came in for great public ridicule for his actions in fleeing the scene on Kennedy's horse and leaving his sergeant to fend for himself. Other officers were quick to defend him, though, including big Frank Hare, who said it actually took a brave man to seize the opportunity and vault onto Kennedy's horse as it passed him.

'He was of no use to Kennedy,' Hare said. 'He had no arms in his possession, and the fact of his bolting off as he did, gave Kennedy a better opportunity of shooting one or two of the bushrangers if they attempted to pursue him. [McIntyre] had seen his two companions shot dead and the third fired at; clearly his best course was to escape and give the alarm. There can be no question that if McIntyre had also been shot (which he would have been, had he not escaped), the world would never have known the fate of the four men. The bush near the spot where the tragedy took place is so dense that, if the bodies had been burned and the ashes covered up, no sign of the bodies could have been discovered.'[56]

Chapter 7

WHILE NED KELLY and his gang spurred their weary horses through the Warby Ranges, there was a noticeable lack of urgency by local police at Wangaratta a few miles to the east. At 12.45 a.m., almost a day after the report that the Kellys had ridden through there, Sergeant Steele arrived in town on a special train from Benalla carrying 14 mounted constables and their mounts, bound for Beechworth and the Sherritt home.

Thirty-year-old Irishman Constable Michael Twomey,[1] a native of County Cork, collared Steele on the platform and told him that the Delaneys had seen four desperate-looking men roaring through town with a team of horses.

Steele said it must be the Kellys but that he was not hanging around to find out, because he had orders to take the train to Beechworth and hunt for the gang around the granite boulders known as the Rats' Castle. Twomey told him the evidence that the Kellys were nearby seemed rock solid but Steele insisted that orders were orders.

Steele seemed to have a permanent hangdog expression but the murders of his three comrades had made him decidedly morose. And afraid.

Kelly had threatened to roast Steele alive for arresting his mother, and the policeman knew Kelly was serious. He told Twomey he should report the matter to the man in charge of the Wangaratta station, Inspector Brooke Smith, even though one of the few things that Kelly and his pursuers agreed upon was that Brooke Smith was a nitwit.

A Royal Commission later declared that, since Steele knew Brooke Smith's personal peculiarities and 'unsuitability' for the work, passing the buck was an obvious 'attempt to evade responsibility'.[2] But Steele protested, saying that he ran a great risk if he disobeyed orders:

> If [the outlaws] turned up at Rats' Castle afterwards, and I had disobeyed any instructions, I would have been in a rather peculiar position with my superior officers. Had there not been a party of police at Wangaratta I would have taken the responsibility on myself, but Mr Smith was there with a large party of men at the time, and I sent up word by a constable to tell him that it was undoubtedly the outlaws, that Steve Hart had piloted them over the bridge; and I added, 'Start at four in the morning, and you are bound to catch them on the Warby ranges.' [But] I could have followed the horses myself without a tracker; the horses were bogging into the ground six inches, the ground was so very soft. We tracked them all about the hills some weeks afterwards.[3]

Inspector Brooke Smith was a curious character who, despite his early promise as a lawman, had spent a few days in jail in 1870 after amassing gambling debts. His reputation for courage established on the goldfields took an almighty battering during the Kelly hunt. Brooke Smith became the model for Purdy Smith, a character in the novel *The Fortunes of Richard Mahony*, as 'a little apple-cheeked English boy, with a comical English accent'.[4]

Kelly wrote that the inspector had a 'head like a turnip' and that he reminded him of 'a poodle dog half clipped in the lion fashion', who 'knows as much about commanding Police as Captain Standing [sic] does about mustering mosquitoes and boiling them down for their fat on the back Blocks of the Lachlan'.[5]

Kelly claimed that Brooke Smith would invade the Kelly shack, where the younger children were largely fending for themselves, and that he would tell the Kelly sisters that they would blow their brothers 'to pieces'. Kelly claimed that Detective Mick Ward and Constable Jim Hayes[6] would take out their revolvers and threaten to shoot the children and were in fact worse than 'the greatest ruffians and murderers'.[7]

Constable Twomey roused Brooke Smith from his slumber at Henry Kett's Royal Hotel at 2 a.m. on 4 November and was told by his sleepy boss to investigate further. So Twomey went back to the Delaney home to interview them again. He inspected the bank of the creek destroyed by the horses' hooves. He returned, wet to the skin, at 5.45 a.m. with all the evidence for Brooke Smith.

The response was deflating. In five years in the force, Twomey had never seen such evasive action from a lawman. Brooke Smith told him 'something about sending a telegram about half-past eight, about the office being open then'.[8] Twomey told his comrades that the inspector's inactivity was 'disgusting'.[9]

In fact, a Royal Commission's investigation into the police's pursuit of the Kellys found Brooke Smith's conduct could not 'be too severely censured' and that his conduct revealed 'culpable negligence and incapacity'.[10]

At midday on 6 November, three and a half days after the gang drove their horses through Wangaratta, Brooke Smith finally saddled up and led 22 men to Peechelba Station, 20 kilometres north of Wangaratta. It was here that the bushranger 'Mad Dan' Morgan was shot dead 13 years earlier. With his knees knocking, Brooke Smith sent 13 of his men with Detective Kennedy to Lake Rowan and the rest to spend the night up on the flooded Murray at Yarrawonga. Brooke Smith was so frightened that he refused to keep a notebook and told his men not to either, for fear 'the outlaws might get hold of it'.[11]

Ned and his gang were nervous, too. They had found their way to the Ryans but knew the police were close behind. Ned had barely slept a wink.[12] On 7 November, late in the day, Brooke Smith led his men towards Lake Rowan and, while he always travelled his 'horses very slowly', this time his officers reported that he rode 'very slow indeed' lest they actually get close to the heavily armed desperadoes. The diligent officers in the party complained bitterly that the snail's-pace pursuit was a waste of time.[13]

The Royal Commission would declare that 'with no other apparent object than that of retarding the pursuit, [Brooke Smith] compelled his men to make unnecessary detours to follow up the tracks; he rode slowly, loitered in the rear, and altogether so conducted the affair that only one conclusion can be arrived at as regards his conduct, namely, that he was determined that his party should not overtake the outlaws'.[14]

The next morning, Friday, 8 November, Irish-born Senior Constable Charlie Johnston,[15] a 38-year-old native of County Tyrone and an expert horseman, came down out of the Warby Ranges and into the Ryans' stockyard.

Big Frank Hare said Johnston was 'a most excitable fellow and bold, and as good a rider as ever sat on a horse'. But he had no safety catch on his impulses and Hare said he would have faced the four outlaws alone if he had had the chance, 'and shot them one after another if it were possible'.[16]

The ground was soft, and Johnston, a 15-year veteran of the force, knew instantly that horses, both shod and unshod, had been there within the previous 48 hours.[17] Johnston decided that there were three men riding singly and another with a packhorse next to him,[18] and he cooeed Brooke Smith to break the news to the reluctant lawman.

Jim Dixon, whose now-bankrupt father once owned the sawmill where Ned Kelly had worked, was riding with Johnston. They found white hairs on a brush fence and guessed that they were from the stocky chestnut police gelding, marked M 42, which had white legs and a white face. Johnston followed the trail of horse hoofs into the Warby Ranges near Morgan's Gap, where convict's son Jim Brien[19] had established the first big orange grove in the area. Beside the hoof prints the area was littered with fresh peel. Brooke Smith managed to extract information from Brien that the killers had been to his house for supplies of tea and the fruit, but he proved 'too experienced a man' to say when.[20]

Johnston urged Brooke Smith that if they hurried they could quickly trap the killers, but Brooke Smith slammed on the brakes. After he had grilled Brien for 15 minutes, Brooke Smith's men had ridden out of sight, and he fired a shot to bring them back. Any element of surprise they might have had was now lost as the shot echoed around the hills like an alarm bell.

It was getting late in the day and if Brooke Smith was trying to sabotage the operation, he couldn't have done much better. With a hot dinner and a warm bed waiting for him at the Royal Hotel back in Wangaratta, he told Johnston the men would continue the hunt at 4 a.m. with Aboriginal trackers.

When Johnston woke his boss early the next morning with the news that the men were ready to ride, Brooke Smith said he'd be up to join them 'immediately'. An hour later he said the same thing. It wasn't until 7 a.m. that the inspector finally emerged and told Johnston to head back to the orange grove and scout around – and that he would join them after breakfast. Six hours later Brooke Smith was still nowhere to be seen and Johnston, ready to rumble, told his comrades they should pick up the tracks again and get ready to fight the Kellys.

Late in the afternoon they found the police packhorse grazing among the trees. Johnston suspected the rest of the horses and the desperate, weary men riding them had to be nearby, but as dusk approached and they prepared to camp out overnight for a full-scale assault at daybreak, Brooke Smith came clip-clopping along for the first time that day and ordered them instead to 'Halt! form up!' and head back to Wangaratta.[21]

While Johnston and the others turned back with anger, the Kelly Gang split up, two heading towards the Murray again to look for a crossing, the others heading towards Ellen's hut on Eleven Mile Creek to see what provisions and support they could rustle up.[22] The police knew the gang were hanging around Greta because they had a spy planted among the family, a man named Bill Donnelly, a friend of Wild Wright's who was said to be a cattle thief,[23] and who was boarding at Ellen's hut and watching Maggie Skilling.

A BARK-STRIPPER CLAIMED to have seen the gang near Beechworth on 3 November and he rode into the town to tell the police. He went on a three-day bender to boost his 'Dutch courage' and drank so much that he had to be carried to the police lock-up 'in a speechless state of drunkenness'.[24] The gang were gone but police moved into the area to investigate all avenues.

There were many others in the area who either sympathised with the Kellys or who were simply scared to death of them. A young worker at Kilfera Station said the police offered him £50 to tell them where the gang were hiding but he refused, 'because I have a mother and father keeping a little farm not far off, and if I told anything they would be murdered and burnt'.[25]

But Sadleir knew someone he could lean on for vital information, and sent out an urgent message for all available officers to meet at Beechworth for a raid on the Sherritts.

Late on the evening of 6 November, Sadleir, sick with rheumatic fever, nevertheless reached Beechworth on horseback alongside Senior Constable Frank James. It was bright moonlight as they entered the police camp, and they were startled at seeing armed young men in rough clothes everywhere. Sadleir warned James in a hushed voice to 'look out', not knowing what they were confronting.

'We were both armed, of course,' Sadleir recalled, 'but as we advanced James recognised the men as residents of the town.'[26] Sadleir then discovered that five-year police veteran Constable Robert Keating,[27] one of the two men at the police station, had quickly organised an eager posse to chase down the killers. Having arranged by telegram for additional police to be sent to Beechworth during the night, Sadleir thanked the volunteers for responding so readily to Constable Keating's call, and let them return to their homes.

A large party of police were now in Beechworth including Commissioner Standish and Superintendent Nicolson along with Melbourne press reporters.

Standish had been in Benalla discussing the hunt with Nicolson over supper when they received Sadleir's urgent message to hit Beechworth. Standish immediately ordered a special train, and proceeded, with Nicolson, nine mounted constables and one Aboriginal tracker.[28]

The party arrived at Benalla's train station at 3 a.m. on 7 November for what was supposed to be a top-secret early morning operation,[29] though two of the Lloyds and Wild Wright were on the train platform acting as spies for the Kellys.

The police party set off on horseback from Beechworth station at 4 a.m. boosted by additional men from there.

Soon 35 or so policemen and a couple of Aboriginal trackers quietly surrounded the house of Sherritt's parents at nearby Sheepstation Creek, waiting and watching to see if there were any police killers lurking there. Nicolson, putting himself in charge of potential arrests, decided to have a closer look and called on a few of his troops to get ready for an attack. He also sent men to guard a large paddock behind the house to ensure that no one escaped. Nicolson was pushing 50 but he was still tough and ready to fight.

The balding Scot barrelled his horse at full speed towards the Sherritts, before throwing his legs off the horse and shoulder charging the front door. As he did so the intrepid Constable Bracken tried to beat his boss inside and they collided at the narrow entrance. Nicolson was livid. He roughly pushed Bracken aside causing Bracken's shotgun to discharge[30] and the blast triggered a police stampede.

Sadleir, sick and weary from the effects of his fever, still eagerly followed the pair into a darkened abyss. He expected one of the Kellys to blow his head off at any moment. It was a 'rambling sort of building without windows, and so dark within that nothing could be seen for the first few moments'.[31] Nicolson raced from room to room throwing off the bedclothes but finding no bushrangers, only indignant Sherritts. Sadleir then entered a dark, dingy room lined with bunks, the top row so high that he couldn't see whether they were occupied without climbing up. Slowly, warily, he waited for the bushrangers to show themselves. He tiptoed carefully round the bunks, with his hat perched on

Livewire Hugh Bracken collided with Charles
Hope Nicolson when trying to beat his boss inside
a house during a raid early in the Kelly hunt.
State Library of Victoria, H96.160/192

the point of his rifle, level with the upper row. He hoped that
any bullets would find the hat when his head was not in it. 'If
[the Kellys] had been at home,' Sadleir theorised, 'most of the
attacking party would have gone down' before they could have
used their weapons. But Nicolson told Sadleir that he was well
used to kicking doors down looking for criminals and he had not
come to any harm.

'It certainly was a plucky bit of leadership on his part,' Sadleir
wrote.[32]

As the police emerged from the Sherritt home with not a
bushranger in sight and just one odd angry shot in vain, a red-
faced Standish watched the debacle unfold from a distance
alongside two Melbourne journalists.

The police then raced a mile towards Aaron's selection, which was sandwiched between his mother's dairy farm and the Byrnes' house. The Kelly hunters visited his 'squalid den',[33] but he was absent. The pursuers pushed on over the range and descended 'a precipitous and dangerous gorge about 800ft [244 metres]', until they came to a green valley and the home of Joe's mother, Margret Byrne, and her younger children, at milking time.

Initially Margret was 'greatly scared at seeing such a large party surround her house' but then became 'very bold and impudent'.[34] She refused to give the police any information and denied all knowledge of the Kellys. The police went through her place to see whether any of the property of the murdered men was there. When the whole thing was over, Aaron Sherritt, 'a very fair and tall, high-shouldered young man'[35] who had been away chopping wood when the police arrived, strolled up to them nonchalantly carrying an axe over his shoulder.

For a hardy bushman Sherritt had the reputation of being something of a dandy, and 'physically a splendid specimen of a man'.[36] He was planning to marry Mrs Byrne's daughter Katie[37] and had spent the night with her family.

Sergeant Steele and Anthony Strahan spoke to Sherritt and then Sadleir had a conversation with him before calling over some of the other police. Aaron had a talent for annoying lawmen and he told Sadleir that the veteran inspector was only a puppy in the case and that he would only deal with the big dog, the man in charge. Standish was summoned, and he and Sherritt had a long chat about what this small-time crook could do for this big-time policeman.

With a large crowd watching, but only a few of the officers, including Detective Ward, able to hear what was being said, Standish promised that if Sherritt betrayed the gang he would pocket a sizeable chunk of the reward. Sherritt said he would only help the police if his mate Joe Byrne's life was spared when the Kellys were caught.

Aaron told him it would take a lot of money, though, to loosen his tongue. Standish agreed.[38] Sherritt was not to go with any party of police, but, 'pretending friendship with the gang and their allies, he was to take his own course as a secret agent'.[39]

Nicolson remonstrated with Standish for making such a proposal with such a shady character, telling the commissioner that 'no person with any experience in police duty would have done such a thing'.[40] It was contrary to all practice to make proposals to 'a man like that', Nicolson thundered, 'especially in the state of terror the country was in'.

INSPECTOR BROOKE SMITH had failed dismally with the pursuit,[41] so by 11 November, the day before Kelly and his accomplices were required to surrender to police at Mansfield station or risk being shot on sight, Nicolson organised a major manhunt. He was following up a report from a railway platelayer who said he saw men answering the description of the suspects crossing the line at Glenrowan, 14 kilometres south of Wangaratta.

Superintendent Sadleir met Nicolson at Glenrowan on the morning of 12 November. Dr Reynolds told Sadleir that having just battled rheumatic fever it was 'highly dangerous for him to go out upon search parties and suffer exposure from the weather and cold night air of the hills'. But Sadleir saw taking a lead in the hunt as a duty to the public and especially the three dead officers. Brooke Smith, Johnston and their search parties were there, too, as well as two Aboriginal trackers, the wily and experienced 'Doctor', rated by Nicolson as 'a very good man', and his young protégé 'Jemmy',[42] who Nicolson regarded as 'perfectly useless'.[43] Doctor hailed from the Coranderrk Aboriginal station to the east of Melbourne, near the present town of Healesville. The trackers took the police to the foot of the ranges and then another mile or two. But then Jemmy and the Doctor got cold feet. They were not about to get their heads blown off for these white men who'd taken over their land. Instead, the two trackers took the police off the trail and on to swampy ground, where there were thousands of tracks and where all the cattle of the neighbourhood came to water.

Sadleir became 'perfectly satisfied' that the trackers were deliberately misleading the police:[44] 'They just took us ... within a short distance of cover, where an ambush might be, and led us clean away from that ... and I do not blame them. They were actuated of the spirit of self-preservation, because they knew they would be the first to be shot.'[45]

Sadleir wrote, 'I heard it reported afterwards as coming from Ned Kelly, that he saw us, and could have shot Mr Nicolson and myself if he liked, of which I do not believe one word; but he must have heard we were there, for he described that we sat in a little open place where there was water; and he stated he could have shot us, that he saw the brands on the horses [and] recognized different men in the party.'[46]

Johnston was so frustrated by police bungling the Kelly hunt that he applied for a transfer the next day.[47]

Sadleir said that, if Brooke Smith had been more energetic at the start of the hunt, the gang would most likely have been trapped, but instead he 'was so dilatory in starting and so bungled the whole business that the pursuit, as he conducted it, was hopeless ... His failure of duty was most unfortunate, since the gang and their horses were at the time completely knocked up, and prompt pursuit could scarcely have failed to effect the breaking up of the gang within a week of the murders at the Wombat range.'[48]

Because of what Nicolson said was Brooke Smith's 'constitutional inability to leave his bed before eight or nine o'clock in the morning', Nicolson posted him to a desk job in Beechworth, with instructions to meddle no more in the Kelly business.[49] Nicolson said Brooke Smith had been 'natty in his person and temperate in his habits' as a younger man but had now become careless and nervous.[50]

Brooke Smith, in fact, became so paranoid that Kelly and his gang would hunt him down and torture him for the persecution of Ned's young siblings that he eventually suffered a nervous breakdown. Within a year his appearance became 'wretched and his memory apparently much gone ... muttering and speaking incoherently about the Kellys'. He talked of suicide, too, and while his friends feared for Brooke Smith's life, Nicolson scoffed.

He was sure Brooke Smith did not have even 'the courage for that remedy'.[51]

Sadleir finally bowed to medical advice and returned to office duties while Nicolson remained 'indefatigable in his efforts',[52] forming and leading search parties, although the dour Scot quickly realised he wasn't as young as he had been when he burst into Harry Power's lair to arrest him a decade earlier.

For the next few weeks there was more searching than chasing, for no definite news came to hand of the Kelly Gang's whereabouts. Parties of police varying in number from six to nine were constantly on the move, scouring the countryside by day and camping out by night. Travelling constantly through rough mountain country, sometimes for as long as two weeks, took its toll.

Nicolson said his police parties, which often included Kelly's enemies Strahan and Flood, would camp at night and eat their dinner, but instead of lying down to rest, some of them would become nocturnal hunters as he led two or three officers at a time on foot to investigate places miles away, such as the huts of suspected persons. Nicolson sometimes would not get back to the camp after visiting those places until 3 a.m. Then he would rest till daybreak, which in November came early. 'This had a serious effect upon me,' he said. 'It reduced my strength. It also affected the whole party; we would come in very much fagged – horses and men. The young men used to recuperate in a couple of days, but it took me, at my time of life, and the other members of the force, mounted constables and others, more than that, but I had to go out notwithstanding at once.'[53]

Anxiety abounded. Search parties were sent out on the slightest information. Night parties watched on roads and at river crossings, and Sadleir wrote that 'timorous travellers, who tried to bolt when challenged, had so many narrow escapes of being shot by the police that these night watches had to be greatly reduced'.[54]

The fatigue and hardship caused by these expeditions, with men out in the wilds through cold, frost and rain, became the most severe Nicolson had endured in more than a quarter of a

Queensland-born Victorian tracker Moses Bulla was described as 'a most active little fellow' in the hunt for the outlaws. Queensland Police Museum

century in the force. Along with the aches and pains in his rapidly aging bones, there was also 'the mortifying consciousness' that so many residents – Kelly sympathisers – were doing their best to frustrate the police efforts.[55]

In Mansfield, one of the Aboriginal trackers displayed a wound under his eye that he said was caused by Ned Kelly savagely striking him with a stirrup iron about 12 months earlier. The tracker was said to be a 'cute fellow' who looked upon the murders as 'something atrocious'. A reporter at the *Mansfield Guardian* quoted the tracker as declaring that if he came upon the gang in the bush he would forget he had 'been civilised, and give the miscreants their deserts in true blackfellow fashion'.[56]

On 14 November, Nicolson wrote to Standish to tell him he would need the services of the Queensland-born trackers Moses Bulla and Tommy Spider to supplement one who was already working well, Jimmy Gublator. Jimmy had come to the Victoria Police most likely after driving cattle south to Melbourne from the Mount Margaret Station near Quilpie in south-west Queensland. He was now anxious to go home.[57]

The following day, in Pentridge Prison, Brickey Williamson was supplying 'certain particulars respecting the gang, their haunts, probable whereabouts, and their mode of obtaining supplies of provisions while hiding in the ranges'.[58]

This time he was spilling his guts to Inspector Reginald Green, who had shown himself to be a first-class 'thief catcher' alongside Nicolson and Sadleir when the three served as cadets way back in 1852.[59]

Brickey told Green the gang needed money for provisions, to provide for their family, friends and relatives, and to pay off sympathisers who were feeding the police with false leads.

In a whisper to make sure no one else could hear, Brickey told Green: 'I reckon they'll try a stick-up to make a haul.'[60]

Chapter 8

EVERY KELLY HUNT was meant to begin in secret but with the gang's spies all through northern Victoria word spread quickly whenever a group of undercover officers rode into the bush.

Consequently, party after party of the police, having spent anything from a few days to two weeks in the mountains, invariably returned exhausted and empty handed to their different stations.

While Nicolson worked certain sections of the ranges, James Whelan at Benalla, Frank James at Mansfield, Sergeant Steele at Wangaratta and Senior Constable Edward Shoebridge[1] at Bright worked other sections of the map Nicolson had divided into sections.

The police heard that the outlaws carried a small tent and about a month's rations, and that Maggie Skilling used a large hollow log about 500 metres from her mother's house as a food drop for them.[2] Senior Constable Flood found it soon enough but there was no sign of the gang.[3] The police knew that Maggie was always busy 'preparing large quantities of food',[4] baking so much bread 'that it could not have been for the ordinary family'.[5] She would signal to the gang when police were about, by hanging a white sheet on a sapling near her house, which could be seen from a great distance.

Maggie also took supplies for them into the bush at night in a well-filled swag on her horse White-foot,[6] and wherever she rode to, it was a long distance because she returned in the morning with the horse 'completely exhausted'.[7] Standish suggested she could be prosecuted under the *Felons Apprehension Act*,[8] which prescribed penalties of up to 15 years' imprisonment for assisting outlaws, but Nicolson argued against that, believing there was insufficient evidence against her to secure a conviction, and that if Maggie was left alone, and unsuspecting, she would either lead police to the Kellys, or the Kellys, confident they had gone undetected, would eventually emerge from hiding.[9]

But while the police attempted to follow Maggie on her nocturnal rides, Superintendent Sadleir said it was impossible for them to do so without being detected.[10]

On 15 November, Brickey Williamson furnished Inspector Green with localities likely to be frequented by the gang. The places he mentioned were deep in the bush, mostly inaccessible heads of various creeks and rivers, some of them 70 kilometres apart, and from where the outlaws could see the police coming.[11] He said they could get food at Merrijig and on the Devil's River, where a relative of the Lloyds ran a store. Jack Quinn, Tom Lloyd and Wild Wright would also give them food and shelter at their remote homes.[12]

The Kellys also used a secret route from Greta to Barnawartha in New South Wales, passing under the railway bridge, but Brickey told Green the gang would almost certainly 'keep to the ranges'.[13]

NED KELLY HAD BEEN planning to rob a bank at Seymour for some time and there was speculation he would give the money to Maggie,[14] though Kelly was soon looking for another target when the police presence in the Victorian town, 100 kilometres north of Melbourne, was dramatically increased.

Police reinforcements also arrived at Beechworth, Benalla and Wangaratta along with Kelly's neighbourhood haunts at Oxley and nearby Milawa. So, Kelly eventually chose as his target Euroa, at the foot of the Strathbogie Ranges, where his grandmother, Mary Quinn, and his young, widowed aunt Grace Farrell both

Maggie Skilling became her cousin Tom Lloyd's lover while her husband was in jail. They were two of the Kelly Gang's major accomplices. Lloyd's son Tom Junior later served as a horse trainer for the Victorian police for almost 30 years. State Library of Victoria, H2003.25/6; Victoria Collections VPM3063

lived. Kelly knew the town well and he told supporters there that he planned the sort of audacious raid Ben Hall used to carry out when he would take over a whole town. Sadleir estimated that at the time Kelly had at least 100 close relatives in that part of Victoria and many more staunch friends.[15]

At just 24, Ned Kelly was already a ruthless and complex criminal, admired by his sympathisers for his physical prowess, his horsemanship and his boldness to stand up for himself at any cost. He had proved at different times that he could be heroic and hard-working, but he was more often vain, violent and megalomaniacal with a pathological hatred for authority.

His good looks, virility and overt masculinity, combined with a rough charisma, would eventually build a cult following for him, but his volatility would also lead to innocent people being killed.

After the discovery of the police bodies, press reports had described Kelly as a murderer and mutilator of the dead with a 'low ape-like forehead and gloomy expression [that was] distinctly animal ... a creature born to crime',[16] but he was preparing something of a charm offensive at Euroa, proclaiming long and loud that he was a victim of police brutality and government lies.

He said he only ever killed in self-defence.

Kelly devised a scheme to rob Euroa's National Bank and take over the expansive Faithfull's Creek homestead on the railway line 6 kilometres away. Faithfull's Creek was part of a half-million-acre (200,000-hectare) pastoral empire controlled by businessmen Isaac Younghusband[17] and Andrew Lyell,[18] a member of the Victorian Legislative Assembly. The gang mistakenly thought one of Lyell's parliamentary colleagues, Donald Cameron, MLA,[19] was sympathetic to their cause after he attempted to embarrass Premier Graham Berry in Parliament on 14 November. Cameron had asked about rumours 'that some members of the police force had been guilty of certain conduct that led to the perpetration of the Mansfield outrage'.[20] Ned mistakenly thought Cameron, a well-known country journalist,[21] could be a channel through which to plead for understanding. So, he and Byrne composed a rough draft of a 22-page[22] letter protesting the law's treatment of Kelly's family and his fury over what he claimed was police corruption.

'I was outlawed without any cause,' Kelly declared, 'and if the public do not see justice done I will seek revenge for the name and character which has been given to me and my relations while God gives me strength to pull a trigger ... For had I robbed, plundered, ravished & murdered everything I met my character could not be painted blacker than it is at present but thank god my conscience is as clear as the snow in Peru.'[23]

He suggested that if he obtained justice – the release of his mother – he would leave Victoria alone: 'For I need no lead or powder to revenge my cause ... With no offence (remember your railroads) and a sweet good bye from Edward Kelly a forced outlaw.'

BYRNE HAD STILL NOT been formally identified as one of the four killers, and six weeks after the Stringybark Creek murders, he strode unchallenged into Euroa's North Eastern Hotel on Sunday, 8 December 1878[24] to meet Kelly's old friend, Ben Gould, who was now running a Euroa store. Gould, who prefaced Kelly's first prison sentence eight years before by writing an obscene note and wrapping calves' testicles for delivery, had been supplying the gang with sausages and other provisions ever since they had gone on the run.[25]

From the North Eastern Hotel, Byrne could spy on the bank and learn that in two days, on Tuesday afternoon, most of the people in Euroa would be occupied either with a sitting of the Licensing Court or with the funeral of a 12-year-old boy named Bill Gouge, killed in a riding accident. On 9 December, Ned's old rival Superintendent Nicolson was promoted to Assistant Commissioner and with the Kellys about to go into full guerrilla mode his job immediately became even more stressful. At 12.30 p.m. on 9 December, the four gang members rode up to the well-built brick house of the Faithfull's Creek Station on new mounts, four of the finest looking horses in the colony. Dan Kelly and Hart were on a pair of magnificent bays, Joe was on Music, a striking grey mare that had just foaled,[26] and Ned was on a big bay mare with white hind feet. He called the horse Mirth, and to most of the colony the police pursuit had become a bad joke.

The four bushrangers reeked from having lived rough together for weeks.

Their trousers were stained with horse sweat and their tweed jackets tattered. Each man had a revolver holstered on his belt and a rifle wrapped in a swag at the front of his saddle. Ned had a pipe in his mouth and Michael Kennedy's watch in his pocket.[27] Some of the people working at the station knew of Kelly's plans and were about to help him as spies embedded with his prisoners.

Kelly marched up to Mrs Fitzgerald, the elderly station cook.

'I am Ned Kelly,' he declared, 'but don't be afraid. We shall do you no harm, but you will have to give us some refreshments, and also food for our horses. That's all we want.'[28]

Two of the gang ate, while the other two kept watch. The prisoners were made to taste the food first, as Kelly and his gang were deathly afraid of being poisoned.[29]

The men working at the station were locked in a slab shed along with a few unlucky visitors who arrived throughout the afternoon, so that eventually there were 14 imprisoned including the station overseer William McCauley,[30] who brought in a mob of sheep and immediately recognised what he later called the 'ugly face' of Dan Kelly from the portraits he had seen in newspaper reports.[31] Forgetting his public relations exercise, Ned told McCauley that 'if you attempt to take me or get away, you will be shot, as I have plenty of men outside. If you do get away, I will burn the homestead and shoot the horses.'[32] Dan Kelly, who everyone agreed had 'a most villainous cast of countenance',[33] asked his brother if he could shoot McCauley but Ned said no.

The Faithfull's Creek groom George Stephens, a former policeman, noticed that Byrne sometimes stood with his back against a small window in their makeshift prison, and Stephens searched among his tools that were about for hay work, hoping to nail Byrne through the window, but none could be found. Then he took an axe, but the window opening was too narrow to allow an effective blow. When the other prisoners, some of them Kelly plants, discovered what Stephens was after, they threatened to hand him over to the gang.[34]

At sunset the station had another visitor in hawker James Gloster,[35] who was riding in a covered wagon with his name emblazoned on the canvas.

Gloster had been a convict with Ben Gould in Van Diemen's Land and was travelling with his 18–year-old assistant, Frank Becroft. To the police and press it seemed just too much of a coincidence that they were carrying sets of new clothes, hats and boots in the very sizes of the four gang members.

As though rehearsed, Gloster made a show of going for his gun in the wagon, only for Ned to point the barrel of his revolver at Gloster's head and tell him: 'I had a good mind to put a bullet through you for not obeying. I am Ned Kelly, son of Red Kelly, and a better man never stepped in two shoes.'[36] With vaudevillian flair Dan Kelly yelled 'shoot the damn wretch'[37] but Gloster's young mate couldn't hide a sheepish grin and seemed 'to enjoy the affair as an amusement'.[38]

The gang burned their old clothes and donned their smart new outfits, helping themselves to Gloster's perfume bottles[39] as well, spraying themselves all over and putting spare bottles in their pockets. They later asked Mrs Fitzgerald to fetch them water, a comb and a hairbrush so they could look their best.[40]

Even as a wanted outlaw with his future in a noose, Ned Kelly knew how to win friends and influence people. That night he told his captive audience of his mother's struggles with a large, hungry family and of how much it broke all their hearts to see her with a baby at the breast being sent to prison on the word of that 'lying, drunken article' Fitzpatrick. He said he would overturn a train if his mother wasn't set free. He had nothing to do with the Fitzpatrick business, he continued, and at Stringybark Creek he was just defending himself against men who had come to kill him. He shot all the policemen himself, he said, none of the others had a hand in it, and it was a fair fight.[41] Kelly's prisoners played euchre and laughed at his jokes, and he let them out now and then for fresh air and a smoke, warning them, though, that he would roast them alive if they tried to run away.[42]

AT DAWN ON TUESDAY, 10 December 1878, Byrne, the most educated of the four, wrote out a copy of Kelly's letter to Donald Cameron, using blood-red ink and 'beautiful handwriting'.[43] He then penned a copy for Superintendent Sadleir.

After a hearty breakfast, Joe, Ned and Steve took tomahawks to break the telegraph wires running beside the nearby train track. Seventeen-year-old Dan, described by one of the prisoners as 'one of those bullying tyrannical ruffians', was left in charge of the captives. He made them call him 'Mr Kelly'.[44] A young labourer named John Carson[45] had a nosebleed and Dan aimed a revolver at his head, saying he would gladly put him out of his misery.[46] When Robert MacDougall,[47] a Melbourne public servant on a

The Kelly Gang's raid on Euroa was a daring robbery and a major public relations exercise. State Library of Victoria IAN27/12/78/216

kangaroo shooting jaunt, objected to his watch being taken, Dan asked his brother if he could shoot him, too. Carson suspected that Dan, already facing a sentence of death, had nothing to lose and was just itching for the chance to kill someone else, only being restrained by his big brother's orders.

While at the station Ned also confiscated a .577 calibre Snider-Enfield rifle, once the weapon of choice for the British Army.[48] He would eventually carve a 'K' into the wooden butt, call it 'Betty', and tell everyone that it was now his favourite.[49]

That afternoon, with Joe Byrne left in charge of the station prisoners, the two Kelly brothers, dressed like wealthy graziers in their new clothes, climbed aboard the hawker's wagon and a spring cart, while Steve Hart jumped on one of the station horses. Together they travelled the 6 kilometres into Euroa, arriving just before 4 p.m. at the National Bank, a one-storey brick corner building on the almost deserted Binney Street.

Most of Euroa's population was occupied preparing for Bill Gouge's funeral or at the Licensing Court, being presided over by the eccentric magistrate Alfred Wyatt. The bank closed at three, but staff were always inside working late. Kelly knocked on the door and told the young accountant, William Bradly,[50] that he had a cheque to cash. Bradly opened the door a little to tell the big, bearded intruder that the bank was closed just as Kelly smashed the door in. Bradly staggered backwards, with Kelly leaping in after him and drawing a revolver. Hart followed and they bailed up the teenaged Bob Booth,[51] the bank clerk. At the back of the building Hart encountered the bank manager's 15-year-old maid Fanny Shaw,[52] who was in the middle of ironing. Fanny was one of Hart's friends from his brief time at the Wangaratta Catholic School. She asked her old schoolmate what he was doing there with a revolver in each hand.[53] Fanny later confirmed Hart's identity to police as the previously unknown fourth outlaw. Kelly and Hart then walked into the manager's office to find a fiery 44-year-old bald Scotsman with glasses. Robert Scott[54] was getting ready for Bill Gouge's funeral, too, but the outlaws called on him to bail up three times before Scott, eyeing his own handgun at the opposite end of his desk, finally raised his arms but only as high as his armpits. Kelly took Scott's revolver and, as Hart guarded the banker, rifled through the teller's drawers, grabbing £400 in notes, gold and silver. Kelly then strode towards the adjoining residence where Scott lived with his pretty, much younger wife and their seven children. Stories of the police murders had sparked terror throughout Victoria and Scott, worried what this cop-killer might do to his young family, declared: 'Kelly, if you go there I'll strike you, whatever the consequences may be.' Hart cocked both his revolvers and aimed them at Scott's head. Kelly kept walking and found the sassy 32-year-old Mrs Susy Scott[55] with her nanny preparing to take her infant daughter for a walk. Mrs Scott had been married to the bank manager since she was seventeen and rather than being the least bit frightened by the handsome, athletic young visitor, she seemed pleasantly intrigued.[56] Susy's mother, Anne Calvert,[57] matriarch of a prosperous farming family from Rochester, 110 kilometres to the north-west, was staying with her daughter and gasped in terror when she realised the identity of this striking stranger with the rusty red beard and hazel eyes.

'Don't be frightened,' Kelly told the old lady. 'Nothing will happen to you. I have a mother of my own.'[58]

Susy was charmed and told Kelly that she couldn't believe such 'a tall, handsome well-dressed man who speaks so kindly' could be 'that bloodthirsty villain' she had read about.[59]

Susy always had a soft spot for Kelly and years later claimed that 'there was a great deal of personality about [him] and he knew how to control men and circumstances … He would have made a magnificent general. He was a good son … and I believe a good brother.'[60] But Kelly had no time for small talk.

Susy's husband refused to hand over the keys when Kelly demanded he open the safe and strong room and, fearing repercussions, Susy dug them out of her husband's desk instead. Kelly took a sugar bag and loaded it with £1433 in notes, £500 in gold sovereigns, about £90 in silver coins and a 31-ounce (900-gram) dark gold ingot belonging to a Dry Creek miner.[61] Only a couple of years earlier Kelly had been working for £2 a week but now he told Scott he was disappointed with the haul and expected £10,000.[62] Kelly ordered everyone to get ready for a drive because they were all going to Faithfull's Creek. Susy astonished Kelly and her husband by changing into an outfit worthy of a royal gala, complete with French muslin, lace, ribbons, a stupendous hat covered in flowers and long white driving gloves.

Kelly had spent the last few weeks living rough with three other men in need of a bath and was gobsmacked by her appearance. But he quickly remembered why he was there. He told Scott to harness his buggy for transporting some of the prisoners, but Scott, still trying to understand his wife's bizarre behaviour, bravely refused and told Kelly 'do it yourself'.

Kelly eyed Scott angrily, but with a shrug of his shoulders said meekly, 'Well, then, I *will* do it myself.' Scott then offered Kelly and Hart a whisky, which they gladly accepted, but only after they made Scott take the first sip, just to be sure. The bushrangers then led their convoy back to Faithfull's Creek, with 14 prisoners including the Scotts, their seven children, Susy's mother and their staff.[63] To onlookers the procession of carts looked like a large family group heading to a picnic. A short distance out of Euroa they passed Bill Gouge's funeral procession and the dead boy's mother was aghast that the Scotts and their friends went by at such a disrespectful pace. Ned had the reins of the spring cart with a crestfallen Robert Scott plonked next to him.

He told Scott that Steve Hart wanted to blow the bank manager's brains out when he was unco-operative and that he'd better not give any more trouble.[64]

Hart rode alone on the way back to Faithfull's Creek and became lost. He came upon a curious old man driving an old cart and wearing an enormous pyramid hat. The angry young outlaw asked him for directions and when the old man told him he was a stranger in these parts, too, Hart bombarded him with 'obscene expressions' before galloping off. Later Hart told the others of his meeting with the 'old buffer' in the funny hat, and when informed that it was the Police Magistrate Alfred Wyatt, he replied, 'By

God, if I had known that I would have popped him.'[65] Wyatt had seen the damage to the telegraph wires while travelling into Euroa on the train that morning and after conducting his brief business at the Licensing Court had borrowed an old cart to drive out to the rail line for a closer look.[66]

THAT NIGHT AT FAITHFULL'S CREEK the Kelly Gang put on a display of trick-riding, with Ned 'maintaining his seat in the saddle in any position, sometimes resting his legs at full length along the horse's neck, and at others extending his whole body till his toes rested on its tail, dashing along at full speed in view of his prisoners'.[67] The gang played with the children and gave some sixpences. When bank teller Bob Booth asked for a souvenir from the gang's visit, Hart gave him a bullet with an 'H' carved into the lead and Ned gave him a bent sixpence.[68] MacDougall, the kangaroo shooter, begged Ned to return the watch Dan stole from him because it was a gift from his mother, and Ned made his furious brother hand it back.[69] Ned even apologised to the prisoners that he didn't pass a hotel on the return journey from the bank or he would have bought them all a drink.

But groom George Stephens would never forget that, despite the moments of Kelly charm and bravado, the gang had threatened to shoot and burn people and that Ned had proudly showed off the gold watch he had plundered from Michael Kennedy's dead body.

Stephens noticed that when they came back from the bank Ned not only gave Gloster's young mate Frank Becroft £2 for doing as he was told, but also gave him Thomas Lonigan's watch.[70] Lonigan's widow and four children were living with grief and poverty only a few miles away.[71]

Kelly put the bank loot onto his horse and the gang packed up all their guns. At 8.30 p.m. they ordered everyone back into the storeroom and announced they were leaving. The prisoners were to stay inside for three hours under penalty of death.[72] Robert Scott remembered that Ned 'did not seem a bit afraid of the police, but, on the contrary, laughed at them and at their efforts to catch him and his mates'.[73] Scott asked Hart where the boys were headed, but before the youngster could answer Ned replied, 'Oh, the country belongs to us. We can go anywhere we like.'[74] Then, in the words of their prisoners, the four immaculately dressed outlaws rode off north towards Violet Town 'at full gallop, on magnificent horses, and in a perfect cloud of dust'.[75]

The raid on Euroa was galling for the police who were finding the Kellys too fast, too clever and too well-concealed in their hideouts. Sadleir lamented that had Aboriginal trackers followed Maggie Skilling's trail to the outlaws' food drop early in the hunt the gang may have already been in custody. He complained that the trackers in Victoria at the time 'were altogether useless for the purpose'.[76]

The trackers working in Queensland had a much better reputation.

Soon Victoria would be looking to the distant north for deadly reinforcements.

Chapter 9

A S THE GANG MADE THEIR getaway from Faithfull's Creek, magistrate Alfred Wyatt was standing on a railway platform at Benalla 40 kilometres to the north with a bunch of torn telegraph wires in his hand, telling Superintendents Sadleir and Nicolson that he suspected it was the work of the outlaws.

The two veteran policemen scoffed. Nicolson told Wyatt that one of Kelly's close friends (Big Mick Woodyard) had grassed on the gang and that they were riding towards the Murray and an escape route into New South Wales.[1]

Nicolson and Sadleir then left Wyatt on the platform with his torn wires like a droopy bouquet as they boarded a train for the river crossing at Albury.

When they arrived at the New South Wales border town, they were met by a curt telegram from Standish telling them that the Kellys were nowhere near the Murray River. Instead the gang had made fools of the police, yet again, with the raid at Euroa, 200 kilometres away.

Having been at loggerheads with the commissioner for years and having nursed a persecution complex for much of that time, Nicolson endured a humiliating return journey on a special train south, finally arriving at the torn telegraph wires beside the Faithfull's Creek homestead at 8.30 a.m. on 11 December, 12 long hours after the gang had disappeared into the bush like mist.

The tough old Scot was half blind and 'suffering great pain' from ingrown eyelashes,[2] and the embarrassment of his tactical blunder compounded his physical and emotional agony.[3] The stress did nothing for Sadleir's poor health either, as he organised a search party to head south from Wangaratta.

At Faithfull's Creek, Nicolson met a seven-man police party led by Detective Ward and Senior Constable Johnston. Peering through his rimless glasses Ward examined the bonfire the Kellys had made of their old clothes and found a woman's hat and fan only partially burned. He told Nicolson that he believed Steve Hart disguised himself as a woman to evade his pursuers.[4]

Mrs Fitzgerald, the station cook, was soon sacked after being found with a large quantity of sixpences believed to have been a payoff from the gang.[5]

With the station's groom George Stephens helping, an Aboriginal tracker led the way as the searchers spent hours under a blazing sun charging about the countryside following the trail of the three bay horses and the one grey until all signs were gone. Most of the men were so exhausted by the day's wasted hunt that, when they returned to their hotel in Euroa, they fell asleep over their food.[6] Johnston, the County Tyrone horseman, 'the strongest and hardiest man of the party, a most energetic man' most of the time, was instead dead to the world on a sofa at the side of the pub. He couldn't be woken even when his comrades poured water on him.[7]

Sadleir's party believed they found traces of the Kellys but their trail petered out, and the frustrated superintendent despaired at 'the character of the forest country, into which each pursuit by the police led. Every part offered hiding places for fugitives … and all search seemed hopeless unless their very footprints could be traced.'[8]

After another futile search in the dark around Faithfull's Creek finished at dawn on 12 December, Nicolson flopped into bed at 6 a.m. 'heart-broken' and unable to sleep despite his fatigue.[9] Standish arrived in Euroa, furious. He said Nicolson had bungled the entire situation by not increasing security at the bank and by not instructing telegraph operators to immediately inform police where lines were broken. As a result, he said, 'a splendid chance of capturing the outlaws at Faithfull's Creek was lost'.[10] He found Nicolson 'very much knocked up in appearance, and his eyes bad',[11] so he sent him back to Melbourne. Standish had claimed that he once had 'perfect confidence' in Nicolson, but he now thundered that he had 'very good occasion to doubt him' because of what he termed Nicolson's 'procrastination and inefficiency'.[12]

Standish then called on his favourite lawman, big Frank Hare – a man whom he said never spared himself in any kind of way, but was most 'indefatigable in the pursuit of the outlaws'.[13] Nicolson and Hare had had long been rivals even before their race to capture Harry Power at his bush hideout and Hare's animosity to Nicolson festered with the knowledge that, while Hare was earning £375 a year, Nicolson was on £500.[14] Now Hare had the lead role in the most important case Australian police had ever undertaken.

THE ROBBERY AT EUROA dominated headlines around Australia. It was 'skilfully planned',[15] the newspapers declared, by young men of 'cool impudence and daring effrontery'.[16] It was also, they said, 'an awful disgrace to the Victorian police system'.[17] The four cop-killers had outwitted Standish's best, despite credible intelligence that a hold-up was imminent.[18]

Reports abounded of the gang's whereabouts, fuelled often by false leads supplied by Kelly's family and friends. Police in civilian clothes, bearded and dirty from camping out, were riding all around the countryside armed with rifles and revolvers, and were often themselves mistaken for bushrangers.

Premier Graham Berry increased the price on Ned's handsome head from £500 to £1000 and across Victoria '700 or 800 calico posters' advertised he was wanted dead or alive. His three accomplices were still only worth half that, making a total of £2500 for the set of four.[19] The price would rise again before long.

Victoria's colonial militia was staging war games amid the constant fear of a Russian attack on Port Phillip, and Premier Berry sent 50 soldiers by special train to Benalla to guard banks

The price on the heads of the Kelly Gang was constantly increasing.
State Library of NSW, DLADD 76/item 19

at Seymour, Avenel, Euroa, Violet Town, Wangaratta, Chiltern and Wodonga.[20] Another 58 police officers were deployed, increasing the number of active Kelly hunters in northern Victoria to 214.[21] Their arsenal included 217 British Beaumont-Adams revolvers in .442 calibre, 70 .442 calibre Webley revolvers, 25 Colt Navy revolvers in the lighter .36 calibre, 62 single-shot Martini-Henry breech-loading rifles in .577 calibre, eight .52 calibre Spencer repeating rifles, three single-shot Snider-Enfield .577 calibre carbines, 62 double-barrelled shotguns and 20 old muzzle-loading rifles.[22]

But all the guns were useless unless there was something to aim at and some of the police were not shy about voicing their concerns.

Four days after the Euroa raid, the Melbourne *Argus* newspaper declared that there was something radically wrong in the organisation of the police force and that the men were dissatisfied with their officers.

'They seem to feel that the routes they are ordered to take in pursuing the bushrangers are not those which are most likely to lead them to where the gang might be found,' the paper reported. 'Whether or not this idea is correct, the search for the outlaws as conducted in the past has been like looking for a needle in a haystack, and the men are naturally disheartened.'[23]

The paper revealed that a day after news of the Euroa outrage was published, 'sixteen well mounted troopers and two very competent black trackers' had been cooling their heels at the Mansfield barracks. One of the trackers was Tommy Spider, from the Cleveland Bay area near Townsville in North Queensland, and the other was 'Harry', 'a valuable horse tracker' from South Australia's Yorke Peninsula.

'Those could have been sent off at once to Euroa, distant only 42 miles, for the purpose of taking up and following the tracks of the desperadoes,' the newspaper argued, continuing:

As Ned Kelly's horse was newly shod, whilst the other three were unshod, a clearly defined and characteristic trail must have been left, one which the blacks could have followed very easily. It is a mistake to suppose that it is impossible to track in the Strathbogie Ranges, for in many places the ground is soft and boggy, and although the marks of the horses' hoofs might be lost on the top of the ranges and in rough country, yet they could be picked up at once in the valleys which would have to be crossed, and where they could only be obliterated by very heavy rains.

Instead of going to Euroa, a Mansfield party under Senior Constable Frank James only went down the Broken River for some distance in the direction of Benalla, and then returned to the township. James, though, would eventually lead a search party that found the Kellys' long abandoned camp near the site of the police shootings.

Thomas Meehan, the policeman who ran away from the suspicious characters when taking the news of the murders to Benalla, re-joined the hunt, partnering Constable Allwood and Tommy Spider on search missions into the Puzzle Ranges between Euroa and Mansfield but with no success.

Queensland's Irish-born Police Commissioner David Seymour offered to send a number of Aboriginal trackers south but Standish was opposed to the idea, convinced that the 'blacktrackers' were best used 'in pursuing and dispersing the native blacks' in large, uninhabited districts of Queensland where there was little or no traffic. He argued that they would be of 'little or no use' in northern Victoria where there was more traffic on all the roads, and where the movements of the outlaws were known to be 'wonderfully rapid', with them often riding 70 miles (more than 110 kilometres) through the night across countryside they knew intimately, and where there were 'numerous sympathizers, who would very soon obliterate their tracks'.[24]

Members of the police force complained that, six weeks after the killings, Bridget Kennedy and Maria Lonigan had still not received a shilling from the government 'and that the hardship [was] aggravated by the fact that arrears of pay were due' to their unfortunate husbands. The press blamed 'sheer red-tapeism' for the lack of support to the families of the dead officers and said the situation disheartened the members of the force who were 'called upon to risk their lives in the capture of the murderers'.[25]

SUPERINTENDENT HARE arrived in the north-east ready to take charge of the hunt, wearing a white sun helmet and brandishing a shotgun. A greyhound enthusiast,[26] he mixed play with work despite the gravity of the situation and brought his favourite dog with him on the train ready for an upcoming coursing meeting at Benalla.[27]

Hare also faced a race to restore public confidence in the law as Kelly's family and friends rubbed the noses of the police in the mess that the gang had created.

While Bridget Kennedy remained seriously ill in Mansfield trying to cope with the shock of her husband's murder,[28] her grief was compounded when National Bank notes suddenly became common around Victoria's north-east as the gang distributed the stolen money 'pretty freely'.[29] Bridget's friends tried to shield her from the newspaper reports that Ned has been flashing her husband's gold watch around Faithfull's Creek like a victory scalp. Bridget was now a widow with five small children and no means of supporting them apart from the charity of Kennedy's brother officers. At Violet Town the pain was just as cutting for Maria Lonigan, with reports that the village was in fear 'of receiving a visit from the marauders' and that two additional policemen had arrived with 'firearms in readiness'.[30]

Ben Gould went on a bender and boasted to Magistrate Alfred Wyatt that he was getting £600 out of the Euroa robbery.[31] Detective Ward dragged Gould into Benalla Court on 14 December and he was jailed in Beechworth on remand, looking 'especially seedy and miserable'.[32] The court heard that following the police murders Gould told fellow drinkers in Euroa: 'Serve the bastards right, there will be more of them shot before Kelly is caught.'[33]

Senior Constable James Gill reported that James Gloster, until recently heavily in debt, was likely in on the Faithfull's Creek operation as well. Despite being robbed of suits and a gun by the Kellys, he now seemed to have 'plenty of money to pay cash for whatever he buys'.[34]

A few days after the Euroa heist, Grace Kelly, Ned's 13-year-old sister, rode into Benalla on her pony, with an old frayed bridle and a makeshift saddle made from cornsacks. She dismounted, walked into a saddler's and, with a bag full of shilling pieces, bought the best bridle and side-saddle he had in stock.[35]

Kelly's two oldest sisters, Maggie and Kate, went on a Christmas shopping spree, buying clothes, hats, household goods, food and toys, and paying for the lot with £5 notes.[36]

Riding home from Benalla, Maggie encountered one of the police search parties. 'Good day, fellas,' she said, laughing. 'Now wouldn't you like to know whether I've got some of those sovereigns yet?'[37]

With her husband, Bill Skilling, locked up for six years over what was likely a mistaken identity, Maggie started sleeping with her cousin Tom Lloyd.

Police kept regular watch on Maggie's house from a distance, but the Kelly girls usually rode with dogs beside them and Hare

This old picture of the 'eighties looks impressive. It portrays Kate Kelly, sister of Ned and Dan, and has been for many years in the possession of the family of Mr. A. Skinner, 309 Sussex street, Merlynston, N.14. 10/6.

Kate Kelly went on a Christmas shopping spree after the Euroa bank robbery, buying clothes, hats, household goods, food and toys, and paying for the lot with £5 notes. State Library of Victoria H23557 lamented that 'sympathizer dogs and the dogs of the relations' are a great nuisance to the investigation. He appointed one of his men to drop strychnine baits to poison as many of them as he could.[38]

The Kelly sisters responded by keeping their dogs muzzled.[39]

Maggie and Kate regularly bought large quantities of food and tobacco in Benalla. Hare recalled that one morning, just after daybreak, Maggie rose early, jumped on the back of White-foot and rode up a steep gully at walking pace. Police followed on foot as quietly as they could, confident that their patience was finally being rewarded with a breakthrough. Maggie had a bundle wrapped and was sitting on the pommel of her saddle. After a long, steep, arduous climb that left the policemen red-faced and sweating, they found Maggie sitting on a log. Smirking, she put her thumb to her nose and waggled her fingers at them.[40]

The police were well used to these humiliations.

Sadleir felt that Hare gave too much attention to sending out search parties 'on the mere hope of their coming across the Kellys'. 'He certainly did not spare himself, and he shared with his men all the discomforts of camping out,' Sadleir recalled, 'but his fault, as I have always thought, was in confining his efforts to this one line and dispensing with the use of secret agents. He did indeed use Aaron Sherritt, if Sherritt did not use him, but he had none of the skill and patience of Nicolson in handling aids of this sort.'[41]

IT ASTONISHED HARE that so many of Kelly's close contacts seemed to regard the hunt for the killers as a lark. The day after Christmas 1878, Kelly sympathiser Andrew Morton, the disgraced son of Beechworth's congregational minister and a twice-convicted stock thief, wrote to Hare asking for a secret meeting with him 'under the culvert at Euroa on the 27th at 11 o'clock'. The two men met and Morton was handed £5 for some information that like so many tips from the public in Kelly Country proved worthless.

Constable Flood, now stationed at Hedi on the King River, reported that a letter had passed through the local post office containing particulars of an arrangement made for a meeting of the Kellys and a Chinese gold-buyer at a remote spot known as Spink's Crossing on the Ovens River. The Kellys wanted to offload the ingot of gold they'd taken from the Euroa bank.

Sadleir reconnoitred the place a day or two before the appointed time, and then, with Hare, arranged for a large party of police to hit Spink's Crossing at sunset on the day indicated by Flood. The men were to approach the place in ones and twos, to avoid observation as much as possible, and were then to await the two senior officers. When Hare and Sadleir reached the spot from another direction just at sunset, they were astonished to hear a tumult of voices from the river, and they immediately rushed forward, certain that some melee was on. As the two superintendents hurried on, a Chinese man, who had been concealed in some bushes overlooking the river, ran across their path, but they paid no heed to him in their eagerness to get to the scene of the tumult. There, to their shock, Hare and Sadleir found several policemen ducking and splashing each other in the water like children.

By this time the Chinese man could not be found, and, with diminished hopes, Sadleir and Hare settled down to keep watch throughout the night. It was a fruitless job, for the Kellys did not show themselves.

The incident did nothing to dent Hare's sizeable ego, which rankled other leaders of the police. Many of them regarded the big bear of a man as 'active, energetic, courageous and popular' but 'too little inclined to credit his brother officers with the possession of the same qualities'.[42]

Standish despaired that the Kellys had an enormous number of sympathisers, and that after their outrages many respectable men 'were in dread of their lives', fearing the consequences if they gave information to the police. Not only their lives and those of their families were in danger, but their cattle, sheep and horses were liable to be stolen or killed.[43]

FACED WITH PRESS and public ridicule, and fears that the Kellys could kill or rob again, Standish took the unprecedented step of ordering that the gang's support network should be immediately dried up. The commissioner called all the local police station chiefs and detectives to a meeting in Benalla and told them to use the *Felons Apprehension Act* to round up and imprison all those suspected of helping the Kelly Gang, even on the flimsiest of accusations.[44] He wanted Kelly's sisters to remain at large, though, still hoping that they might one day slip up and lead police to the outlaws.

Sadleir said apprehending sympathisers was an 'unwise step' and 'unlawful'[45] but Standish insisted the plan had the government's backing. So, on Wednesday, 2 January 1879, the commissioner issued warrants for the arrest of 20 of the so-called 'Kelly sympathisers'.[46] Hare insisted that they would all have to be brought in on the same day or that there would be 'just as much difficulty in catching them as the Kellys'.[47] So the next day police began a three-day strike that initially rounded up 18 friends, relatives and 'suspected associates'[48] to join Ben Gould behind bars. Many of the men were out in the fields cropping but the police showed no regard for their circumstances. They even handcuffed Ned's old workmate from the sawmill, Jack McMonigle, who insisted he was no sympathiser and in fact was appalled by the gang's crimes.

The police took Ellen's brother-in-law Old Tom Lloyd when they really wanted his nephew of the same name. Old Tom convinced the police to let him send a telegram home to tell his family of the arrest. He sent a message to Greta that said, 'Turn the four bullocks out of the paddock',[49] a warning for Ned, Dan, Steve and Joe to run. The alleged sympathisers were all handcuffed in pairs and taken to Beechworth Gaol, where 12 troopers from the Garrison Corps in Melbourne had just arrived with rifles and bayonets to repel any attempts at a rescue mission or mass breakout.

Most of the accused would spend three months behind bars and these 'witch hunts' created enormous resentment against the law and sympathy for the gang as neighbours and other family members had to harvest the prisoners' crops, feed their livestock and keep their farms going. Eventually there were 23 arrests, with little more evidence for most than an anonymous tip. Beechworth spent £790 on new iron gates to make the jail Kelly-proof.[50]

ONLY TEN WEEKS AFTER helping to find the bodies of the murdered policemen at Stringybark Creek, Constable Tom Kirkham endured another, far more personal, horror. Kirkham was back in Melbourne, stationed at the Richmond Depot and encouraging the budding talents of his wife, Ada, just 21, who was forging her own career as a dancer. By the night of 14 January 1879 Ada was into her third week as a ballerina in the musical extravaganza 'Alfred the Great' at the Academy of Music on Bourke Street. 'Alfred the Great' was co-written by the celebrated Australian author Marcus Clarke, who was still celebrating the success of his novel *His Natural Life* (later called *For the Term of His Natural Life*), and Melbourne society was enthralled by the musical's drama and splendour. It was totally unprepared for disaster.

Ada was passing a gas light outside a dressingroom on her way to the stage when the gauze of her costume suddenly erupted in flames. She screamed in terror and anguish, and as the flames quickly enveloped her, she ran toward the stage in a frenzy. The stage manager bolted towards her, wrapping the terrified young woman in a blanket as she rolled about the floor wailing to the heavens. Although the flames were quickly extinguished, the damage was already done. Ada had sustained severe burns to more than half her body and despite rallying a little in the Melbourne Hospital, Ada died from her wounds a week later.[51] An inquest found that the use of a wire cage around the gas burner, or a fireproof chemical for her clothing – a chemical that would have cost less than a penny – could have prevented her death. The whole theatre would be gutted by fire a decade later.

EARLY IN FEBRUARY 1879, a week after the first round of hearings for the sympathisers began, Detective Mick Ward was recovering in Beechworth's Ovens and Murray Hospital with fractured ribs and a banged-up knee after accidentally falling into a pit. According to rumours circulated by the Kelly sympathisers, Ward was 'tomcatting' among Beechworth's womenfolk. Aaron Sherritt, who had never had cause to wish Ward well before, sauntered into the hospital for a bedside chat. Ward was immediately on guard, since he had sent Sherritt and Joe Byrne to Beechworth Gaol on a six-month lag over stolen cattle two years earlier, and Byrne had let it be known that 'he would swing easily if he could shoot Ward and put his body in a hollow log and burn him to ashes'.[52] Sherritt told Ward that he had vital information for the police. He said a day earlier at about 2 p.m., Byrne and Dan Kelly came riding out of the hills to his selection. Byrne had jumped off his horse, a magnificent grey, and, after telling Sherritt that they had always been best friends, sat down beside his old chum on the grass and asked him to ride away with them across the Murray because the gang were heading for Goulburn, where the Kellys had a cousin.[53] Sherritt's story was that Byrne told him that the gang needed Sherritt to scout for them and watch for police patrols. Sherritt said he told Byrne that he had enough problems without putting a price on his own head. Ward was dubious about the story and why Sherritt had headed straight for him with the news. He became even more suspicious when Sherritt leaned in and said 'come with me, Mick, and we'll be able to get them before they cross the river'.[54] Not wanting to end up as ash in a hollow log, Ward begged off but said he would send two good men in his place. 'No deal,' Sherritt replied, 'the only bloke I'll take is you.'[55] Ward reached a compromise and organised a meeting between Sherritt and Standish in Benalla the next night. Standish was away so Frank Hare took his place.

Hare had never met Sherritt before but was immediately impressed by the fine athletic specimen before him, 'tall, strong, hardy but an outrageous scoundrel'.[56]

'[Sherritt] was a remarkable looking man,' Hare later recalled. 'If he walked down Collins Street, everybody would have stared at him – his walk, his appearance, and everything else were remarkable.'[57] Hare pretended he wasn't interested in anything

Sherritt told him about how the gang were heading to Goulburn but he kept him at the station until he was convinced he had all the information he needed to finally hunt down the gang.

He gave Sherritt £2 and told him there would be plenty more coming with every bit of information he revealed.

Sherritt left the Benalla police station smirking.

The Kelly Gang were indeed about to cross the Murray for a raid in New South Wales. But they were going nowhere near Goulburn.

On the afternoon of Friday, 7 February, while a large party of police watched the Murray near Corryong, the Kellys were 260 kilometres west, crossing the river halfway between Mulwala and Tocumwal.

They were on their way to Kelly's old horse-stealing haunt at Jerilderie. He had talked about shooting police there.[58]

JERILDERIE HAD A POPULATION of about 500 and was a thriving community with six hotels, three large general stores and its own newspaper. There was no church yet but Catholics held their divine service in the courthouse.[59]

Some of Kelly's supporters had already crossed the river, planning to act as scouts, decoys and plants among the townspeople. The Riverina was hot and dry but as the gang camped overnight in a thick, scrubby forest near Berrigan, there was a forecast of rain to break the drought.

The police murders continued to have every lawman and their families either side of the Murray in a state of high anxiety and at the Jerilderie Police Station, a three-room bark slab tenement on the edge of town,[60] Mary Devine[61] was shaken from her sleep by a terrifying dream in which the Kellys bailed up her family. She fretted for her husband, Senior Constable George Devine,[62] and their three children, two girls and a boy all under the age of seven.[63] Later that night, when her husband and his assistant, Probationary Constable Henry Richards, who also lived at the station, arrived back from patrol, Mary told George of her nightmare.

'You're always dreaming up some rot,'[64] he said with a laugh, trying to calm her. The next day George suffered a 'severe rupture', colliding with the pommel on his saddle, and had trouble walking, but he and Richards arrested an old drunk and put him in the log-cabin lock-up in the middle of the police paddock. The only light in the small cell, 3 metres square, was a 25-centimetre square opening in the massive door, through which food and water were passed.[65]

At about the same time, the Kelly Gang were spelling their horses in a pine forest 8 kilometres east of Jerilderie. At sunset, they reached Mrs Davidson's Woolshed Inn. There was a constant stream of passing travellers, drovers, dealers and station hands, so the arrival of four men posing as squatters went unnoticed.[66] The gang gleaned all the information they could from other drinkers about Jerilderie, especially about the number of police stationed there. Ned Kelly rebuked Byrne for drinking too much[67] and shortly after 10 p.m. gave the barmaid Mary 'The Larrikin' a tip of a florin (2 shillings) because she stopped giving Byrne whisky.[68]

A full moon was shining as the four horsemen began their ride to Jerilderie.[69]

Late on Saturday night, 8 February, Mary Devine climbed into bed beside George and realised that she hadn't emptied the bathwater from the tin tub in the kitchen.

She was tired and decided to leave it until the morning when she was due to take flowers to the courthouse to prepare it for the Sunday Mass being performed by a visiting priest. Then, at about midnight, the drunk in the log cell peered out of the opening in his door to see three shadowy figures creeping in the moonlight towards the police station.[70] A fourth figure rode to the front gate of the police paddock, opened it and rode on to the front door of the station.

Devine, still in great pain with his injury, was ripped from his sleep by a booming male voice.

'Devine! Devine! Are you inside?'

The weary policeman stirred uneasily, and without rising yelled back: 'Who is this? What's the matter?'

The gang bailed up lawmen George Devine and Henry Richards at their police station in Jerilderie. State Library of Victoria, IAN21/02/79/17

'Devine, where are you?'

'I'm in bed. What do you want?'

'For God's sake, man get up. There is a row going on up at Davidson's hotel. They're fighting. If they are not stopped there will be murder before the morning! Get up at once and bring Richards with you!'

Devine sprang out of bed, quickly pulled on his trousers and socks and, with Mary watching on warily, hurried out onto the veranda.

'Who's fighting?' he demanded of the bearded stranger on horseback in the street.

'A lot of drunken fellows. Where's Richards?'

The constable, who had been in his bed inside the office, opened the door of his quarters. 'I'm here,' Richards said. 'What's up?'

'Is there only two of you? The men are mad with drink!'

'Yes, just the two of us and that will have to do.'

With that, the man on the horse drew a revolver and, levelling it at the stunned officers, said: 'Throw up your hands! I'm Ned Kelly!'

Totally flummoxed, the two officers obeyed.[71]

Byrne emerged from the east end of the veranda, and Dan and Hart from the west, all with guns trained on the policemen.

Ned Kelly dismounted and ordered both his captives to march into the dining room.

He had heard that Richards, the taller of the two policemen, recently shot at a group of horsemen he thought were the Kellys.

Ned planned to teach him a painful lesson.[72]

Chapter 10

NED KELLY PUSHED THE two policemen through the
front door of the senior constable's home. He had his finger
on the trigger of his revolver as Mary Devine, dressed in her
nightgown, rushed out into the dining room. She saw the big,
bearded stranger with a gun pointed at her husband and fell to her
knees, pleading with him not to shoot 'for the sake of her little
children'.[1]

Ned told her to shut up.[2] As a man already under sentence
of death he had nothing to lose and had been contemplating
ridding himself of two more of his enemies. Perhaps he was only
grandstanding. He now said that Mrs Devine's entreaties saved
the lives of the two men,[3] and that if they did as they were told
no one would get hurt. 'But,' he insisted, tapping his revolver, if
he saw any signs of 'hanky-panky work … their blood will be
on their own heads'.[4] Ned asked Mary to make the gang a late
supper as Dan Kelly and Hart took their horses to the stables and
turned the police mounts into the paddock. Ned and Byrne then
marched the policemen to the lock-up and put them behind bars
with their drunken prisoner.

Devine was terrified. Not for himself, but for his wife.

'Please,' he begged Kelly, 'don't interfere with my wife.'
Ned was genuinely insulted. The man who had been portrayed
as a monster and mutilator by sections of the Victorian press
indignantly replied that he and his mates 'had always treated

women with the greatest respect and courtesy'. He might have shot armed men dead but he insisted no matter what the law or anyone else could say against the gang, 'they could not truthfully charge them with any disrespect to women'. And Kelly wasn't finished with that, declaring that it was more than could be said about many of the Victorian police, 'whose cowardly conduct to defenceless women was well-known'.[5]

Even Superintendent Hare would agree years later that the gang 'never behaved badly to, or assaulted, a woman but always treated them with consideration and respect ... In like manner they seldom, if ever, made a victim of a poor man. And thus they weaved a certain halo of romance and rough chivalry around themselves.'[6]

'Rough' was the word. Still trying to overcome the trauma of seeing a killer aiming a gun at her husband in the middle of the night, Mrs Devine was forced to take a candle and, with hands shaking, surrender all the weapons in the house.[7] All four outlaws then sat down to eat a supper she made for them, though Ned carried out the bathwater for her, saying it was no job for a lady in her condition. After supper, with the plates cleared away, she was allowed to retire to her bedroom, where her children were asleep. The outlaws lay down on the floor in the dining room but there was no rest for Mrs Devine, worrying about the safety of her husband and children.

The next morning she made the gang some breakfast and Devine and Richards were allowed back into their home to have theirs. The drunk ate in his cell.

Then Ned donned Richards's police uniform and Dan tried on the smaller one belonging to Devine. Mary told Ned that Mass was to be celebrated inside the courthouse 90 metres away[8] in an hour – at 11 a.m. – and that she always prepared the altar. Ned realised her absence from the service would create suspicion, so he told Hart, dressed in a spare uniform, to go with her.[9] The young Irish priest Father Richard Kiely had only been to Jerilderie once before, and like the rest of the Catholic flock he assumed the new uniformed troopers around the police barracks were reinforcements to guard against the Kellys.[10] Hart followed Mrs

Devine to the courthouse, poking her in the back with a revolver when no one was looking and telling her he would shoot his own mother if she did not do as he said. When Mrs Devine had to hurry home before Mass began, the parishioners and their priest assumed she had 'extra household duties to attend to' with the additional police in town.[11] That afternoon, Joe and Steve, wearing the police uniforms, took Richards for a walk, telling him to introduce them as new constables. For an hour or so the three strolled about the town as the outlaws made notes on the positions of buildings. The Bank of New South Wales was housed in a converted assembly room[12] in the eastern portion of the Royal Mail Hotel, where Ned had previously stayed. Back at the police station Ned took from his saddlebag a 56-page letter he had been working on for weeks: an expanded version of the letter he sent to Donald Cameron and Sadleir. He had dictated all his rage and irrationality to Joe, whose penmanship and vocabulary were the most polished of all four outlaws, though the competition wasn't fierce. Kelly gave Mrs Devine a taste of some of the 8300 words in his 'Jerilderie Letter'. In it, he threatened more slaughter if his mother wasn't released, tried to explain what happened at Stringybark Creek and hinted at an uprising against British rule by Australia's Irish.[13]

'This cannot be called wilful murder,' he wrote of the police killings, 'for I was compelled to shoot them or lie down and let them shoot me. It would not be wilful murder if they packed our remains into a mass of animated gore to Mansfield ... certainly their wives and children are to be pitied but they must remember those men came into the bush with the intention of scattering pieces of me and my brother all over the bush ... and is my brothers and sisters and my mother not to be pitied also who has no alternative only to put up with the brutal and cowardly conduct of a parcel of big ugly fat necked wombat headed big bellied magpie legged narrow hipped splawfooted sons of Irish bailiffs or English landlords which is better known as Officers of Justice or Victorian Police.'[14]

To Ned, 'The Jerilderie Letter' was a declaration of independence for all the downtrodden in Victoria, an Irish call to arms against tyranny. But with her husband locked up and a triple murderer prattling on in her parlour, Mary Devine had other things on her mind than his grudge against society. Two days later she couldn't remember a word of what this most unwelcome guest was jabbering on about.[15] She did remember 'very well' that Dan Kelly placed her son on his knee and played with him for some time, and that, while 'Ned Kelly and Joe Byrne were quite good looking … Dan Kelly and Steve Hart were more like Chinamen than white men'.[16]

The next day, at about 10 a.m., Ned ordered Constable Richards out of the lock-up, told him to put on his police jacket, and gave him an empty revolver to put in his leather holster.[17] He then warned Mrs Devine not to go outside until they returned. Though Kelly claimed to have always treated women with respect, he threatened to burn her house down on top of her and the children if she raised the alarm.[18] With Dan and Steve following on horseback at a distance, Joe and Ned, now in the police uniforms, walked with Richards between them to the bar of the Royal Mail Hotel. Ned told the startled publican that he was robbing the bank and turning the hotel into a temporary prison. Any trouble would result in bloodshed.[19] Every thirsty patron who came into the pub had a revolver put to their head before being marched into the holding pen inside.

John Sadleir lamented that just one 'bold man, armed with say a double gun' could have picked off the outlaws. Instead, he said, Jerilderie had the 'indignity of having their town laid under tribute by four hooligans'.[20]

Kelly and Byrne entered the adjoining sitting room of the bank through the back door 10 minutes after midday.[21] Ned made straight for the manager's room while Byrne entered the door to the teller's office and safe. The gang made prisoners of the bank's athletic young accountant, Edwin Living,[22] and the junior staff member, 17-year-old James Mackie.[23]

The bank manager, John Tarleton, was bailed up in the bath. The local schoolmaster, Bill Elliott,[24] who only a year earlier had encouraged the parents of his star pupil John Monash to send the

The Jerilderie branch of the Bank of New South Wales was the site of another audacious robbery by the Kelly Gang. murrumbidgee.nsw.gov.au

boy to a top school in Melbourne, walked into the bank to deposit the takings from the collection plate of Methodist missionary Reverend John Gribble,[25] only to end up staring down the barrel of Joe Byrne's revolver. Ned ordered the manager to open the inner drawer of the safe and to throw together the chamois leather bags of coins, rolls of notes, deeds, mortgage documents, jewellery and precious heirlooms that would never be returned. He told Elliott that he would burn all the bank's mortgage documents because 'the bloody banks are crushing the life's blood out of the poor struggling man'.[26] Among his loot was the watch of a deceased young girl, a family keepsake. The mother's distress later at a second cruel blow for the family was 'very great'.[27]

HAVING SEEN FOUR NEW policemen wandering about and Trooper Richards looking decidedly nervous, the local newspaper editor, Samuel Gill,[28] headed to the police barracks to quiz George Devine about what might make a scoop for his readers. He knocked at a window, heard a child crying and then saw a haggard Mary Devine with the weeping infant huddled in a corner. Mary had trouble forming the words but finally blurted out: 'Run. Your life is in danger!' Gill bolted down Jerilderie Street and into the store owned by John Monash's father, Louis, and breathlessly told him and his assistants what he'd seen.[29] Gill kept running and rounded up Monash's rival shopkeepers and Justices of the Peace James Rankin[30] – all 140 kilograms of him – and Hugh Duffin Harkin.[31] The three headed to the bank to let John Tarleton know there was danger lurking only to hear Ned Kelly cocking his handgun inside. All three turned to flee but the corpulent Rankin fell over as Ned leapt onto him. Gill ducked behind a brewery wagon to hide[32] and then bolted through the scrub for 10 kilometres, looking over his shoulder every few steps. He finally reached the Carrah homestead to raise the alarm late in the afternoon. When Rankin told Ned that the man who got away was the newspaper editor, Ned had trouble stopping himself from exploding. He had wanted Gill to publish his 'Jerilderie Letter' – the 'history of my life'[33] he called it – and run off copies for mass distribution. With his plans thwarted, his face became 'distorted with the violence of his passion'.[34] He and Hart said they would kill Rankin. 'Put the bugger on his knees,' Hart roared 'and I'll put a bullet through him.' But the prisoners, now 30 or so strong, begged for Rankin's life.

Bill Elliott thought Kelly's show of strength 'was a matter of bluff', knowing that if one shot were fired the whole party of captives would rush the outlaws, even if there were Kelly supporters planted among the genuine prisoners.[35] Ned called Hart by the nickname 'Revenge' and told him to shoot the first person who tried to escape and to keep the first bullet for 'Fatso'.[36] Hart asked the prisoners about the local auctioneer Michael Curtin, with whom he once argued over stolen horses and whom he promised to deal with when he returned to Jerilderie. Curtin had gone to Urana on business.[37]

'Bugger,' Hart said. 'I wanted to shoot him. We would have shot Devine and Richards if not for Devine's wife pleading for them.'[38]

Still in police uniform, Joe Byrne cantered over to the Jerilderie Post Office to bail up postmaster Henry Jefferson.[39] He stole his watch, dismantled the Morse key and pointed a revolver at James Rankin's frail and sickly 14-year-old son James junior who was working there. Byrne ordered the telegraph poles to be cut down and threatened to shoot anyone who touched the wires before 9.30 the next morning.[40] Ned, meanwhile, marched Edwin Living and Trooper Richards to the house of the newspaper editor. He knocked on the Gills' door and was again surprisingly polite when a cautious Mrs Gill answered it, telling Ned she knew who he was but that she had been told her husband had run away. Kelly showed her the Jerilderie Letter and said he wanted Gill to publish it and run off copies for distribution.

'Look here, Mr Kelly, if you shoot me dead,' Mrs Gill replied, 'I still don't know where he is. You gave him such a fright. I expect he is lying dead somewhere.'[41]

The letter was Kelly's way of communicating all his troubles and making his impassioned plea for his mother's release. Disgruntled, he instead gave the letter to Living, who promised to get it into print.

Kelly then took Richards across to Thomas McDougall's[42] Traveller's Rest Hotel[43] and, revolver in hand, demanded the famous black racing mare Minnie. He returned the horse later in the day, though, when Reverend Gribble, a fearless and pious man devoted to helping Aboriginal people in remote corners of Australia,[44] told him that McDougall's young daughter was 'inconsolable' about the theft of her pet.[45] Then calling Hart a 'thing', Kelly made his young accomplice give back the reverend's watch that he had stolen earlier.[46] Gribble described Kelly as 'a fine, noble-looking fellow, tall, and well-proportioned, with a long, flowing brown beard'.[47]

Back in the Royal Mail, Kelly delivered a farewell speech. Only a few people in the crowd, his planted sympathisers, applauded as he outlined all his grievances – that Constable Fitzpatrick was a 'low, drunken blackguard' and that with few exceptions most of the police were a 'lot of lazy, loafing scoundrels, always ready to swear a man's life away, if they thought it would gain them promotion'.[48] He gave them a long rundown on the killing of the police that made most in the crowd shudder, and then he declared with theatrical pomp: 'Now, I am going to shoot Constable Richards before I leave.' There was a deathly silence. Ned ordered

Richards to step out from the group and face him. Richards was one of the policemen involved in the recent Tocumwal fiasco, when New South Wales police shot at Victorian police across the Murray, each suspecting the other were outlaws. Richards nervously stepped through the crowd to the front.

Ned looked him dead in the eye, pointed his revolver at him and snapped: 'You were one of those who fired, weren't you?'

Richards stood firm. 'Yes, I fired across the river at them.'

'You aimed to hit them?'

'Yes, I did.'

'You did your best to bring us down?'

'Yes, I did my best. I fired two shots before we found out they were police we were firing at.'

'You did not know me, and yet you tried to kill a man you never saw before, or who never did you any harm?'

'I was doing my duty. You were outlawed at the time.'

'You would have taken my life if you could, so you now cannot blame me for shooting you?'

'Yes I can. We were both armed then and had an equal chance in the fight. If you shoot me now, you shoot an unarmed man who has no chance of his life. I was doing my duty; but look here, Kelly, you are now armed and I am not. Give me a loaded revolver and I'll fight you now, and if you shoot me, it will be in a fair fight.'

Kelly had already booked an appointment with the hangman or a bullet, so it mattered not if he had another murder on his record.

But he wanted everyone to believe that he was a widow's son wronged by unjust laws and that the killings at Stringybark Creek were done in self-defence.

After a slight pause, as Richards's heart raced madly and beads of sweat pooled on his forehead, Ned told the young policeman, 'All right, you can go now, for I'm damned if I don't like your pluck.'

After a day of humiliation, Richards refused to give ground.

'That's all right, Kelly,' the trooper said, 'so long as the two of us are armed it will be you and me for it.'[49]

Kelly let him have his moment. Then he told Richards, postmaster Jefferson and his young assistant that he was taking them to the lock-up but that all the other prisoners could go 'when you like'.[50] He returned Jefferson's watch that Joe Byrne had stolen and made Hart give back the saddle he'd taken from Edwin Living.

Back at the police lock-up George Devine was in severe pain from his rupture.[51] Kelly gave Devine's 'poor, terror-stricken'[52] wife the lock-up key but told her not to let anyone out until 7.30 p.m. or her house would burn.[53]

Altogether the gang stole £2100 in cash and jewellery, but just like in Euroa Kelly had expected more. They also took two revolvers from the bank and two from the police, plus the policemen's pair of .539 bolt-action Calisher and Terry rifles. Hart took Devine's striking grey horse.

When Kelly's spies told him that John Tarleton and Edwin Living had bolted to get help, he said the gang would return to shoot the pair of them and anyone who tried to fix the telegraph lines.[54]

Living and Tarleton rode hard for almost 100 kilometres to Deniliquin, and then caught a train from the new station there to Melbourne so they could report the robbery in person at head office.[55] Instead they were treated like imbeciles when they arrived for letting the Kellys run roughshod over them.[56]

The four gang members rode out of Jerilderie to Wunnamurra Station, 8 kilometres out of town, suspecting that Living and Tarleton might be hiding there. Bank clerk James Mackie's brother was the manager of the property. But after causing a degree of terror with interrogations, the gang rode on towards Tocumwal and the Murray.

Kelly's threat to return to Jerilderie that night was an idle one. Mackie, schoolteacher Bill Elliott and the town's chemist, Rudolph Gartman, ran down to the police station to liberate the policemen and telegraph operators, but despite her husband's physical and mental anguish, Mary Devine was still in 'terror at the outlaws' threat' to return and refused to hand over the key until 7.30.[57] Four men defied Kelly's orders and began restoring the telegraph poles strewn along the road, while Louis Monash and others hunted around for guns, ready for a shootout if the bandits returned.

Many of the townspeople were reluctant to produce weapons because they feared the sympathisers still in Jerilderie, but Louis Monash found a rusty old revolver. He brought it over to the post office and raced around for ammunition. James Rankin provided four double-barrelled, breech-loading shotguns and plenty of cartridges. A carpenter lent Bill Elliott his shotgun and the new recruits stood guard in the post office as the alarm was finally sent down the telegraph line just after 8 p.m.

Rain began to fall and it pelted down for hours, obliterating any tracks as, once again, the Kellys vanished like ghosts.

WITH THE CLUMSY MANHUNT an embarrassment to his force, Commissioner Standish was now under pressure from politicians, his senior officers and a sarcastic press to employ the best trackers on the continent.

Kelly and his gang had barely time to divvy up their loot when the governments of New South Wales and Victoria announced a combined reward of £8000 for the outlaws, dead or alive. Appalled that the police killers had now invaded his patch and indeed commandeered one of his own towns, New South Wales Premier Sir Henry Parkes gained immediate support for his proposal that his colony should kick in £3000 towards their capture or death, with another £1000 supplied by Sydney banks.[58]

A surveyor named H. Curzon Allport, who had spent some years working in North Queensland, approached the inspector general of the New South Wales Police, Edmund Fosbery, suggesting he go up to Queensland to bring down 'six or eight natives who have either been in the police force, or have had the experience in bush fighting, and who can track a bare footed man over the hardest ground'.[59]

Curzon knew the Riverina country well, having been a surveyor around Echuca and Wagga, and he said he had spent many years 'in some of the least civilized parts of Australia, and had carried arms and used them in some warm affairs, both here and in the South Seas'.[60]

He only asked for expenses and a share of the reward and offered to arm his trackers in Sydney at the Lassetter's store where Winchester repeating carbines were on sale at £8 10s each and Colt army revolvers at £4 10s.

Curzon was ready to start at a day's notice and his Queensland trackers would require no supplies for the field, he said, 'beyond a pound of tobacco and a handful of salt, which is often all men have to help through a four or five weeks patrol in North Queensland. They trusting to their tomahawks for the rest.'[61]

The New South Wales Police were interested in the idea but believed the gang had recrossed the border, and were therefore once again Victoria's problem.

Standish also read Curzon's request with interest but he already had a better idea.

Five days after the Kellys had ridden out of Jerilderie, Standish had a rethink about the Queensland trackers and had fired off an urgent telegram to Commissioner David Seymour in Brisbane.

From Benalla 15.2.1879
Confidential. Can you send me down a party of Black Trackers say eight with some one accustomed to manage them they might come by sea to Sydney whence Mr Fosberry [sic] would have them forwarded to Albury the country where outlaws hide is very mountainous in places covered with dense scrub very rocky with deep gullies quite inaccessible to horsemen inform me rate of wages any expenses you may incur sending them to Sydney will be at once remitted if you can do this endeavour to send them off as quietly as possible so that it may not appear in newspapers.

(Sd) F.C. Standish
CC Police[62]

Seymour met with Queensland's colonial secretary and former premier Arthur Palmer, another Irishman, who was a pastoralist from central Queensland.

Two days after receiving Standish's plea, Seymour told his Victorian counterpart that the colonial secretary had approved of sending trackers provided they volunteered for the service, received extra pay and were assured of a fair share of the reward being offered. Their rate of pay was £3 per month.[63]

Standish immediately sent word:

> Confidential will pay your trackers any sum per day you may fix also find provisions when in the bush. They will receive a fair proportion of Government reward should they succeed in leading to capture or death of the outlaws.
>
> (Sd) F.C. Standish
> Chief Comr. of Police[64]

Seymour told Standish there was no hope of keeping the matter from the newspapers. He and Palmer saw the opportunity for all of Australia to know that Queenslanders were coming to the rescue and would hunt down the most feared criminals in the country.

Seymour was a hard man, a strident proponent of flogging to keep order and a police chief who, in a Brisbane riot twelve years earlier, had ordered his officers to fix bayonets and load live ammunition to disperse a large crowd near the Treasury Hotel in Queen Street.[65] He was sure his Aboriginal trackers and their commander Stanhope O'Connor would show the Kellys no mercy.

Chapter 11

ON THE DAY THAT commissioners Standish and Seymour reached agreement for Queensland to send trackers to Victoria, Stanhope O'Connor was with six of his Native Police on the northern bank of the Endeavour River near Cooktown, lighting a large bonfire to signal the success of their latest manhunt.

According to press reports that would soon circulate around Australia, O'Connor and his troopers had massacred at least 28 Aboriginal men as punishment for wounding Captain Sykes and William Hartley with their shower of spears 11 days earlier on 6 February 1879.

Queensland was a colony where the lives of Indigenous people were often given less value than that of the profits from sheep and cattle.

Archibald Meston,[1] a journalist, explorer and politician, once wrote that in Queensland 'white men shoot blacks for fun, to try the range of their weapons, to teach them a lesson, or from a general idea that, like snakes, they should be wiped out'.[2]

Another journalist who had been in Cooktown for some time wrote that squatters in Queensland's north had deemed it necessary to use Aboriginal trackers to drive what he called 'wild blacks' away from their native land.

These 'blacktrackers', he said, formed the nucleus of the Queensland Native Mounted Police, which was composed exclusively of young Aboriginal men in the prime of life, and generally taken from the 'Southern tribes to be employed against their Northern brothers'.[3] It was a common occurrence, he wrote, to see a white officer riding through Cooktown at the head of a dozen Aboriginal troopers in uniform, with Snider-Enfield carbines slung across their shoulders, and their ammunition belts stocked with cartridges. Sometimes they would depart in the dead of night on secret missions and return a few days later, covered with dust and fatigue, their ammunition belts empty but their hands full with spears that they brandished as war trophies. On the wooden butts of their rifles some of the troopers carved notches, and some of them had many notches, each one for a man he had killed.[4]

Early in 1879 O'Connor told authorities he had brokered a truce with the Guugu Yimithirr people after repeated spearing attacks on horses and cattle. O'Connor said he had made the Guugu Yimithirr 'acquainted with the friendliness of the whites', promising not to 'disperse' them so long as they did no harm to the settlers or their stock, and stopped cutting the telegraph wire.[5]

He also promised them that if they were hostile again in any way to the white men, he would come down on them. Hard.

So it was that on 14 February 1879, four days after the Kelly Gang rode out of Jerilderie, O'Connor and his six Native Policemen, along with two Chinese labourers carrying their rations,[6] crossed Cooktown's harbour in a boat at night and by moonlight picked up the tracks of those believed responsible for wounding Sykes and Hartley.

The hunted, though, were not easy to catch and, sensing the approach of the lawmen, they were said to have retreated with a group of women across the range to an ocean beach.

But O'Connor was not about to let them escape. He divided his hunters into two, and with one party made a detour in the direction of Cape Bedford.

Now advancing on two fronts, O'Connor and his men finally hemmed in their targets inside a narrow gorge on Sunday, 16 February.[7]

According to newspaper editor William Henry Campbell, who became a Member of the Queensland Legislative Council, the only two escape routes were secured by the troopers, who lifted their Snider-Enfield rifles and took aim.[8]

The Guugu Yimithirr people were trapped. O'Connor wasn't sure these were the people who had almost killed the two white men but they might have been.

Screams of terror tore through the bush as the desperate prey raced for their lives. Wide-eyed and with hearts pounding, they ducked and darted this way and that, trying to dodge the bullets and get away through the gorge.

According to Campbell, 24 of the 28 men were shot down. The other four and one of the women made it to a nearby beach and dived into the boundless sea. No one recorded how many women died during the roar of the gunfire. They almost never did. But with bodies all around and the sand red with blood, O'Connor and his men were said to have sat down on the beach, keeping the surviving, wailing women prisoners under penalty of death. Together they all waited for the five ocean-going escapees to return. They waited and waited while the police cleaned their rifles and prepared to finish their day's shooting.

After four hours in the water, the head of the Aboriginal woman was spotted emerging from the waves and one of the Native Policemen dived into the water and swam out to her. Four hours in the ocean made resistance futile and she was dragged back to the beach.

O'Connor conjectured that the other four men had drowned.

The troopers hunted up the remainder of the Aboriginal women and searched them. After finding Hartley's meerschaum pipe and tomahawk, O'Connor said he was satisfied that he had not made a mistake in killing at least 28 people.

He told one of his troopers to explain this to the shattered, bedraggled women, who numbered 13. After this was done, he let them go away to lick their wounds and mourn their men.

O'Connor and his troops then returned to the north shore of the Endeavour River the next afternoon and lit their large fire 'as a signal of success'.[9]

NED KELLY'S RAGE OVER the plight of his mother and baby half-sister locked up together in Pentridge Prison bubbled over. Despite the haul from Jerilderie his hopes to have his 'Jerilderie Letter' circulated around Australia to plead his case had fizzled into nothing. Edwin Living had taken the letter on his escape from the town and stopped to revive himself at John Hanlon's hotel, 13 kilometres from Deniliquin. Hanlon made a copy of the letter and Living took the original to the Bank of New South Wales in Melbourne.[10] When Living returned from there, he asked Hanlon for the copy, promising to give it back to him, though he never did.[11]

Jerilderie schoolteacher Bill Elliott read the Hanlon copy and, calling it the 'emanations of wild fancies from a disordered brain',[12] summarised it for newspaper editor Samuel Gill, now back out of hiding after hearing that the Kellys were long gone. Gill sent a summary to *The Age* in Melbourne, which published a 3600-word article called 'Ned Kelly's Letter' on 18 February. Other newspapers also published long summaries of the document, but its entire contents were not publicly revealed for 51 years,[13] such were government fears about its revolutionary tone and Kelly's criticism of the police.

NEW BANKNOTES FROM Jerilderie were soon circulating around Greta. The McAuliffe family of Greta, close friends of the Kellys, seemed to have a sudden turnaround in their fortunes. Sergeant James Whelan reported that, while Mrs McAuliffe had been penniless before the Euroa and Jerilderie raids, she was now renting 300 acres (121 hectares), 'had bought £60 or £70 worth of cattle, a £12 horse and a £10 side-saddle, employed four men on fencing, had sent a son to Tasmania and bought home a daughter who had been "in service"'.[14]

Much of the money also went on lawyers for the alleged sympathisers, who had been thrown into Beechworth Gaol and were being remanded there week after week.

A Royal Commission later declared the arrests of the sympathisers were counter-productive and said they only 'did violence to people's ideas of the liberty of the subject; they irritated and estranged probably many who might have been of service to the police ... and, what was of more significance, the failure of the prosecutions led the public to believe that the conduct of affairs was mismanaged'.[15]

STANHOPE O'CONNOR had no intention of mismanaging his next assignment. There were rumours that Queensland would send a party of trackers to Kelly Country under the command of the 'The Black Avenger', English-born policeman Tom Coward, whom the press said was reputed to have killed more Aboriginal people 'than any ten men in Australia'.[16] But David Seymour and his police chiefs in North Queensland had other ideas.

Just after O'Connor returned to Cooktown from Cape Bedford, his boss, Inspector John Isley, handed him a telegram from Seymour stating that the Government of Victoria, now desperate to destroy the Kelly Gang, required a detachment of Native Police, and an officer capable of commanding them. Isley had chosen O'Connor for the duty, and wished to know if he would go. He would receive double his Queensland wage plus an allowance of 12 shillings a day.[17] O'Connor first saw the telegram at about 4 p.m. and within the hour had accepted.

Travelling to Victoria was just what he wanted. His 19-year-old fiancée, Louise Smith,[18] was the daughter of a seven-times mayor of Melbourne[19] who had just died of cancer at his mansion in Flemington, leaving behind a fortune of £42,500 that included property and stations on the Darling River in New South Wales, and in the Warrego District of Queensland.[20] A share of that inheritance would certainly clear up O'Connor's massive debts. Louise's much older sister Helen was married to Assistant Commissioner Nicolson and that represented a sterling opportunity for O'Connor to press for a well-paid posting in Victoria.

Just two days after agreeing to the assignment, O'Connor and his team were on their way to Brisbane aboard the SS *Alexandra*, with newspapers declaring that he had 'every confidence in his boys', believing they would hunt the gang down day by day, and 'could no more be shaken off than bloodhounds'.[21]

As Victorian police scoured the mountains around Mansfield and Mrs Kelly's home in Greta, O'Connor was in Brisbane on 27 February showing off his team of trackers to Seymour who sent out an official police memo that day stating:

A Detachment of Native Police consisting of one Senior Constable and six troopers under the command of Sub Inspector O'Connor will proceed to Sydney tomorrow by the *Alexandra*, and thence by train and coach to Albury where instructions will await them from the Chief Commissioner of Police of Victoria, under whose orders they will consider themselves while on duty in that Colony.

Sub Inspector O'Connor will obey all instructions given him by the Chief Commissioner and will co-operate cordially and cheerfully with the members of the Victorian or New South Wales Police with whom he may be required to serve. He will also from time to time as opportunity occurs communicate with the Commissioner of Police, Brisbane.

He will look carefully after his troopers and be particular about their arms and ammunitions – see that they are properly clothed and fed and are always in the charge of either himself or the Senior Constable.

... Sub Inspector O'Connor must recollect that he merely goes as an assistant; that the conduct of affairs is entirely in the hands of the Chief Commissioner and his officers, and therefore that in obeying any orders given him he frees himself from responsibility for anything beyond his own acts.

(Sd) D.T. Seymour C.P.[22]

O'Connor's second in command was fellow Irishman Senior Constable Tommy King,[23] from Maryborough, Queensland. Their six wiry Aboriginal trackers were mostly from Mackay and Fraser Island, or K'gari, as they called it. They were 'specially

Jack Noble, from Fraser Island, with his wife Alberta.

Trooper Jimmy, who would be shot by the Kelly Gang. Queensland Police Museum

Gary Owens, known as Trooper Barney. Queensland Police Museum

Trooper Johnny had a long history of violence. Queensland Police Museum

selected' by O'Connor for their work alongside him in North Queensland.[24] Their names were Jack Noble, his brother 'Corporal Sambo', three other men known as 'Jimmy', 'Johnny' and 'Hero', and Gary Owens, whose tribal name was Werannallee,[25] but who the police referred to by the nickname 'Barney'. They were aged from 16 to 24 and most had been riding with O'Connor since he sailed into Cooktown three years earlier. They called him 'Marmie', which he explained was 'an old Queensland black word, meaning "Mister"'.[26]

Jack Noble, a Butchulla man[27] whose Aboriginal name was Wannamutta,[28] was the tallest of the trackers. He was born at Sandy Cape on Fraser Island but taken from there at the age of 14 or 15 by Tommy King and pressed into service for the police.

Noble's brother, who was known as Quambo or more often by the common racist term 'Sambo', was the oldest of the trackers. He was said to have earned a reputation with the Native Mounted Police as a 'good tracker and splendid fighter' but in his younger days was known as a 'notorious rascal who had committed every sort of crime, including being a bushranger'. It was Tommy King who had captured him and brought him into Maryborough after a long and difficult search, only for Sambo to be duly acquitted at trial due to a lack of evidence.[29] King thought that with his bush skills Sambo would be the perfect fit for O'Connor's team at the Lower Laura in North Queensland.

Tracker 'Johnny' was also known as 'a notorious character' who had been accused of killing an Aboriginal woman a year before in Charters Towers. Some of the police who knew him actually thought that he was insane.[30] But O'Connor reckoned Johnny was the best tracker he had ever met, recalling that on the hunt for a murderer in North Queensland that involved two detachments of eight men each, Johnny was the only one who could find the killer's tracks.[31]

Not all of O'Connor's men were able to speak English when they enlisted, but while the young Irishman understood some Aboriginal languages, one of the rules of the service was to never allow men to use their native tongue.[32]

He was adamant that his men were far more efficient in groups of five or six and that if they were sent out in just ones and twos, they became 'thoroughly demoralized'. They were peculiar men, he told his colleagues, and required a 'great deal of drilling to keep them up in a good state of efficiency ... They require to be kept together, to have their friends and connections in the same barracks to make them contented. Some were natural enemies away from the force, he said, and sometimes it resulted in murder.'[33]

The solidly built Tommy King was born at Kerry, Ireland, 27 years earlier and had come to Queensland as a boy. At 17, he followed his father and brother into the police force and was originally stationed at Ipswich.[34] He had earned acclaim as a member of the first gold escort from Gympie and, as he prepared for his meeting with Ned Kelly, the press described King as 'the best man, on horseback or as a tracker, that Queensland can produce'.[35]

'There certainly is no give–in or back–out with Sub–inspector O'Connor or our Tom King,' one paper said. 'Many fervent wishes for success follow Senior–constable King ... the cause in which he risks himself is a righteous one, and a more honest or brave heart than his has never trod the path of duty.'[36]

O'Connor was not so impressed with his assistant, remarking that 'the very best white tracker I ever knew could not come up to the worst black tracker I ever had'.[37] King drank heavily, too, and O'Connor quickly wearied of him.

WITH A MIX OF SHOCK AND AWE, Ned Kelly read the unsettling newspaper reports that O'Connor's men had been ordered not to eat the bushrangers when they finally caught and killed them, 'although most of the natives of northern Queensland to which these men belong are cannibals to the extent of eating enemies slain in battle'.[38] Looking smart in their blue uniforms and caps with red facings, the troopers were all heading to Kelly's known haunts armed with revolvers and Snider carbines, but it was their unseen weapons that sent a chill through the outlaws. Kelly had feared Aboriginal trackers since his childhood. He was 'astounded and terrified'[39] by them, because he knew they could follow a trail no one else could see, and he called O'Connor's troopers 'those six little demons'.[40]

As the *Alexandra* headed south, there were reports around Albury that the Kelly Gang were hiding in the mallee scrub on the New South Wales side of the Murray, waiting for a favourable opportunity to cross the river near Balranald. Kate Kelly was said to have arrived in the town and secured apartments at Edmund Powell's Rose Hotel, with the 'evident intention of remaining there for some time'.[41]

Ned Kelly knew, though, that he could not stay in one place for long.

As the *Alexandra* carried the latest Kelly hunters south to Sydney, reports of the massacre at Cape Bedford sparked outrage. While O'Connor was lauded as 'one of the most experienced officers in the Queensland Native Force' and a man always 'selected for dangerous duty in that colony',[42] the *Brisbane Courier* asked whether the Cooktown killings were 'Swift Punishment, or Wholesale Massacre'. It said O'Connor's action appeared to be 'a strange and awful violation of all the principles of justice' and 'out of all proportion to the offence'.[43]

The *Maryborough Chronicle* said such qualities as 'mercy' were absent in the Native Police, 'a force ostensibly established to protect blacks and whites alike, but whose cold-blooded cruelties have long stamped it as a damning blot on the fair fame of the colony'.[44]

Another newspaper pointed out that there was so little love among the white community of North Queensland for their Aboriginal 'brothers' that if 'fifty or a hundred blacks had been shot, the popular verdict there would have been "good job"'.[45]

Commissioner Seymour brushed off the controversy, though, saying he had received a telegram from John Isley in Cooktown stating that O'Connor had made no official report on the subject, and that since no white man had accompanied the sub-inspector on the mission to confirm the details, what happed in North Queensland stayed in North Queensland.[46]

The Brisbane *Telegraph* scoffed at this explanation saying the killings were 'unnecessary and disgraceful barbarity' and that:

Mr. Isley has not the least idea of what Mr. O'Connor and his troopers were doing on the north shore of the Endeavour … Mr. O'Connor may have given his immediate superior a graphic description of his triumphant raid, but officially – oh, no, such things are never mentioned. Only every man in Cooktown knew exactly what had happened … Officially, we never shoot blacks – we send our troopers to 'patrol' a district, we 'disperse' a tribe that proves troublesome … the consumption of cartridges by the native police may be accounted for entirely by their activity in keeping down the number of marsupials. Some time ago an abominable outrage was explained away by an official story of a kangaroo hunt … The shame is that we compel the force to act in such a furtive manner and bury all their proceedings in such profound secrecy, that under cover of it they are tempted to do deeds for which no possible justification can be offered.[47]

When the aging Bishop Mathew Hale, who headed a Queensland government commission for Aboriginal welfare, asked the Colonial Secretary Arthur Palmer whether the reports of the slaughter were true, Palmer refused to deny them, but replied that he was 'not in the habit of taking any notice of absurd paragraphs in newspapers'.[48]

Hale had laboured to improve the lot of Aboriginal people in South Australia and Western Australia before arriving in Queensland. As a result of his pressing Palmer about the massacre, funding to his commission dried up and it eventually died.[49]

O'CONNOR WAS FROM WESTMEATH, the same Irish county as the late Michael Kennedy, and he had revenge to score and the double pay to make.

After arriving in Sydney he and the trackers stayed for a few days, before O'Connor finally shook hands with Commissioner Standish at Albury Station at 7 p.m. on 6 March.[50] It was the high point of a relationship that deteriorated quickly.

The brothers Jack Noble and Sambo had become seriously ill on the voyage south and Standish gave permission for the party to stay and eat at Albury's Rose Hotel until the two trackers were well enough to continue their journey.[51]

At 9 a.m. on 8 March 1879, Standish accompanied O'Connor to Benalla and two days later Tommy King and the six troopers joined them by the afternoon train.

The Queenslanders took up their quarters at the police camp. Then they visited the barber, apparently to look their best when they shot it out with the outlaws, and then they went shopping. There was much speculation in the press about their chances against Ned Kelly and his men. The trackers were described in the newspapers as 'a small, slight looking body of men, more intelligent than our own natives' but so slim that they would not cause the Kellys to shudder 'if they meet them … They are reticent, but apparently confident and self-reliant, and thoroughly under the control of their leader.'[52]

It was a different story with O'Connor who looked to be 'a fine, smart, dashing-looking young man'.

He carried a belt round his waist full of rifle and revolver cartridges and had the 'appearance of one who would care very little whether he met one or half-a-dozen Kellys'.[53]

That would soon be tested.

Only hours after the trackers had arrived, Standish ordered that they lead the hunt into the mountains the very next morning.

Chapter 12

A S STANHOPE O'CONNOR and his men prepared to invade the densely forested lairs of the Kelly Gang, sightings of the outlaws were reported all over New South Wales and Victoria. There were reports that Hart had been treated by a St Kilda doctor for syphilis;[1] a magistrate swore that he saw Ned, wearing a short jumper with a pocket full of apples, getting into a horse-drawn cab in the middle of Melbourne; and Joe Byrne was rumoured to have visited his mother's farm repeatedly.

At another time it was claimed that the gang had hidden in the head of a fallen tree to escape a search party.[2] Despite Aaron Sherritt's hot tip that they were heading to Goulburn, there was no sign of them there or at Corryong where the large party of police waited forlornly.

On 12 February, two days after the Jerilderie robbery, a man reported to Beechworth police that he saw Dan Kelly near Taylor's Gap. Detective Ward and two constables investigated but found nothing.

Frank Hare then drove his buggy out to Beechworth, and quizzed Aaron Sherritt to explain his false information.

Sherritt's first words were: 'Did I not tell you they would stick up a bank in New South Wales?'

Hare replied, 'Yes, but you told me they were going to Goulburn.'[3]

148

'Well, they will be back probably tonight, to Woolshed,' Sherritt said, knowing they wouldn't be.

For a time Sherritt and the Kellys laughed at the games their mate was playing with the police, and the gang planned to send him £100 of the Jerilderie money, through Joe's brother Paddy, though the money was never delivered.

Sherritt told Hare to meet him at a place in the ranges, known to Detective Ward, and he would then show the officers where the Kellys tied up their horses, while they went into Mrs Byrne's house for supper.

Ward had known Sherritt for years and told Hare that, while the notorious larrikin could put them in a position to capture the Kellys, he was most likely taking the 30 pieces of silver from the police while playing them for fools.

Still, Hare's faith was boosted by the fact that Sherritt's father, Jack, had been a constable in Ireland.

At 8 p.m. that night Ward and Hare met Sherritt at the appointed spot in the ranges and waited anxiously for a party of back-up mounted police from Eldorado. After an hour Sherritt told Hare, 'You will be late, Mr Hare. We should have been nearly three miles from here by this time.'

Hare told Ward they should follow Sherritt on horseback to the Kellys' secluded camp. The night was terribly dark, and Sherritt took the two veteran lawmen at a dangerous pace over rough ground, living up to his reputation for being tough and fearless. He might have taken Hare over a cliff if he chose as the superintendent could see nothing.

Suddenly in a whisper Sherritt told Hare: 'This is the bushrangers' country; no one ever comes in here but them.'[4]

They were then high in the mountains about 16 kilometres from Beechworth at the back of Woolshed. Hare and Ward rode along with their chief informant, winding round a treacherous creek one minute, and over logs and rocks the next, trusting entirely to their horses.

Suddenly Sherritt pulled up. 'They are back from Jerilderie,' he said almost inaudibly. 'Do you see that fire in the distance?'

All three men dismounted.

'What do you want me to do?' Sherritt whispered, 'I will do whatever you like.' In the remote, dark, dense forest, so silent that Hare could almost hear his racing heartbeat, the big superintendent told Sherritt he needed to know if the bushrangers were sitting or sleeping near the fire.

Sherritt removed his boots and, without hesitating, set off crawling along the ground like a snake, aiming to get as close to the fire as he could. Ward and Hare were now alone, prepared for 'do or die'. They stayed in the same spot for about ten minutes, deciding how they would make the attack, though outnumbered. Then they heard footsteps coming towards them at a quick pace.

Ward hissed: 'He has sold us; who is this coming towards us?'

Both lawmen, with revolvers in their hands and ready to shoot, remained perfectly still until the footsteps came within a yard. A voice they recognised as Sherritt's said, 'Mr. Hare, we have been deceived. That fire is on the opposite range and some miles away.' Hare's first thought was that Sherritt had gone to the fire and warned the bushrangers to escape but Hare and Ward investigated and found Sherritt was telling the truth.

Sherritt then told them they must hurry on to Margret Byrne's house because the gang were always a chance to be there.

The policemen followed Sherritt down a fearfully steep range until he said: 'I am afraid to go down here tonight, it is so very dark. Be careful not to move from your saddle, for this is a terribly steep range, and if you attempt to get off you will roll down hundreds of feet.'

He told the 130-kilogram Hare and Ward to dismount, and they led their horses round and came down another gap in the mountains. They followed Sherritt down the ranges until they came to Mrs Byrne's.

Sherritt crawled up to the house. Everything was quiet and there was a candle burning. Sherritt returned and told Hare and Ward to wait in a stockyard overlooking a clump of trees at the back of the house, where the outlaws generally tied up their horses. It was then about 2 a.m. The three sat and waited and waited and waited until daylight, and then, with nothing happening, the lawmen started forlornly back to Beechworth, arriving at 8 a.m.

Soon Sherritt suggested that Hare should bring a party of men and camp in the mountains at the back of her house. He said he could put the superintendent in a blind gully that was like a cave and was unknown to anyone except the bushrangers. The only danger of being discovered was by them. He said Hare could stay in the mountains by day and take up his position in the stockyard behind Mrs Byrne's at night. That evening Hare arrived with his men – his 'cave party' – carrying blankets and provisions, intending to stay there for as long as it took to catch the Kellys.

Hare stayed for 25 days straight, waiting and watching as the nights grew longer and bitterly cold. He and his men had to be careful where they trod, for fear of their tracks being discovered. They dared not make a fire for fear of the smoke being noticed. For three and a half weeks they lived on water, cold preserved beef and bread.

Sherritt, who always wore the same outfit – a white shirt, trousers and long boots, with his trousers tucked inside – would spend his evenings inside Mrs Byrne's, courting her daughter Katie, and telling police that he was constantly gathering information on the Kellys. He generally bade the Byrne women farewell after midnight and came to lie down beside Hare on watch, whispering to the superintendent his latest intelligence, usually all kinds of encouraging reports. Hare fought his exhaustion in the stockyard night after night, expecting four armed horsemen to suddenly appear like phantoms in the moonlight. He was constantly disappointed.

As each dawn broke, the police would creep back to their camp in the mountains, disappointed, avoiding the paths or soft places so as not to leave tracks.

At the same time, Hare placed four men in a spot pointed out by Sherritt as one of the remote bush camps used by the Kellys, 'a wonderfully romantic spot, on the edge of a precipice, and only approachable on one side'.[5] It was here that the gang had

Veteran policeman Joseph Ladd Mayes was
regarded by Superintendent Frank Hare as
'a bold, trustworthy, well-tried man'.

stayed after the murders, while Sherritt supplied them with
food. Hare regarded it as a defensive stronghold where two men
could hold off a dozen. The camp was placed under Irish-born
Senior Constable Joseph Ladd Mayes,[6] a 21-year veteran of the
force regarded by Hare as 'a bold, trustworthy, well-tried man,
in whom I had the utmost confidence'.[7] But the police presence
was discovered by the ever watchful Mrs Byrne, who came upon
a spot of flattened grass where an officer had been sitting and
'whittling' a stick. Margret told Sherritt to go and have a look,
but Sherritt, instead, immediately told Hare of her suspicions.

Police also put feelers out in the Chinese community around
Beechworth, a community that had once welcomed Joe Byrne,
taught him Cantonese and encouraged his use of opium. Informers
Ah Man and Ah Toy gathered information for Detective Ward,
and Ah Man earned £8 18s from the police after spending 27 days
sussing out information around the Buckland River.[8] The police
also rented a paddock from which a spy, posing as a 'broken-down

selector', could keep watch on Jim Brien's orange grove, which the outlaws visited back in November.

STANHOPE O'CONNOR was confident that his men would not let the Kellys escape once they found any sort of trail and were allowed to hunt the gang on their terms.

He wasn't anticipating interference from Victoria's commissioner, who seemed to believe that he knew more about tracking in the bush than the Aboriginal manhunters.

On the night of 10 March 1879, O'Connor, Sadleir and Standish sat in the commissioner's office in Benalla.

'Now, O'Connor, what is the way you work?' Standish asked.

'Well, sir, I would like to take two white men, Victorian constables; I would like them for watches at night. I can trust everything to my boys with that one exception.'

'You do not know what kind of men those outlaws are,' Standish replied. 'If you leave your horses anywhere, they will turn round and hamstring or shoot your horses. You must not think of such a thing. I would not allow it. You must take not less than six or seven men.'[9]

Standish insisted O'Connor take half a dozen Victorian officers with him and O'Connor protested that the large hunting party was far more likely to send an early warning to the gang. But Standish was unmoved.

O'Connor was angry, but he obeyed Standish's orders and, as Frank Hare remained hidden above Mrs Byrne's property with his cave party,[10] O'Connor, Tommy King and their six trackers rose early on 11 March, the day after they'd arrived in Benalla.

At 11 a.m., with Corporal Sambo still feeling ill in the much cooler climate of Victoria, Standish dispatched the newly arrived Kelly hunters with Superintendent Sadleir and six Victorian policemen for a week-long search in the mountains.

They were to make a wide circle on the north side of the Wombat Ranges in the hope that they might cut the tracks of the Kellys passing to and fro between their various haunts.[11] Five packhorses carried their supplies.

They searched the mountain tracks along what was known as Harry Power's route and found some stale tracks of horsemen. O'Connor doubted that they were tracks of the Kellys, but the men followed the faint trail for a day until nightfall, riding down to Holland's Creek and past Fern Hill Station. In some places the fallen leaves, blown about by the wind, covered all traces; in others where there was stony country, tracks were few and far between, and then little more than an occasional scratch of a horse's shoe on a surface rock.

The men they were tracking along Power's route were revealed as stockmen searching for sheep.[12]

While O'Connor's relationship with Standish quickly deteriorated, he maintained a close friendship with Sadleir, who had always been intrigued by the trackers' hunting methods and watched them intensely on their first mission.

Sadleir said their skills derived from their 'manner of life before they were drawn into the service of the white men' and that the life of their tribes 'depended on the skill exercised in the pursuit and capture of the wild creatures that provide its food. In their wild state each and every individual is continually on the lookout.'[13] Sadleir was especially impressed with the fact that, while previous trackers had taken police off the trail when they sensed danger near Lake Rowan, these men were always eager for a shootout.

Still, the cold and severe weather of the high country played havoc with their health, and O'Connor complained that Standish had not supplied them with sufficient food and bedding for difficult and unfamiliar conditions in the mountains. Sambo's throat burned and his coughing and spluttering would have alerted the Kellys from a mile away. The corporal became so sick that O'Connor sent him back to Benalla four days into the mission.[14]

The rest of the Queenslanders kept hunting for the gang but when O'Connor and his troopers returned to Benalla at 5.50 p.m. on 18 May they were met by Constable William Bell, who told them that Sambo was on his deathbed. He died in the police barracks the next night at 8.30.[15]

'Sambo had one regret paramount to all others,' the newspapers said, no doubt stretching the truth, 'and that was the leaving of his master, Inspector O'Connor, whose life he saved in Queensland on two occasions.'[16] The other trackers cried when they heard of Sambo's death, but only one of them, his brother Jack Noble, went to Benalla Cemetery with O'Connor for his funeral. Sambo was buried in what Standish called the 'most economical manner' under his direction.[17] The 20 shillings spent on the grave was taken from a government fund for destitute persons but Standish said that was a mistake since 'this Queensland native trooper was doing regular duty as a Constable with the Victorian Gov't and his illness was contracted while he was on active duty in the ranges'.[18]

Following Sambo's death, Hero was promoted to corporal and Moses Bulla, who had grown up on the Coranderrk mission, approached O'Connor and purportedly said, 'I am a Queensland boy, and I would like very much to go back to Queensland with you.'

Inspector William Montfort, who had helped to hunt down bushrangers Mad Dan Morgan and Harry Power, considered Moses 'a most active little fellow and more intelligent' than the other trackers.[19]

O'Connor asked Standish for permission to include Moses in his team and Standish, who never participated in the search parties, preferring comfortable digs in Benalla, replied: 'He is no good to us, and you had better take him if you like.'

Moses became the source of much bitterness for O'Connor, who later called him 'a good-for-nothing fellow'.

O'Connor said he mentored Moses in police methods and that 'when he got of some use Captain Standish [tried] to get not him only, but another of my men'.[20]

ON THE DAY AFTER SAMBO'S DEATH, Ned Kelly and Joe Byrne were reported to have been among a crowd of 150 prizefighting fans on the New South Wales side of the Murray River, just downstream from Echuca.[21] The mob had gathered at dawn to watch a much-anticipated bareknuckle bout on 20 March in which Australia's most famous boxer, another pugnacious Irish-Australian Catholic, Larry Foley, won a brawl against Englishman Abe Hicken.[22]

The reports only confirmed the police frustration over the support the Kellys were getting from sympathisers.

O'Connor informed Commissioner Seymour in Brisbane of Sambo's death and gave him a detailed report on their first mission:

> The gang are supposed to be near about here, but nothing reliable has been heard about them since the Jerilderie affair … You can have no idea of the sympathy shown to these ruffians, even ladies look upon them as heroes, and all the lower class unite in trying to fool the police.[23]

Bishop Moorhouse was just one of the many onlookers in Benalla amazed at the 'little people' leading the manhunt, and O'Connor's trackers were glad to put on an exhibition for the cleric. Their boomerang throwing astonished him. A crowd of onlookers watched the bishop as he dodged the return flight of the boomerangs, sometimes flinging himself flat on the ground in what Sadleir regarded as a 'very unepiscopal way', and 'tipping' the trackers with coins after every throw'.[24]

ON 16 APRIL 1879, O'CONNOR and his remaining troopers started out for the Wombat Ranges again, but once more with about an equal number of Victorian policemen. Again, O'Connor protested that the party was way too large to be effective in hunting bushmen as skilled as the Kellys.

There was a credible report from the Upper King River of traces of a horseman who might be one of the Kellys. A 60-kilometre ride brought O'Connor and his team to the place the suspicious character was seen. Although the signs were not easily noticed by the white officers, O'Connor's trackers quickly spotted a sweat mark where the man had shaken a loose rail and the mark of a spur strap where he had dismounted to drink from a creek. They pressed on and the signs became visible to all.

They found a sheath-knife and horse-dung that was still warm. O'Connor told the men to leave their horses and follow on foot as the nostrils of the trackers distended with excitement. They crept forward on their heels. Then one of the trackers suddenly drew back, beckoning to the rest of the party to follow. On hands and knees, they crept to a hut 60 metres away. There were a few whispered words, and then a silent rush of police through the door of the hut, and suddenly a sleeping figure was being held down by eight pairs of strong, heavy hands.

'By God, it's Dan Kelly,' cried one of the triumphant police. He was mistaken. The man was John Morphy, the son of a goldfields commissioner Sadleir knew. Morphy was scared witless but recovered and shared with his visitors a hunk of corned beef that he had prepared for his dinner.

O'CONNOR AND SADLEIR did their best to circulate stories of the trackers' uncanny skills, knowing they would quickly reach the Kelly Gang's ears and heighten their feelings of terror.

Sadleir always thought it strange that Frank Hare, who had urged the Victorian government to obtain the Queensland trackers, showed little interest in their work. Sadleir surmised that the big man was looking forward to the Kellys being captured by the white police alone.[25]

Hare continued to use Sherritt – who he codenamed 'Tommy' and 'Moses' in police correspondence – as his key to unlocking the riddle of the Kellys' whereabouts, even though officers, such as Daniel Barry,[26] a County Kerry Irishman who spent 45 days watching the Byrne house, were not convinced Sherritt was trustworthy.[27] Hare intercepted a letter from Joe Byrne, written in peculiar slang-like code, to Sherritt telling him to meet him a week later at the Whorouly Races, about 40 kilometres from the Kelly home in Greta.

Byrne wanted to meet his mate at the back of the course and ordered him not to say a word about the rendezvous. He said that he had a black mare that Sherritt had ridden in a steeplechase race previously, and that the mare was in good order and sure to win.

THE KELLYS' GANG—QUEENSLAND NATIVE POLICE SEARCH PARTY.

Stanhope O'Connor's six Queensland trackers were the subject of much media interest before their first mission in Victoria on the Kelly hunt. State Library of Victoria, IAN12/04/79/52

O'Connor pleaded with Commissioner Standish to allow the trackers to tail Sherritt from a distance, but Standish refused. O'Connor bristled.[28]

Hare sent mounted constables in uniform, but selected his three most daring officers to send separately in plain clothes – Tommy Lawless,[29] Alf Falkiner[30] and Charlie Johnston, who were unknown in the district. All were crack riders mounted on the fastest horses the police could find and according to Hare 'pluckier fellows never trod the earth … The men and horses could have been backed against the Kelly Gang, man for man, at anything.'[31]

Lawless was a small, wiry Irishman, and from a distance was sometimes mistaken for Steve Hart in build and appearance.[32] He broke in horses for the police at the Richmond depot along with his brother. Alf Falkiner had been part of the Benalla search party sent to find the bodies of Kennedy and his men, while Johnston was a hothead ready to shoot the Kellys at any moment.

Hare also rode out to Whorouly, pretending to take great interest in the races.

Johnston saw three men riding outside the course. Taking it for granted they were the outlaws and without a moment's consideration, he galloped off alone towards them. Hare watched him return, terribly ashamed. All Johnston could mutter was that he could not help himself.[33]

Byrne's brother Paddy[34] had been with Sherritt for much of the day, but the subject of Joe was not mentioned by either of them and the bushranger and the black mare never made an appearance. Despite hopes for a gunfight, Lawless instead rode in the steeplechase himself and won it, for what was the most exciting incident of the day.

WITH THE QUEENSLAND trackers on their tails, the Kelly Gang now hid in different locations in the most rugged country they could find, moving constantly and using calls in the night like animal sounds as signals. Their rest became infrequent, their moods more despondent, their actions more frantic. They could only risk lighting small fires and had to remove all ash and cover the black spot before riding off.

Such was the gang's caution over the trackers that, with winter approaching, they moved to a hut above the snowline, hoping it would thwart men used to working in tropical Queensland.

As Frank Hare and his cave parties battled the cold, dark nights above Mrs Byrne's farm, and the constant frustration of not seeing their quarry, Sherritt confessed to the superintendent that he had been mixed up in 'all the crimes with the Kellys for years past'.

Hare came to regard Sherritt as 'an outrageous scoundrel'[35] but he had great respect for his toughness and 'most wonderful endurance'.

'He would go night after night without sleep in the coldest nights in winter,' Hare reported. 'He would be under a tree without a particle of blanket of any sort in his shirt sleeves whilst my men were all lying wrapped in furs in the middle of winter. I saw the man one night when the water was frozen in the creeks, and I was frozen to death nearly. I came down and said, "Where is Sherritt?" and I saw a white thing lying under a tree, and there was Aaron without his coat. The men were covered up with all kinds of coats and furs, and waterproof coatings, and everything else, and this man was lying on the ground uncovered. I said, "You are mad, Aaron, lying there"; and he said, "I do not care about coats."'[36]

Hare asked him once, 'Can the outlaws endure as you are doing?' Sherritt replied: 'Ned Kelly would beat me into fits. I can beat all the others; I am a better man than Joe Byrne, and I am a better man than Dan Kelly and Steve Hart. I can lick those two youngsters to fits; I have always beaten Joe, but I look upon Ned Kelly as an extraordinary man; there is no man in the world like him.

'He is superhuman.'[37]

As winter approached, the plight of the freezing policemen only worsened their reputation as fools among the local populace. Hare confessed that one night while he was hiding in the grass behind the Byrne home, Joe Byrne may have stepped right over the top of him, with Hare believing it was one of the family's friends.[38]

Mrs Byrne became increasingly suspicious of Sherritt, convinced he was lying to her when he said he could find no traces of the police around her farm. Despite the withering gaze of the weathered matriarch, he continued his visits to the house, and his romance with Katie Byrne continued. He was still providing Hare with information, none of it particularly helpful. He was convinced that, when the gang were caught, Joe would be spared. Standish, though, had already told Victoria's Attorney-General that such mercy was a 'course which I should be unwilling to recommend'.[39]

Between January and April 1879, the Sherritt family received £74 15s from the police, with some of the money going to Hurdle Creek headmaster Jimmy Wallace,[40] codenamed 'Bruce',[41] a childhood friend of Joe and Aaron. Like Sherritt, he was also providing a good deal of false information.

One evening Detective Ward came to Hare's cave party and told him that Dan Kelly had been seen near Myrtleford, riding in the direction of Beechworth. Sherritt convinced the police to camp at the home of Sherritt's mother, Anne, because the gang were sure to call there. Hare rode over to Anne Sherritt's and secreted himself inside their barn – a large open building within a few yards of their house.

Hare said that the two nights he spent in the barn with two officers beggared description.

'The pigs slept in the straw,' he said, 'and the fleas beat anything I ever felt in all my life; the mice, also, were running over me, and I really believe that a snake went over me also … I had arranged with Mrs Sherritt that if she heard footsteps, or anyone coming to the place during the night, she would call out, as a signal, "Is that you, Jack, or Willie? [Sherritt's brothers]" and I could hear their reply.'[42]

Aaron stayed all night in his mother's house, in case the outlaws called to see him. Once or twice during the night Hare heard footsteps approaching the house, but the outlaws never showed, and all Hare had for his time among the pigs were nightmares and a smell that seemed to linger forever.

The 25 days and nights Hare spent around the Byrne house played havoc with his health and morale. Sherritt suffered, too.

On one of Hare's last mornings there, he and Sherritt ate a breakfast of sardines and bread, and each of them lay down and fell asleep. At about 8 a.m. the Irish-born police sentry, Senior Constable Luke Mills,[43] told Hare that Mrs Byrne was on the prowl.

Hare sat up in his cave, looked out and saw Mrs Byrne climbing up to a high place where the police had breakfasted. 'She used to go crawling along like a rabbit, and only show her head over the rocks,' Hare recalled.[44] Margret noticed a sardine tin shining on a rock and looked down in the direction of where one of the men was lying, then halted for a moment, and retreated. Hare watched the tough old lady from his hidden vantage point.

As Margret left, Hare jumped up and went to see who it was she had spied, and to his horror found it was Sherritt.

Hare told Mills, 'Go up and give the old woman a fright,' hoping it would chase her away. So, Mills crept up behind her and gave Margret 'a tremendous yell'.[45]

Margret almost fainted but then she gathered her composure and fire, and roared back, 'I will get my son to shoot the whole bloody lot of you.'[46]

Hare was not certain Mrs Byrne could have recognised the person she saw sleeping in the grass because Sherritt was lying partly on his side. But Hare told Sherritt about what had happened, and the tough bushman turned deathly pale.

Huge drops of perspiration dripped down his face.

He could scarcely speak, but Sherritt finally gasped, 'Now I am a dead man.'[47]

Chapter 13

THE TOUGHEST PART of life for Ned Kelly and his gang was constantly keeping guard against a surprise raid by police. Victorian officers spoke of the Aboriginal trackers' 'wonderful skills' and word quickly passed down to the gang through their network of spies, so that Ned became 'dreadfully afraid' of Stanhope O'Connor's men.[1]

But while O'Connor and Commissioner Standish should have been focused on the outlaws, they spent much of their time loading bullets to fire against each other.

On their second hunting expedition, O'Connor, Sadleir and their men rode along the King River, and on the fifth day out, 21 April 1879, arrived at De Gamaro station. Workers there told them that they had seen a horse matching the description of one of the police mounts taken from Jerilderie. They offered to show O'Connor the horse and its tracks, but just as they were arranging for an early start for the next morning a constable galloped up to the sub-inspector with a letter from Standish, saying his men should return to Benalla. Frank Hare was pursuing a lead in the Warby Ranges instead.

O'Connor and his team returned to Benalla on 23 April, and it wasn't until months later that two police horses taken from Jerilderie were found in the King Valley.[2] O'Connor told Standish he had erred by not letting him follow the horse's trail. Dissension and bitterness arose, and Standish began to find the young Irishman 'insolent in his manner'.[3] O'Connor became increasingly irritated by the way Standish treated him, saying the commissioner did not believe anything that the Queenslanders uncovered.

'When we gave information about it, he laughed at it,' O'Connor said, 'and took no more trouble about it. Up to about this time, and a little later, Captain Standish was upon the most intimate terms with me, and often expressed a wish that I would join the Victorian force after the Kellys were taken.'[4]

O'Connor accused the commissioner of being jealous that his men would find the outlaws.[5] Standish wanted to take O'Connor's men from under his command and place them in different townships, but O'Connor told him that such action was in direct violation of the orders O'Connor had from Brisbane on 13 May that he was not to separate himself from the troopers and not to allow any to be detached from him.[6]

Standish was soon saying the trackers and O'Connor had been 'sent for against my recommendation',[7] and he pinned all his faith on Frank Hare, even though Sadleir often remonstrated with Hare over what he said was the folly of spending days and valuable resources on speculative missions.[8]

After Hare left the cave party above Mrs Byrne's home, he was constantly on the move. His object was to harass the outlaws as much as possible and he sent out parties of policemen – 'a splendid lot of fellows' he called them – in every direction, going all day, and watching for fires at night.[9]

His right-hand man was Joseph Mayes, who acted as his sergeant, and next to him was Luke Mills.

The others included Charlie Johnston, Tommy Lawless, Alf Falkiner, Daniel Barry, Tom Kirkham, still grieving terribly for his young wife, an Irish-born probationary constable named William Canny[10] and sometimes Moses Bulla, who Hare regarded as a 'capital tracker'.[11] Hare's deployment of Moses without O'Connor's permission was a continuing source of fury for the Queensland officer but the big superintendent lived in hope that Lawless, Falkiner or Johnston might have a chance to show the

Kellys that they were their superiors on horseback by eventually running them down.

'There was not a weak spot in any of them,' Hare said. 'I felt that I could at any moment have said, "I think the outlaws are in that cave, go and pull them out," and they would have been proud to have been selected for the purpose. No work was too much for them, day or night, and I never heard a grumble.'[12]

In May 1879, Standish received a letter from a well-to-do farmer, informing him that four persons answering the description of the Kellys were using a hut near Benalla. Keeping the news from O'Connor, Standish told Hare to get cracking with his own team. When he heard about it, O'Connor said Standish was foolish in refusing his men permission to follow Hare, but Standish replied, 'I will endeavor to get the Kellys without your assistance.'[13] Standish claimed that with all their horses and baggage, O'Connor's trackers were too slow, but O'Connor said that was nonsense and in fact the Victorian policemen could not stay with his 'boys'.[14]

Standish 'was in great glee' when he received the report that the Kellys were hiding near Benalla, and he and Hare sat up half the night talking about their next move.[15]

At midnight, Hare went round to his men in the Benalla barracks, waking them and ordering them to be ready to follow him into battle at 4 a.m. At 3 a.m., they all rose, readied their horses and provisions, and rode out at daylight. Afraid word of their mission might leak out to Kelly's sympathisers, Hare took his men in the opposite direction for miles before filling them in on the plan.

They camped at eight that night, tied up their horses and, after having some water, bread and beef, laid down until 1 a.m. As the men got out of their hammocks, Lawless cried out, 'I say, Mr. Hare, I think some of these hammocks will be for sale to-night.' He meant that some of the lawmen would likely be shot, as all were convinced they would fight the outlaws that morning.

The officers were in great spirits as they passed through the railway gates at Glenrowan. They often found great difficulty in crossing the railway, for many of the gatekeepers were in league with the Kellys. Hare always found that the Glenrowan gatekeeper required a lot of calling before he rose. Riding among the farmhouses required the police to travel quietly for Hare looked upon every farmer in remote areas as a Kelly sympathiser.

After travelling about four more hours through the night, the police came upon the hut where the Kellys were said to be hiding.

The lawmen dismounted and left their horses on the road under the watch of one officer. The rest approached the house cautiously and were in front of it half an hour before daybreak. Hare told Mayes to take three of the men and cover the back of the house, and that he would, when it was clear daylight, put his hat on his rifle as a sign for Mayes to approach. The troopers were so eager that Hare feared he could not restrain them from rushing ahead.

At the appointed time, half an hour later, Hare gave the signal and they started for the house. They had to pass a window before getting to the door, and one of Hare's men stepped in front of him to protect him in case a bullet was fired from there. Hare and his officers burst into the hut and ransacked it, but the gang were not there.

The police then searched the haystack, outbuilding and every place they could think of, but all to no purpose. The men became downhearted.

On 6 June 1879, O'Connor wrote to Commissioner Seymour in Brisbane to say that despite four months of searching there had been no credible information about the Kellys since the raid on Jerilderie.

'Any news we have ever got was three or four weeks old, and always came through three, four, or five people, and, when sifted, turned out to be lies,' O'Connor told his boss. 'Standish will not listen a moment to the idea that they are in N. S. Wales but persists in asserting that the outlaws are in Victoria ... Twice we have had information that they were in N. S. Wales ... I think you will admit that what I say is feasible, or else how is it nothing can be heard of the dogs?'[16]

MARGRET BYRNE'S SUSPICIONS about Aaron Sherritt's dealings with the police became contagious and Katie Byrne broke off her engagement with him, handsome and virile and flash as he was.

Sherritt told Hare that he might try Kate Kelly for a wife, even though one press report said that, despite the romantic legend growing around her as an accomplice for the gang, she was a 'heavily-featured evil-eyed woman' right at home among the Kelly sympathisers who were 'certainly villainous-looking scoundrels'.[17]

Sherritt went to the Kelly house at Greta and started going for walks with Kate, but her older sister Maggie objected.

Maggie had her own problems with men. Her husband, Bill Skilling, was doing six years in Pentridge and still claiming he had nothing to do with the Fitzpatrick business. If that wasn't bad enough, on 28 April 1879[18] her cousin and lover Tom Lloyd was skylarking with another cousin 'Fat' Jack Lloyd[19] and some mates at O'Brien's hotel in Greta, celebrating their release from Beechworth Gaol as Kelly sympathisers. Dennis 'Dinny' McAuliffe, whose family seemed to have more spending money after the bank robberies, challenged Tom to 'hit me on the chest, and see if you can knock me over'.[20] Tom punched Dinny 'in a friendly way' and his mate didn't move. Nineteen-year-old Jack then jumped up and said, 'you can have a smack at me, too – you can't shift me'.[21] Tom unleashed another blow at his cousin, 'but with greater violence' and the punch landed with a sickening thud. Jack stood dead still, stunned, for about half a minute and then fell 'all of a lump forwards',[22] his forehead striking the doorstep. His friends picked him up and put him in a chair, but he never spoke again, and died a few minutes later. Tom broke down weeping.[23] Over the next few days Tom made two attempts to drown himself.[24] He was charged with manslaughter, but though the Kellys and their supporters often complained of not getting a fair shake from the courts, Judge James Stephen told the jury that in his opinion death was caused by 'misadventure'. The jury returned a verdict of not guilty. Another prisoner accused at the same court and on the same day as Tom did not fare so well. Judge Stephen sentenced Tom Hogan to hang for shooting his brother. Ned Kelly and the gang read that Hogan's body hung from the gallows for an hour … and while 'the face of the deceased was neither disfigured nor discoloured, as is often the case … the skin of the neck had been cut through by the rope from ear to ear, the wound, being about an inch in width'.[25]

NED WAS STARTING to share Margret Byrne's suspicions about Sherritt and demanded that he prove his loyalty. Joe Byrne slipped a note to his boyhood pal, telling Aaron to stop playing both sides – even if he was giving the police misinformation.

June 26 1879

Dear Aaron

I write these few stolen lines to you to let you know that I am still living. I am not the least afraid of being captured. Dear Aaron meet me, you and Jack, this side of Puzzel Ranges. Neddie and I has come to the conclusion to get you to join us. I was advised to turn traitor but I said that I would die at Ned's side first. Dear Aaron it is best for you to join us. Aaron a short time and a jolly one. The Lloyds and Quinns wants you shot but I say no you are on our side … We sent that bloody Hart to your place twice. Did my mother tell you the message that I left for you? I slept at home three days on the 24 of May. Did Patsy give you the booty I left for you? … I told Hart to call last Thursday evening. I would like to know if he obeyed us or not. If not, we will shoot him. If you come on our tracks, close your puss. You know you were at Kate's several times. You had just gone one night as we came. We followed you four miles but returned without success … You know I will riddle that bloody [Constable] Mullane if I catch him. No more from the enforced outlaw till I see yourself.

I remain yours truly
you know[26]

Sherritt had given a horse to Katie Byrne as an engagement gift, and she decided to keep it. So, Aaron stole another one, worth £4, from Margret Byrne, and bizarrely sold it to Maggie Skilling. Even though Mrs Byrne's son was an outlawed murderer and Maggie was supplying the gang with provisions, Margret went straight to the police to have Aaron arrested.

At Beechworth, before Police Magistrate William Foster, Sherritt was remanded for four days on a charge of horse stealing. Reporters said 'he appeared quite confident as to his defence',[27] and four days later the case was dismissed, but not before Margret told the court she had a falling out with the Sherritts over Aaron 'giving the police assistance … in the pursuit of the bushrangers'.[28] Somewhere in the mountains Joe Byrne was cocking the hammer on his shotgun.

One of the new police recruits, lanky, sharp-faced marksman Charlie Gascoigne,[29] believed that Sherritt's information was all bogus. Gascoigne's father had been in charge of the mounted police on the Ovens goldfields and Charlie had grown up around the Kellys. He recalled having a conversation with Sherritt for an hour, and coming away thinking that his information was 'a lot of nonsense'.

He told Standish that he would not like to follow Sherritt into the ranges because it would most likely be a trap and that most of the informers were taking police money and laughing all the way to the bank.

'What information we got was from friends of the Kellys,' Gascoigne said. 'Some of them might give a little information if it was very safe – if they thought they could get away after they gave it.

'If a party of police went out as they used to go, they would be starting through the town; there would always be someone watching. A search party like that would be a laughing stock to the outlaws.'[30]

THE FINAL GROUP OF Kelly sympathisers had been released from Beechworth Gaol on 22 April, but the government immediately began a program of denying land ownership to anyone suspected of being Kelly associates. Sadleir supplied names to the Land Board and applications for selections were blackmarked. One man, William Jacks, a bullock driver from Lake Rowan, was denied land because he had once lived in Wallan, hometown of Kelly's grandparents, the Quinns, 14 years earlier.[31] These new economic sanctions caused even more resentment.

The resentment Stanhope O'Connor felt towards Standish was just as chafing, even though on 4 June they posed together for a photograph in Benalla with Sadleir, Tommy King and the five surviving trackers from Cooktown.[32]

O'Connor would later claim that Standish treated him in an 'ungentlemanly, ungenerous, and discourteous manner' for the whole of his stay in Victoria and that the commissioner had 'made some reflections about my private character'.

'But,' O'Connor retorted, 'I do not care a fig about it from a man of his private character.'[33]

Standish said he had found out things about O'Connor that made him keep out of his company.

The trouble apparently started when Standish objected to O'Connor co-habiting with Louise Smith in Benalla a few days after he arrived from Queensland. Louise's sister Helen was married to Charles Hope Nicolson, a man constantly at loggerheads with the commissioner. O'Connor claimed that he and Louise had actually been married in a private ceremony.[34]

When Standish told O'Connor, 'I noticed you were making love to a certain young lady,' O'Connor replied, 'That is nonsense, it is only fun.'

Standish never fully trusted O'Connor again.

O'Connor would later tell a Royal Commission into the Kelly outbreak that 'Captain Standish's knowledge of my private character is very limited, and all I can say is that if he has so low an estimate of my character, I care very little about it, considering the character of the man who judges. He said I was not a fit and proper person; I say that of him.'[35]

At the same time as Standish and O'Connor were going to war, the Aboriginal people around Maryborough, Queensland, were beginning to congregate about the town in anticipation of the charity that was doled out to them each year on Queen Victoria's birthday. About 200 trooped into town as the local paper ruminated on the recent proposals by the Catholic Missionary Father Duncan McNab to settle what it called 'the unfortunates' on freehold land of their own, as a preliminary step towards 'civilizing them'. 'The blanket and tobacco distribution,' opined the *Maryborough Chronicle*, 'stops a long way short of this thorough paced method of dealing with the "native difficulty",' but it was 'preferable to Inspector O'Connor's [bullets] still so liberally and indiscriminately prescribed in the Far North'.[36]

STANDISH TRUSTED HARE more than any of the other Kelly hunters. The big man was willing to endure all manner of privations in pursuit of the gang, setting off into the wilds with his men and packhorses at the vaguest of rumours for eight or ten days at a time.

Hare was almost 50, but his bones ached like he was 100.

'Our life was a very hard one,' Hare recalled, 'sleeping in the open without tent or fire, living on potted beef, and biscuit, and sardines. Bushmen think nothing of camping out for months but ask any of them in the winter months to camp out without a fire and see how long they will stand it.'[37]

All the time in the bush, Hare was anxious that the Kellys might be nearby, ready to surprise him and his men in the dark and shoot them all.

On one of their missions Hare was riding ahead and, hearing a terrible noise, looked round and saw that one of the packhorses had slipped and fallen over a cliff. It was rolling down, turning over and over like a barrel, the stones and rattling of the pack on his back making such a noise that Hare thought half the men had also gone down. The track was too narrow for Hare to turn his horse around, but he jumped off and looked over the embankment. He saw the old horse lying on his side eating grass.

'I expected to see him smashed to pieces,' Hare wrote. 'Strange to say, with the exception of a few cuts, the horse was all right.'[38]

The tracks in the mountains were mostly made by wild cattle, and Hare thought it a marvel that his men were not all killed rolling down the narrow ridges they traversed. One night a party of police arrived at the foot of a steep mountain, and Hare told the men to camp there. He then took three men with him and ascended the mountain on foot. It was a fearfully wild place. Hare went up to see if he could observe any signs of fire in the distance. The officers stayed on the top of the mountain for an hour or two, and then descended, but they had a terrible time getting back with their rifles in their hands. It was pitch dark, and the difficulty of their precarious position, as they called out to each other to find a safe route down, caused much amusement among the other officers listening below as they imagined their huge superintendent tiptoeing over boulders and crags with all the grace of a circus bear.

Once Hare finally reached the camp, exhausted, he ate some meat and bread, and jumped into his hammock, which had been slung between two saplings. Two or three koalas began to sing out in a piteous manner, like children crying. Hare stood this for a short time, and then called out to one of the men to cut the tree down, to get rid of the animals. When Hare awoke in the morning his rug was frozen, the country around was white with frost, and the men told him the creek close by was covered with ice.

Once in the Strathbogie Ranges, Charlie Gascoigne heard dogs barking at the crossing of a creek but Hare concluded that tracks nearby were of someone looking for cattle. A day later, a publican's wife told Gascoigne that Kelly's uncle Mad Jimmy Quinn came there the very night that he heard the dogs barking and bought four bottles of brandy.[39]

On another evening in the Warby Ranges as the policemen were preparing to eat their dinner, rifles by their sides, everyone jumped to his feet as four riders galloped towards them. It was the habit of the Kellys to 'ride like demons through the country'.[40]

The whole police party rushed to a brush fence and got behind it.

When the riders were within a few yards the police all jumped up, pointed their guns at the intruders and confronted them. They were not the outlaws but were well-known Kelly spies. Reining their horses in at the prospect of being shot, the riders started abusing the lawmen with the most frightful curses. Sergeant Mayes gave as good as he got and told the men they were under arrest.

Hare directed that he and three of his men should watch the pass leading into the mountains while Mayes, Lawless and Falkiner took the four spies and detained them. They took their prisoners to the home the spies were using and, from a distance in the dark, an elderly man called out to them obviously thinking that two of the plain clothes policemen were Ned Kelly and Steve Hart.[41] The house was the same place where the outlaws had breakfasted after riding through Wangaratta, shortly after the murders.

About a mile from the house there was also a good stable, all alone in a paddock, with an abundance of feed in it, evidently left there for the outlaws, along with four saddles made in Wangaratta. Mayes told the inmates of the house that they were not to come out during the night, as he and his men intended keeping watch over the place, and they might be mistaken for someone else and be shot. So the inmates danced for half the night, which Hare believed was a sign for the outlaws, if they were about, to keep away.

Hare and his men remained in the bush without covering of any kind until daylight. The night was bitterly cold, and Hare, being in the most exposed place, became nearly frozen. At about 2 a.m. he and Mayes decided to send Falkiner and Canny into Wangaratta to bring out three additional constables under John Kelly.

On their arrival, Hare went to meet the officers at the rear of the house. It was still pitch dark and Falkiner ducked away and yelled, 'Who are you?'

'Don't you know me?' Hare shouted back, and when Falkiner heard his voice, he replied, 'Is that you, Mr. Hare? You are so white with the frost I did not know you.'[42]

Hare ordered John Kelly to guard the house, to stop anyone leaving and to stop any signals being put out, especially any sheet being thrown over a bush in the garden, this being a well-known warning sign for the Kellys. When the people of the house had finished breakfast, one of the girls brought out a tablecloth, shook it on the veranda and threw it over a bush in the garden but John Kelly removed it at once.

At daybreak Hare set off to follow the horse tracks into the mountains, led by his guide 'Kangaroo Jack' Bellis,[43] a Liverpudlian by birth, who was a professional kangaroo shooter, knew the ranges well and was regarded by Hare as 'a capital bushman, a good shot, a fair tracker, and a thoroughly trustworthy man'.[44] For a mile or so the tracks were very distinct, but after some distance they appeared to separate, going in different directions. Some of the men fancied they heard voices ahead but they 'were much excited from want of sleep, and they appeared hardly to know what they were doing'. Hare made them rest.

They then searched fruitlessly for the rest of the day. The next morning Bellis drew Hare's attention to what they all thought were the heads of four men looking over a hill at them. Without a moment's consideration, the whole party started to get up the hill as fast as they could. It was a difficult job for the horses, but the police spurred them on. The only thing they found, though, were four goats feeding quietly.

On nearby mossy rocks Hare found the footmarks of a man in the green moss. One of the men spied a cantering horseman in the distance. The rider was a well-known squatter living close by. He told Hare that, when he was in the mountains the previous day looking for sheep, he saw a tent and he guided the lawmen some 8 kilometres until they saw it in the distance.

The police dismounted, surrounded the tent and then rushed down on to it. It was empty.

Some time afterwards Hare learned that the tent belonged to a party of honey gatherers who were friends of the outlaws and used to leave horse-feed and provisions in their tents for them.

Hare and Sadleir constantly received information that the Kellys were likely to be hiding among their friends and cousins on the low land below Euroa. The police undertook several missions there but, despite the efforts of Moses the tracker, the forays found nothing. And the police suffered heavy casualties.

One morning Hare's team made an early start to search a place belonging to a connection of the Kellys. They travelled lightly, leaving their packhorses behind along with bedding and provisions, intending to go across country, jumping over fences the best way they could. After riding two or three hours they came across a high fence. The men went over it with the greatest ease, but when the bulky Hare and his weary horse approached, Hare's mount baulked.

Hare wheeled the horse around and put him at it again. Summoning all his strength under such a heavy load, the horse made a tremendous spring and got over. But something gave way in Hare's back, just above the right hip, and the agony he went through was beyond anything he ever experienced.[45] His pain was worsened when Charlie Johnston leapt into a giant haystack where the Kellys were thought to be hiding and uncovered only an angry sow.

Hare lay down in the bush in great pain. The next day his men organised a buggy for him, and he drove himself to Euroa.

With a degree of embarrassment, Hare told Standish that the hardships he had experienced in the bush – camping out for eight or nine months since the police murders – had damaged his constitution. He was 'thoroughly beaten'[46] and not fit to go out with a search party again.[47]

Hare's old rival Charles Hope Nicolson was back at the helm.

Chapter 14

COMMISSIONER STANDISH had become so stressed by the failure of the Kelly hunters that he had lost 'upwards of a stone weight' by the middle of 1879[1] and appeared to be spending more time fighting with his subordinates than planning the capture of the killers. O'Connor said the commissioner had made several trips home to Melbourne but never stayed long, always being hunted out of there and back to work in Kelly Country by Sir Bryan O'Loghlen, the Acting Chief Secretary at that time.[2]

Sadleir often told O'Connor that he could never get two minutes' conversation with Standish 'upon Kelly business; that the moment he began to talk upon the subject Standish would take up a novel and commence to read'.[3] Hare also complained that Standish had become indifferent to his work.[4]

Charles Hope Nicolson arrived in Benalla on 3 July 1879 with a totally different approach to the hunt than Hare had pursued. Nicolson hardly ever sent out search parties, preferring to court spies and to make deals with anyone likely to have the ear of the Kellys or their friends, especially Aaron Sherritt.

The Garrison Corps was gradually withdrawn, while the strength of the police in the district was also considerably reduced.

And while the alarm caused by the gang's crimes had to some extent subsided, there was a strong feeling of indignation throughout Victoria that four wild young men were making a mockery of all the resources and powers of the government, remaining undisturbed in their mountain lairs despite a staggering £8000 reward for their heads.

'Few countries in the world,' thundered the press, 'have witnessed such a failure to punish evil deeds as those of the Kellys.'[5]

One Queensland visitor to Benalla was aghast at the support for the bandits, the fear they created and the general contempt for the police among many residents. 'The active sympathy with the outlaws, the terrorism, and demoralisation are serious,' he wrote. 'I saw Miss Kate Kelly and her sister Mrs [Skilling] ... riding on 20 guinea saddles and making extensive purchases right under the nose of Captain Standish, the black trackers, and the troopers.'[6]

To the public, the prospect of capturing the outlaws appeared more remote than ever, but experience had taught Sadleir and Nicolson that it was useless to continue scrambling through the rugged and mountainous country in search of the four outlaws

V. R.

£8000 REWARD

ROBBERY and MURDER.

WHEREAS EDWARD KELLY, DANIEL KELLY, STEPHEN HART and JOSEPH BYRNE have been declared OUTLAWS in the Colony of Victoria, and whereas warrants have been issued charging the aforesaid men with the WILFUL MURDER of MICHAEL SCANLON, Police Constable of the Colony of VICTORIA, and whereas the above-named offenders are STILL at LARGE, and have recently committed divers felonies in the Colony of NEW SOUTH WALES; Now, therefore, I, SIR HERCULES GEORGE ROBERT ROBINSON, the GOVERNOR, do, by this, my proclamation issued with the advice of the Executive Council, hereby notify that a REWARD of £4,000 will be paid, three-fourths by the Government of NEW SOUTH WALES, and one fourth by certain Banks trading in the Colony, for the apprehension of the above-named Four Offenders, or a reward of £1000 for the apprehension of any one of them; and that, in ADDITION to the above reward, a similar REWARD of £4000 has been offered by the Government of VICTORIA, and I further notify that the said REWARD will be equitably apportioned between any persons giving information which shall lead to the apprehension of the offenders and any members of the police force or other persons who may actually effect such apprehension or assist thereat.

(Signed) HENRY PARKES,
Colonial Secretary, New South Wales.

(Signed) BRYAN O'LOGHLEN,
Attorney General, Victoria.

Dated 16th February, 1879.

By 1879 the reward for the Kelly Gang had reached what would be a multi-million-dollar sum in 21st century terms. National Archives of Australia, 11443582 when numerous friends and relatives were alerting the gang to every move the lawmen made.

Nicolson believed the best way to catch the Kellys was now to wait for them to make a mistake.

With Standish leaving the trackers idle much of the time, they were reduced to dreading the winter, occasionally giving public demonstrations of their tracking skills to kill time, and even playing cricket with the youngsters of Benalla.[7]

Standish soon asserted that Nicolson was bungling the hunt; that he 'frequently received reliable information as to the whereabouts of the outlaws', but unlike Hare 'took no steps whatever to act on the information'. If he had, Standish asserted, there was a good chance the Kellys would have been captured or killed. Nicolson would often reassure Standish: 'I have the outlaws surrounded by my spies and have my hands upon them. It is not a case of months or weeks, but of days and hours.' 'That was his favourite utterance to me on every possible occasion,' Standish recalled, 'and from information which I have received from time to time, I believe there is no doubt whatever that nearly the whole time Mr Nicolson was in charge the outlaws were hanging about Greta and Glenrowan.'[8]

There seemed proof of that on 17 July 1879, when Standish, Nicolson and O'Connor kept watch in Benalla as Maggie Skilling came into town, accompanied by Tom Lloyd and a young woman, said to be Ned Kelly's wife, who paid a visit to Noble's photographic studio.

Standish and Maggie glared at each other in a long stare-down.[9]

Nicolson maintained that he should have led the police taskforce all along and said that the pursuit had been bogged down for half a year by that blowhard Hare and his constant chasing of rumours, shadows and wild geese. He said Hare had been hunting the Kellys 'with the largest body of police that ever was in the districts and with the artillery force at his command', yet, he said, the whole colony was sneering at their efforts.[10]

Standish finally returned to Melbourne for good about the same time as Hare was injured, claiming he was going back because his head office was being 'frightfully muddled'.[11] He had to admit, though, that after a year of his men searching, he had no idea where the outlaws were, even whether they were still in Victoria or had gone north towards Queensland.

TWO MEN MATCHING THE descriptions of Ned Kelly and Steve Hart[12] stormed into the Commercial Bank at Lancefield, north-west of Melbourne, on the morning of 15 August 1879. With revolvers in hand, they scooped up £665 and were gone as swiftly as they had appeared. It was rumoured that Dan Kelly and Joe Byrne were waiting in ambush to protect their getaway.[13]

As soon as the telegraph clattered the news to Commissioner Standish, now back domiciled at the Melbourne Club, he directed a police swoop on the town 70 kilometres away. He wired Nicolson to organise a special train for O'Connor, the Queensland trackers, and a team of local police including Sadleir and Alf Falkiner, as well as their saddled horses.[14] The men at Benalla had been practising with their large-bore Martini-Henry rifles and their service revolvers almost daily at a little rented paddock near the station, anticipating just such an opportunity.[15]

Even though he was back behind a desk in Melbourne after injuring himself on the Kelly hunt, Frank Hare organised a special train for himself and another police team, journeyed up to the nearest station to Lancefield, got his buggy and horses out of the train, and drove 25 kilometres to the bank alongside his men as quickly as he could.[16]

He arrived late in the afternoon but immediately made inquiries, and found that, beyond a doubt, it was *not* the Kellys who had robbed the bank. Waiting impatiently in Lancefield for O'Connor and his trackers, he sent a telegram to Kilmore, asking when O'Connor had left the town. The reply was, 'he has not left yet, and will not start before morning'.[17] The next day, at 9 a.m., O'Connor finally arrived at Lancefield. Hare told him of the latest report and castigated him for his tardiness. The young Irishman lost no time in joining the hunt this time; but a terrific storm of rain came down, obliterating all the tracks, and O'Connor

Tommy King (right) was sent home to Queensland
in disgrace from the Kelly hunt after going on a
huge bender that left him violently drunk. He is
pictured with brother Nat and Bulyul, one of the
so-called 'Dora Dora Blacks', arrested by the brothers
in Queensland in 1893 and convicted of murder.
Queensland Police Museum, PM0076

remained that night in Pyalong with his men. The next day the
Queenslanders proceeded towards Heathcote, but while they
found no tracks, one of the bandits was seen and arrested in
Sandhurst, and the other was taken at Eaglehawk, asleep in bed,
drunk, with the banknotes lying beside his bed.[18]

O'Connor was quick to take the credit for the arrests, though,
writing to his boss in Brisbane that it was his information that
allowed the police in Sandhurst to pounce. 'From the chief down,
we have been praised,' O'Connor wrote, '... I have nothing to
feel but joy, except for the conduct of Senr.-Const. King. I can
well do without him and hope you will wire to me to order him
back to Brisbane.'[19]

Tommy King, O'Connor's second in command, had gone on a colossal bender in Lancefield and had ended up at the Heathcote watchhouse, shaking, confused and in the grip of hallucinations brought on by delirium tremens.[20] He became so violent that he was charged with lunacy and remanded for medical treatment, spending three days in police custody.[21]

King returned to Benalla in disgrace and, on O'Connor's recommendation, was sacked from the force. David Seymour ordered him to return to Brisbane immediately and Tom Kirkham took over as O'Connor's offsider, though Standish would try to place him in charge of the Aboriginal trackers at different times.[22]

Kirkham would later give advice on how to deal with the Indigenous policemen, the advice including such direction as ensuring that they do not make 'too free and familiar with white people', and that 'they should not be allowed to mix with constables or their families either inside or outside the police depot'. He recommended, though, that police should speak to them in 'a kind tone of voice' and should give them a few shillings two or three times a month to buy sweets and scent because it made them 'more cheerful'.[23]

Reports of Tommy King's drunken rage made the newspapers[24] and was a further embarrassment to Standish, who now had to admit the outlaws had been on the run, unchecked, for almost a year since the murders.

Standish used the Queenslanders as scapegoats to a point, saying that his doubts had been confirmed and they were now 'utterly useless' against men riding up to 70 miles a day, 'and that their engagement was an idle expenditure of money'.[25]

O'Connor's 'boys', Standish asserted again, were 'wholly unsuitable for tracking in broken and mountainous country, more especially as they required a considerable quantity of impedimenta, could work but slowly, and were therefore the more liable to attract observation'.[26]

Hare and O'Connor had feuded in Lancefield and Standish took Hare's side. O'Connor said Standish made 'a series of communications to the Queensland government, tending to depreciate' O'Connor and to take the men from his supervision, putting them under Kirkham.

IN PENTRIDGE PRISON, Ned Kelly's mother shared a cell with her infant daughter and worked in the prison laundry, stoking the fires under the big copper tubs and spending hours drying clothes and ironing. Nicolson called her 'the notorious Mrs Kelly', mother of the outlaws,[27] but the prison staff treated her well and she gained 'the reputation of being the best behaved and most cheerful of the prisoners'.[28] She still fretted every day about the fate of her sons Ned, Dan and Jim, though, and by the middle of 1879 she lost another child when Alice turned 12 months and was deemed old enough by the law to be taken from her mother.

Maggie Skilling and Tom Lloyd caught the train down to Melbourne to take Alice home to Greta. Soon after that the press reported that 'it was pretty certain that one of the brothers visited the family residence ... to see the infant Kelly',[29] but added that once again the police 'know nothing definite in spite of their numbers and the tremendous expense to which they are putting the country'.[30]

Alice was not all that Maggie and Tom brought back from Melbourne. Increasingly desperate and frustrated by life on the run, Ned was planning a full-scale war with the police, and his sister and cousin secured a huge load of ammunition.[31] Early on a winter's morning, Tom and Maggie visited the gunsmith James Rosier[32] in Elizabeth Street.[33] Rosier supplied the Victorian police with Webley revolvers, as well as the double-barrelled .50 calibre rifles that were often mistaken for shotguns,[34] and Ned knew the store would have plenty of bullets for the gang's police-issue firearms.

The lovers bought up as many bullets as they could and returned to the store that afternoon to say they needed more for a hunting party.[35] They left a £2 deposit and promised to return the following day.

Rosier immediately notified the police that he had sold 'a large parcel of ammunition' to a pair of strangers. As Maggie and Tom expected, a big police contingent staked out their hotel all the next day, so they gave the police the slip and caught the Benalla train from Essendon. They were detained at Benalla and their luggage was searched, along with the luggage of Bridget O'Brien, a friend of the Kellys,[36] who had taken over the Victoria Hotel following the death of her husband Laurence.[37]

No ammunition was found, though, because Maggie and Tom had given it to another sympathiser to transport on the previous night's train.

THE POLICE SOUGHT more help from Victoria's Chinese community.

A hundred copies of a reward poster were printed in Cantonese and circulated through northern Victoria proclaiming: 'A reward of £8000 will be given to any Chinese who gives information to the police by which the offenders are captured or £2000 if only one of them is found – for it is known that they obtain food from the Chinese on the Upper Murray River and along Woolshed Creek.'[38]

Detective Mick Ward, busy co-ordinating police spies and informers, made careful inquiries and found two Chinese men likely to assist the outlaws – Ah Ping and Ah Soon – and others who were friendly with Byrne's mother.

By September 1879, Ward informed headquarters that a Chinese police agent, Ah Yips, was 'going to the upper King and he has promised to make further inquiries for me'.[39]

Ward's chief informant, though, remained Aaron Sherritt. They would regularly meet in the evenings at the bottom of a waterfall about 3 kilometres from Sherritt's home. While many doubted the veracity of the information provided by Byrne's mate, Constable Falkiner was convinced that Sherritt was doing his best to betray the gang, given the hatred shown to him by Byrne's mother.[40]

In October 1879, the trackers Moses Bulla and Corporal Hero, accompanied by Constable William Phillips, were dispatched to Sandhurst via Melbourne for a tracking job, despite O'Connor's protests. Nicolson sent a telegram to Standish asking him to keep the trackers' 'skill as dark as possible as the outlaws are anxious to find out'.[41]

EVEN WITH POLICE PATROLS everywhere, Ned Kelly emerged from hiding towards the end of 1879 to confront Aaron Sherritt over Mrs Byrne's suspicions. He rode up to Anne Sherritt's farm. Only Anne's younger children were home, and the bushranger took the Sherritt baby Hugh, in his arms.

Kelly said he was hungry. There was some bread in the oven baking, and some dough in a dish, and he took some of the dough, flattened it on the table and cooked two or three pieces. Then he made some tea, and he said he was sending the tea up to his men that he had on the hill. He told the children that the best thing that their brother Aaron could do was to come along with them; that he was accustomed to cattle and had been in the bush a long time and would be of use to them. He nursed the baby and made one of the little girls put the kettle on for another cuppa, before riding off.[42]

The gang continued to hide in mountains and caves above the old Chinese diggings of the Woolshed Valley. Snow on the ground made it easier to track them and, while they'd been used to dashing 70 miles during summer nights,[43] they now had to rein in their horses.

It became a lonely, miserable, maddening existence for the four young men, the oldest still just 24. They made their home in a small low tent at night.[44]

Joe Byrne, who had developed a taste for opium during his youth among the Chinese miners around Beechworth, became fretful and emaciated; much troubled by Kennedy's murder, and by life on the run.[45] He now weighed under 10 stone (63 kilograms).[46]

Known around the north-east as a ladies' man, Byrne's romantic adventures had been stymied. Ned Kelly was said to be fond of the widowed Bridget O'Brien, Steve Hart's sister Ettie,[47] and especially his 16-year-old cousin Kate Lloyd,[48] but he knew any hopes of a

Above: Some of the Kelly hunters after bringing down Ned Kelly at Glenrowan: (left to right) Daniel Barry, Hugh Bracken, William Phillips, Jim Arthur, John Kelly, Charlie Gascoigne and William Canny. All but Bracken were in the first rush of gunfire. *State Library of Victoria / H96.160/178*

Left: The first photo of Ned Kelly when he was 15 and an apprentice bushranger. *Public Record Office Of Victoria*

The confronting photograph of Kelly that was circulated after the police murders at Stringybark Creek. It was taken at Pentridge Prison just before his release in February 1874. *Public Record Office Of Victoria*

Ned Kelly's mother Ellen photographed in 1874, not long after her marriage to George King. At the time she was pregnant with John King who would serve as a policeman in Western Australia, and become world famous as the horseman Jack Kelly.

Alexander Fitzpatrick had a high opinion of himself as a good-looking lady-killer and horseman. His attempted arrest of Dan Kelly ended with a bullet wound and in two years of unprecedented violence in Victoria. *Victoria Police Museum*

Ned's younger brother Dan Kelly was just 16 and wearing hand-me-down clothes when Fitzpatrick tried to arrest him, but according to Superintendent John Sadleir he was already a 'ferocious little savage'. *State Library of Victoria / H2001.161/1*

Horse thief Steve Hart is said to have thrown down an axe at his father's farm and declared he wanted 'a short life and a merry one' as he rode off to join the Kelly Gang. *State Library of Victoria / H96.160/194*

'Bullet eyes' Joe Byrne was the best educated of the Kelly Gang but regarded as a dangerous man even before the police murders. *National Archives 11453328*

The Kelly Gang cut down Sergeant Michael Kennedy and Constable Michael Scanlan. *State Library of Victoria / IAN28/11/78/193*

Father of four, Constable Thomas Lonigan was the first man Ned Kelly killed.

Kelly chased father of five Michael Kennedy through the bush and killed him with a blast at point-blank range. *Victoria Police Museum*

Michael Scanlan asked a mate to take care of his dog if he did not come back from the Kelly hunt. *Victoria Police Museum*

Thomas McIntyre was the only survivor of the four policemen ambushed at Stringybark Creek. *Victoria Police Museum*

Victoria's Native Police created terror among the gold miners, as reflected in William Strutt's watercolour sketch of them escorting a prisoner from Ballarat to Melbourne. *State Library of Victoria*

Police endured months of hardships searching for the Kelly Gang, combing remote and difficult terrain in all weather in places such as the Wombat Ranges. *State Library of Victoria / IAN21/02/79/21*

Frederick Standish, Victoria's long-time police chief, was heavily criticised for mishandling the Kelly hunt.

Big burly Frank Hare survived a bullet from Ned Kelly to take the lion's share of the reward for the destruction of the gang.

University of Melbourne Archives / 1979.0078.00055

Charles Hope Nicolson was a tough Scot usurped in the Kelly Hunt when he claimed he had his hands upon the gang's throat.

While chasing the Kelly Gang, Stanhope O'Connor also waged war with Victorian police chiefs Standish and Hare, and a Queensland press that hounded him over a massacre of indigenous men near Cooktown.

State Library of Victoria / H96.160/193

The surviving five Queensland trackers photographed at the Benalla Police Paddock on 4 June 1879. Standing at left: Senior Constable Tom King; seated: Sub-inspector Stanhope O'Connor; sitting on fence L–R: Troopers Jimmy and Barney; standing: Jack Noble; seated on ground L–R: Troopers Johnny and Hero; standing with arms folded: Victorian Police Superintendent John Sadleir; standing far right: Police Commissioner, Captain Frederick Standish. *State Library of Queensland 109905*

Police and Aboriginal trackers in their positions for the shootout at Glenrowan. *State Library of Victoria / H96.160/175*

IRONCLAD BUSHRANGING.

Above: Ned Kelly emerged from the early morning mist at Glenrowan, dressed in his iron armour, to shoot it out with the police. Images of the gun battle quickly appeared in the *Illustrated Sydney News*. *State Library of Victoria / ISN00/08/80/SUPP*

Left: Ned Kelly posed for prison photographer Charles Nettleton the day before his execution in the hope that he would leave a powerful impression on his family and friends. *State Library of Victoria / MS9298/6/PHO1*

wife and family would be ended by a bullet or noose. The gang were worth a fortune to anyone who killed them.

Ned wanted to rob another bank, but police and eager volunteers were on guard everywhere. There was even a new telegraphic alarm system linking Beechworth banks with the police station.[49] Paddy Byrne and Aaron Sherritt's brother Jack scouted out other targets but Nicolson ensured that Jack relayed the information that 'even £20 would not at any time be found in the Eldorado or any other small post office'.[50] Byrne came up with an alternative plan to bail up a Beechworth bank manager at night and force him to open the safe, 'even if blood was shed over it'.[51] The plan went nowhere and Jack Sherritt revealed all to the police.[52]

JIM KELLY was released from Darlinghurst Gaol in January 1880. He was still only 20. Despite the Kelly family's relationship with the police, the sins of his brothers were not counted against him in Darlinghurst, and he not only had six months shaved off his sentence but emerged from prison having learned the trade of boot-making. Jim spent the last few weeks of his sentence imprisoned with the eccentric former convict and Irish preacher Andrew Scott, better known as the bushranger Captain Moonlite. Superintendent Sadleir related a dubious tale that Moonlite, while on the run, had sent word to Ned Kelly that he wanted to join forces and create a 'super gang', and that Kelly replied he would 'shoot him down' if Moonlite or his band ever came near him.[53]

In a gun battle between Moonlite and police in Wagga, Senior Constable Edward Webb-Bowen, a married officer with a young child, and 15-year-old Gus Wreneckie, one of Moonlite's sidekicks, were killed. James Nesbitt, a young petty criminal who was Moonlite's lover, had also been shot dead while attempting to lead police away so that Scott could escape. Moonlite was said to have wept over Nesbitt like a child 'and kissed him passionately'.[54]

Moonlite was wearing a ring woven from a lock of Nesbitt's hair on his finger[55] when he went to the gallows at Darlinghurst with another of his followers, Thomas Rogan, on 20 January 1880.[56]

While police in both colonies circulated Jim's photo in case he become a fifth member of the Kelly Gang, he was exhorting his brothers to get out of Australia any way they could.[57]

Ned Kelly had other plans.

By the beginning of 1880, Standish wanted to get rid of Stanhope O'Connor and organise his own team of Aboriginal trackers for the Victorian police. In January 1880 the Victorian force was given government approval to retain a permanent detachment of six Aboriginal trackers. Standish made a request to the Queensland government that O'Connor's five men from Cooktown be allowed to remain in Victoria and work under his officers. But on 20 January the Queensland government refused permission to do this, insisting again that O'Connor and the trackers not be separated.[58] O'Connor was staying put. He had married Louise Smith in private not long after arriving in Benalla a year earlier and on 10 February 1880 went through a public ceremony before family members in Benalla.[59]

AARON SHERRITT had married 15-year-old Ellen 'Belle' Barry on Boxing Day 1879, just two months after meeting her,[60] and they were now living with her parents in the Woolshed Valley.

While Belle's family has been on good terms with the Byrnes, her father, Edmund, sat on juries that convicted 13-year-old Jim Kelly for horse stealing, and Mad Jimmy Quinn for assault.

Policemen remained camped in caves overlooking the Byrne house and Detective Ward now wanted to create as much friction as he could between Aaron and the gang in the hope of forcing a violent and careless reaction. He knew Ned and his men were becoming paranoid and he hoped they would soon make fatal errors.

On 5 March 1880, Dan Kelly came out of hiding to attend the Moyhu Races, watching from a distance as his sister Maggie came second to Kate Lloyd in the Ladies' Hack Race.

'The ladies are to be praised highly for their judicious riding,' Beechworth's *Advertiser* reported. 'They sat with graceful and firm seats low in their saddles and handled their respective nags better than many paid [jockeys] that we have seen. The fair winner and her competitors were loudly cheered.'[61]

Kate Kelly didn't contest the 'honours of the turf with her sister and cousins' but instead remained on guard for Dan, who, 'mounted on a splendid bay thoroughbred ... enjoyed the sport in safety from a thickly timbered corner of the course'. Kate took care that no police or people likely to betray him could approach without plenty of warning.[62]

But spies were everywhere.

Daniel Kennedy,[63] the brother-in-law of the Victoria Hotel's Bridget O'Brien, had become one of the chief undercover men for the police, sending them reports under the alias of 'Denny'. Police listed him as 'The Diseased Stock Agent' because his coded messages referred to the gang as 'diseased stock'.

Denny reported that the gang has become 'very suspicious and wary yet exhibiting a certain degree of carelessness'.

'Ned Kelly trusts much in Byrne,' he noted. 'They often ride together at night, leaving Steve Hart with Dan Kelly following, one or more of the Lloyds or McAuliffes with them, the latter giving signals if anyone appears, whom the gang then avoids. Denny will furnish further definite information as to their action, whether they settle down again, or plan a raid. They are very short of money and becoming suspicious of their friends.'[64]

All four outlaws knew that with dwindling funds to pay sympathisers the £8000 reward would become all that more enticing to any potential Judases among their family and associates.

From 22 March 1880, police began receiving reports that plough mouldboards, the broad twisted blades that turn the sod from the furrow, were going missing from around Glenrowan.

Joe Byrne had reportedly been at a parade in Beechworth six years earlier that featured a colourful display of costumes including a Chinese gold miner wearing a Japanese samurai suit of armour.

Ned Kelly's favourite book was *Lorna Doone*, with its thrilling account of the reckless outlaw band the Doones of Bagworthy heading to their mountain hideout with plunder heaped behind their saddles: 'heavy men and large of stature' in their suits of armour, 'iron plates on breast and head'.[65]

Ned began to imagine that suits of armour would protect the gang in a shootout with police, though Byrne cautioned that they would only 'bring us to grief'.[66]

Ned Kelly got his wish, though, and the gang began acquiring the necessary metal. Some plough mouldboards were donated by family and friends, and some bought by Jimmy Wallace, the headmaster turned double agent. He visited farms in his buggy claiming to be buying them for his father, 'a dealer in old metals'.[67]

Sergeant Arthur Steele warned his police colleagues that in their next encounter with the gang, the Kellys were likely to be wearing iron suits.[68]

What Steele didn't know at the time was that Ned was planning to use the suits for an act of unprecedented terrorism in Australia: premeditated, cold-blooded mass murder.

POLICE REPORTS NOW indicated that the gang had been 'reduced to the last straits, and without means of carrying on longer'. Their movements had become 'circumscribed, and they were unable to find an unguarded bank to rob'. On 27 March 1880, four horsemen, believed to be the gang, were seen at Broken Creek and Lake Rowan, and on the afternoon of 23 April Dan Kelly was sighted near the Eleven Mile Creek, galloping towards Maggie Skilling's place at Greta.

In a secret memo to Standish, Nicolson noted that, while the trackers were a major expense, they were 'indispensable' in constantly frustrating the outlaws, who were afraid to do anything lest they leave a trail.[69]

Constable Hugh Bracken, who had seen the gang at a distance through the rain just after the police killings 18 months earlier, was transferred to the small Glenrowan station, officially for regular police duty, but really to spy on Maggie Skilling's house during the night.[70]

Spies also reported suspicious movements of Dick Hart, Steve's elder brother, whom Sadleir regarded as an 'unconscionable young scoundrel'.[71] Nicolson told Standish that the outlaws had 'never shown themselves openly ... since the arrival of the Queensland native trackers' and that their presence along with extra security at banks throughout the north-east was a constant thorn in the side of the gang.[72]

In May 1880, Detective Ward[73] cajoled Jack Sherritt into stealing a saddle from his sister-in-law Belle and planting it in the Byrne house so that Margret Byrne and Joe's brother Paddy would be arrested for theft.[74]

Rumours spread that Aaron had said he would shoot Joe 'and f— him before his body gets cold',[75] but Ned suspected that the police had been torturing Aaron to get information.[76]

Joe gave his old friend a chance to get away. One morning Byrne rode down the steep gullies to meet Aaron's young brothers and sisters heading to school and told them that Kelly was coming to shoot Aaron.[77] That didn't work, so Byrne hounded Mrs Sherritt in the middle of a horse paddock near her home, telling her that Aaron and Detective Ward had been starving the gang and that Ward 'went about the hills like a black tracker'. He said that if Ward, Aaron and Senior Constable Mullane were dead, he would be a free man and could go where he liked.

Anne Sherritt begged Joe not to take her son's life.[78] But Byrne was emotionless as he rode away.

A few days later Nicolson sent for Anne.

She went to his headquarters in Benalla and told him what the bushranger had said.

She told Nicolson that her son would be murdered if the police did not remove him from Kelly Country.[79]

Chapter 15

WHEN THE FIRST PLOUGH mouldboards were stolen, Charles Hope Nicolson told Stanhope O'Connor to be ready with his trackers at a moment's notice, as he knew that the Kellys were within a tight radius around Greta. Nicolson said he was only waiting for information that would point to the exact spot where they were last seen to enable the Queenslanders to pick up their trail.

The gang were still well short of the quantity of metal they needed for the bulletproof suits, so the sympathisers began to steal more mouldboards from farmers around Oxley and Greta. Battling locals reported the thefts,[1] and one complained that the hungry culprits had also swiped two sides of bacon.[2] Two of O'Connor's trackers investigated and found footprints with the distinctive narrow 'larrikin heel' from the type of riding boots the gang favoured.[3]

The Kellys shaped the mouldboards into a solitary breastplate. They rested it against a stump and took a Martini-Henry rifle that had been dropped by a nervous constable, Robert Graham,[4] during a night-time vigil at Mrs Kelly's house. Ned fired a heavy calibre bullet at the armour from 10 metres[5] and, while the slug left a sizeable dent and made an almighty clang, it failed to penetrate the metal.

Blacksmiths from around the district – believed to be Jim Brien, Patrick Delaney, William Culph, Charles Knight and Tom

Straughair[6] – then created four full sets of armour in a secluded mountain spot called the 'Devil's Basin'.[7]

The front and back plates were joined at the side with straps and there was an apron to protect the upper parts of the legs and shoulder plates, too, though the lower legs were dangerously exposed. Ned's suit weighed 97 pounds [44 kilograms] and the others about the same.

While the gang were busy plotting mayhem and murder, Standish was back in Victoria's north-east with a parliamentary delegation on Wednesday, 21 April 1880, to honour the policemen the gang had slain. In appalling weather, Standish and his party travelled by coach from Benalla to Mansfield under an armed guard for the unveiling of a £950 monument to the three murdered policemen. As the coach passed between the mountains, near where Kennedy, Lonigan and Scanlan were killed, the rain descended in torrents, just as it had done when the search party entered the mountains to recover the bodies 18 months earlier. Because of the downpour the coach did not arrive in time to permit the unveiling ceremony of the 8-metre-high monument in the town's centre, and it was postponed until the next morning.

The rain still fell steadily as Standish told the crowd gathered around the monument that he sincerely hoped that 'the mellowing hand of time would soothe the great affliction which [had] befallen Mrs Kennedy and Mrs Lonigan'. He thanked the town for their generous support of a 'handsome memorial in honour of the brave men who were murdered in the Wombat Ranges by the gang of outlaws unfortunately still at large'. He said there were 'many combined causes' that had prevented the capture of the 'cowardly assassins' but, to polite applause and a few 'hear, hears', Standish expressed the hope that the day was not far distant when 'justice would be satisfied'.[8]

While it was still the case, he said, that the police in the area took their lives in their hands each day, it was shocking to him that the 'perpetrators of the fearful crime had met with so much strange sympathy and material assistance from many persons' of the district.[9]

THE KELLY GANG POLICE MURDERS—MEMORIAL ERECTED
BY THE POLICE AT MANSFIELD.

Commissioner Standish spoke of the heroic qualities of Michael
Kennedy and his men at the official opening of a monument to the slain
officers at Mansfield in 1880. State Library of Victoria, IAN08/05/80/69

Melbourne's *Illustrated Australian News* told its readers that, despite 'a reward of £8000 offered for them dead or alive, and notwithstanding the expenditure of nearly £30,000 in their pursuit, the authorities are today as far off as ever from capturing these brutal murderers'. The newspaper blamed assistance to the gang given by the district's 'many Irish families of the laboring class ... who, as in many rural districts in Ireland, were ready at any moment to make the Kellys' quarrel their own, even against the authorities'.[10]

The press roared that there had been no reliable public information concerning the gang in a year. The police force in north-eastern Victoria had been reduced by 60 men, or more than a quarter of its strength, but in Benalla, Wangaratta and other police stations in Kelly Country, mounted men readied themselves for any emergency as the law waited for the Kellys to come out of hiding and make their next move.[11]

On the night of 14 May 1880, Steve Hart's brother Dick was seen lurking behind Ann Jones's Glenrowan Inn and disappearing into the bush for two hours. The next night he came out in front of his house near Wangaratta and cracked a stockwhip three times, like a signal.[12] Sadleir directed that Sergeant Steele have Hart's house watched. The McAuliffe family was said to have provided the gang with mouldboards and to have told Ned that if the gang required further support from sympathisers, they would have to rob another bank.[13]

On 20 May 1880, 'The Diseased Stock Agent' warned Nicolson in a coded message that the outlaws were preparing another raid in armour: 'Missing portions of cultivators described as jackets are now being worked and fit splendidly. Tested previous to using, and proof at 10 yards. A break-out may be anticipated, as feed is getting very scarce.'[14]

Support for Nicolson, in the upper reaches of government was getting very scarce, too. Stanhope O'Connor said Standish always had it in for him and his brother-in-law and that the commissioner often spoke of Nicolson 'in the most disparaging terms'.[15]

'Hardly a fortnight passed but Captain Standish was ordering and counter-ordering Mr Nicolson,' O'Connor recalled, 'sometimes demanding him to reduce the number of his men, at other times he was not to employ such and such a person, or not to put police here and police there, until I often wondered Mr Nicolson did not pitch the whole thing up; but, as he often said to me, all his private feelings were sunk out of sight, and therefore, for the public good, he stuck to the work.'

Standish had told Nicolson on 3 May 1880 that he was again being 'superseded' by Hare.[16]

Nicolson was furious and sought an urgent audience in the office of Victoria's Chief Secretary Robert Ramsay,[17] but Standish took a ringside seat.

'Nothing personal, old chap,' Ramsay told his fellow Scotsman, 'I just feel we need a change, like in a game of cricket, you know – a change of bowlers.'[18]

Nicolson protested. Standish interjected with, 'But you are always saying you are going to arrest them.'[19]

Nicolson bristled and the tough Scot fought back. He argued his case and gained a month's extension. He told Ramsay the 'beginning of [the] end' is approaching.[20]

Nicolson believed the gang were hiding in a gully around the Greta Swamp, near the Kelly home, camping in a tent about 4 feet high. He predicted that 'in a very short time' police would have their hand 'on their throats without any trouble'.[21]

A female informer at Beechworth had not only seen Joe Byrne but had spoken to him. Heavy rain thwarted police efforts to follow her lead, though, as Nicolson, Sadleir and O'Connor trekked out there. They interviewed Sherritt, who said Byrne had been at Margret's home. Sherritt told the police that if they did not catch the Kellys soon, the Kellys would kill him and other informers.

Nicolson was anxious to chase Byrne but Sadleir, O'Connor, Mullane and Ward all told him that acting on that information immediately would put the lives of many police spies at risk.

On 31 May, an agent sent word to Benalla that he had seen Byrne up a gully about a mile from Mrs Byrne's house. O'Connor and his men set off at once and took a train to the nearest point at Everton, where they met Sherritt. Then they rode on horseback to an isolated paddock. Rather than Joe Byrne they found his brother Paddy, who looked very much like him.

It was Nicolson's last throw of the dice.

FRANK HARE WAS BACK in Benalla in charge of the hunt from 2 June 1880 and confident the gang would soon show themselves, even though he had fought hard not to return to Kelly Country after the pain the chase had given him.

When Standish ordered Hare to relieve Nicolson, the big superintendent had 'protested in the strongest manner possible at the injustice of being sent up there again'.

He said there were officers senior to him – Fred Winch, Hussey Chomley and David Chambers – who did not have to lay their weary bones on the ground in the cold mountains night after night. Hare was especially angry that, as an assistant commissioner, Nicolson was on a higher pay grade than him. Hare had not seen a promotion since before they had captured Harry Power together, though Hare said that arrest was all down to him and not the sour, dour Scot.[22]

The battle between O'Connor and Standish was also reaching a point of no return. Hare had always objected to having a large party of trackers kept at Benalla and wanted to split them into smaller groups with some posted to Wangaratta and Beechworth.[23] O'Connor again refused to divide his men, but Standish took Moses, the man O'Connor had enlisted to replace the late Corporal Sambo. O'Connor knew Standish was now making plans for other trackers to replace his men. Standish had given Superintendent Hussey Malone Chomley the task of finding a new team of Aboriginal trackers for Victoria, and Chomley had headed off to New South Wales and then Queensland.

O'Connor wrote to David Seymour from Benalla on 2 June to say that

> ... under the present aspect of affairs I am afraid that there is very little chance of us gaining any credit. I am convinced of this, as the Chief Commissioner told me that he could do the work without our assistance and tried to do it upon one occasion when he thought he had received the straight tip. This and other matters, some of which you are aware of, strengthens me in my opinion. It is publicly known that the moment a few scrubbers of boys can be collected, we are to go. Also, one of my men have been taken from me to make a beginning of a new team. I think you must agree with me that the sooner we leave for Queensland the better; in fact, I strongly recommend that you should take the initiative by recalling us at once, or we will be told to go as soon as the other boys arrive. I will require a month's leave to

arrange my private affairs in Melbourne; for this period I can retain the boys, as they really deserve a spell from their good conduct; or, if you like, I could put them on board a steamer for Brisbane.[24]

DETECTIVE WARD HAD paraded Aaron Sherritt among a group of 14 police and trackers investigating a sighting of Byrne near his mother's house.[25] Ward made sure as many people got a good look at Sherritt helping the police as possible. Then to make Sherritt's betrayal even more glaring, Ward stationed four policemen inside the tiny two-room hut Aaron now shared with Belle on his selection.[26] Sherritt slept in his bed with Belle during the day, with the police lying by the fire in the next room, waiting for the couple to rise so they could lie on the narrow bed. At night, as the freezing winter set in, Sherritt led the police to watch the Byrne house.

Police parties were patrolling around Wangaratta and Glenrowan, close to the Kelly home at Greta, and were cutting off the gang's lifelines of communication and supply, forcing them into the open.

From early June, Constables Alf Falkiner and William Canny were on patrol, using borrowed horses rather than branded police mounts, and posing as drovers. Canny, another Irishman from County Clare, had known the Kellys since they were children and had just been recruited into the force at the age of 26, having worked as an overseer at Clear Creek and Edi stations.[27] He was a crack shot and would soon need to be. The two undercover men were away 17 days gathering information and travelled about 800 kilometres through unforgiving country.[28]

On 17 June, Falkiner wrote to Hare from Cotton-tree, about 30 kilometres beyond Bethanga on the Murray, that the Kellys had been seen around there frequently and were getting provisions from a Chinese store, coming down from the ranges two at a time with packhorses. They ingratiated themselves with the Chinese by buying 100 cabbage plants. One of the Chinese told Falkiner that Kelly had warned him if they spoke to the police they would be shot and then burned.[29]

The four young outlaws were frenzied by living on the run, and Hare's spies told him that rumours were coming in from all directions that the sympathisers were very active, that something was about to happen. Old Mrs Byrne was said to be 'very jubilant',[30] and her daughter Katie had told the anxious Anne Sherritt to get ready because the gang were planning something big; something that would 'astonish not only Australia, but the whole world'.[31]

The gang wanted the best fresh horses they could find for what they had planned. Two horses were stolen from Michael and James Ryan of Dookie some time between 17 and 20 June.[32] Ned took a bay mare of 16 hands, 'a fine jumper and hunter', while Byrne grabbed a magnificent chestnut half a hand shorter.

Hare had noted that there was a full moon rising, and because the gang rode during the night a full moon was when they were most likely to strike.[33]

THE QUEENSLAND government approved the immediate withdrawal of Stanhope O'Connor and his five trackers from the Kelly hunt for what O'Connor called Standish's 'act of discourtesy'[34] in taking Moses from his command. He and his team left Benalla for Essendon Station on the morning of 25 June 1880.[35]

Hare was not sorry to see them go.

He believed that the outlaws were afraid to show themselves because of the trackers, and that the sooner O'Connor and his men left the better 'because, should the gang make a raid, there would be a probability of capturing them, but as long as they remained in the mountains, we had little chance of finding them'.[36]

As a full moon loomed on the evening of 25 June, Hare was in no mood to listen to the Diseased Stock Agent, who arrived at Benalla Police Station expecting to see Nicolson, the man he normally dealt with.

The informer told Hare and Sadleir that the Kellys were 'now entirely out of funds', that 'a fresh exploit was to be expected immediately', that they now had 'bullet-proof armour' and were planning 'to affect something that would cause the ears' to tingle.[37]

Probably because the informer had been close to Nicolson, Hare scoffed and told Sadleir, 'If this is the sort of person Nicolson and you have been upon, it is no wonder you have not caught the Kellys.'[38]

Yet the information was spot on.

Ned Kelly was planning a mass murder of Victorian police and it would start with the killing of Aaron Sherritt.

While Kelly had tried to fashion a romantic portrait of himself as a victim of police brutality who only killed in self-defence at Stringybark Creek, he now planned rivers of blood in an ambush that would cut down as many of his enemies as he could.

The gang had carefully thought out and 'matured their plan'.[39] In his letter to the politician Donald Cameron from Euroa, Ned had sent out a warning to 'remember your railroads'.[40] He meant it. By killing Sherritt the gang believed they would not only have wreaked vengeance upon a man they were sure had betrayed them to the police, but at the same time they would induce the authorities to despatch a special police train to Beechworth and into their trap.

By wrecking this police train before it reached its destination, they would then descend over the carnage in their suits of armour and shoot any lawmen who might have somehow survived the crash. Then in a district where the law had been destroyed, they planned to ride down to Benalla or one of the townships in the district, rob a bank, and retrace their steps into the ranges with their loot.[41]

The suits of armour were tested and ready, and with 56 pounds (25 kilograms) of blasting powder[42] in a drum on one of their packhorses, it was time for the gang to act. Ned had his hair cut short for battle and dressed for war 'in the dandy bushman style'. He put on honey-coloured cord trousers and waistcoat, a white Crimean (flannel) shirt and a slate-grey checked jacket.[43] He pulled on a pair of mounted police riding boots with 'very thin soles and very high heels', and removed the lining to make them more subtle.[44] Around his waist he wrapped his green sash with gold fringe – the bravery award given to him by grateful parents for saving Dick Shelton from drowning all those years earlier. He also had a tartan silk quilted skull cap stuffed with cotton wool to wear under his bulletproof helmet. Ned and Hart rode with their drum of gunpowder, two coils of fuse and two Chinese rockets, to signal the start of war at Glenrowan, just up the road from Mrs Kelly's hut at Eleven Mile Creek. Byrne and Dan Kelly rode towards Sherritt's hut 50 kilometres away. It was a dark, icy night and their ghostly ride was lit by a full, ominous moon that cast them in an evil glow.

ON THE NIGHT OF FRIDAY, 25 June 1880, Aaron was at home with Belle, who had just turned 16 and was expecting their first child. The hut was dominated by a wide stone fireplace and had one room for sitting and eating and one bedroom partitioned with calico. As usual, there were four policemen stationed inside. Detective Ward had them ready to pounce at the first sign that the Kellys were coming to confront Sherritt over his betrayal. Sherritt told everyone he could that, rather than the police keeping an eye on him, he was keeping an eye on the police, making sure they didn't get too close to real information on the gang's movements. Ned, though, had devised a plan to show the police not 'what cold blooded murder is but wholesale and retail slaughter'.[45]

Joe and Dan arrived at rocks overlooking the Sherritt hut and kept watch all through Saturday, 26 June. Joe had an old crocheted scarf around his neck and on his fingers he had the rings taken from the corpses of Lonigan and Scanlan. He was carrying the Mansfield vicar's double-barrelled shotgun, which he took at Stringybark Creek. Instead of birdshot, he had loaded each barrel with a fat lead bullet. In the pockets of his dark-striped shirt he had a Catholic prayer book and a brown paper packet labelled 'Poison' because he had no intention of being taken alive.[46]

If everything went as planned, though, the Kellys expected a great day of celebration[47] and Ned and Steve spent Saturday with Jim Kelly and sister Maggie. In the late afternoon Ned visited his beautiful young cousin Kate Lloyd to whom he was said to be 'deeply attached'[48] and who was adorned in a stylish hat and coat.

Sherritt was having Saturday night dinner with Belle and her mother, Ellen Barry senior, a lively redhead who had often nursed Joe as a baby. They ate on a rough tabletop perched upon a packing case.

The log fire was raging and, perhaps thinking of hell, Aaron told his teenage bride that, while he had no religion, he had been thinking about God for a long time and was ready to join her in her faith, to 'turn a Catholic' as he put it.[49]

One of the policemen, Constable William Duross,[50] was finishing his supper by the log fire while the other three rested in the small room behind the calico screen.

Sherritt had told the policemen that no party of men on horseback would ever catch the Kellys. The police did not have the men or the horses to match it with the gang, he said. 'There are a few men in the force, such as Johnston and Lawless — they could ride them on level ground, but they cannot gallop down ranges like the Kellys.' Sherritt said Byrne used to practise riding down steep ranges at breakneck speed. As the officers listened wide-eyed, Sherritt told them if a large party of police was sent into the bush, the outlaws would hear them coming and keep out of the way. If a small party, such as four, like the men under Kennedy were sent after them, the Kelly Gang would surprise them and shoot them down.[51]

Just after 6 p.m. on a bush track 100 metres from the Sherritt hut, Joe Byrne and Dan Kelly waylaid a 54-year-old German miner and market gardener named Anton Wick,[52] who had once tried to have Joe done for stealing his horse.[53] Byrne told Wick if he did not follow their orders, they would hurt him in the 'most drastic fashion'.[54]

The bushrangers handcuffed Wick and forced him to go with Byrne to Sherritt's back door, next to the chimney, while Dan Kelly went to the front door, revolver in one hand, rifle in the other.[55] At about 6.30 p.m. Joe made Wick rap on the back door with his cuffed hands.

Joe and Dan could hear Constable Duross scurrying into the bedroom, where he joined the three others on the floor.

Joe made Wick call Sherritt.

Wick barely whispered, 'AR-Ron' in his thick German accent.

'Call loud,' Byrne said, poking him with the rifle.

Wick called again.

Sherritt was cautious as Belle and her mother clasped their hands to their mouths.

'What do you want?' the tough bushman demanded.

Byrne hissed another command: 'Say "I have lost myself"!'[56]

'AR-Ron, I have lost myself. I cannot find der vay home. Please you show me der road.'

Sherritt finally came to the door and unlocked it, laughing about his neighbour's predicament as Belle called out behind him to give Wick assistance.

Before Sherritt even noticed the handcuffs on his neighbour's wrists, Joe shot his childhood friend through the throat. Sherritt staggered backwards, blood gushing from a huge hole in his neck. As he fell, his head crashed into the table where he had just eaten. Byrne blasted another huge hole through his chest and, as blood erupted all over her husband's white shirt and face, Belle and her mother screamed in terror.

Byrne stepped into the house and roared at the stupefied women, 'That bastard will never put me away again.'[57]

Aaron's dog, chained nearby, started a mournful howl.[58]

Then Byrne grabbed the pregnant Belle as a human shield and sent Mrs Barry to unlock the front door for Dan.

Just 19, Dan smiled as he looked down at Aaron's bloodied corpse on the floor. He gave a slight bow to the horrified ladies and a polite 'Good evening'.

Then Byrne fired into the calico curtain. The four policemen – Constables Duross, Robert Alexander, Harry Armstrong and Thomas Dowling – were hiding under the bed. They cocked their weapons as the bullets blasted through the cloth and out through the boards of the little shack.

THE MURDER OF SHERRITT.
(FROM A SKETCH TAKEN IMMEDIATELY AFTER THE DEPARTURE OF THE KELLY GANG.)

The murder of Aaron Sherritt sparked the Kelly Gang's last stand. State Library of Victoria, IAN03/07/80/97

Byrne roared at Belle, 'Get in there and tell them all to come out.'

Belle scampered in petrified, only to have the police grab her and hold her to the floor.

Joe and Dan then grabbed Mrs Barry and dragged her outside.

They piled kindling against the slab walls as Mrs Barry pleaded for them to stop.

Byrne threated to 'roast'[59] everyone inside and asked Mrs Barry if there was kerosene in the house.

'No please, please, Joe,' she said. 'For God's sake, my girl's in there.'[60]

'Then get her out and bring those bloody traps with her,' Byrne snarled.

Mrs Barry was sent running back into the hut, but behind the curtain police pulled her to the floor as well.

Hearing the howls of the women inside, Byrne eventually thought better of burning alive a woman who once rocked him to sleep as a boy.

Instead, the two killers unlocked Wick's handcuffs and allowed him to run home.

As Sherritt's dog continued its mournful howl under a bad moon rising, Joe Byrne and Dan Kelly climbed onto their horses and galloped away into the inky blackness of the forest.

Their killing spree had begun, and they were eager to kill again.

Chapter 16

WHILE JOE AND DAN were busy murdering Aaron Sherritt, Ned Kelly and Steve Hart had donned their armour under white oilskin coats and ridden into Glenrowan.[1]

They tethered their four spare saddle horses and a packhorse[2] carrying the drum of blasting powder in the bush behind McDonnell's Railway Tavern and, under the shining moon, surveyed their targets in the small town below. On the other side of the railway line from the tavern was the railway station, and beyond that about 400 metres south-west was the Glenrowan Inn, a whitewashed weatherboard cottage with a corrugated-iron roof. It stood between the railway line and the Warby Ranges.

The inn was run by Ann Jones,[3] a plump 50-year-old from Tipperary. Ann's 13-year-old son Jack was playing a concertina on the front veranda, and Ned Kelly and Hart watched the last train from Benalla pass through on its way north to Wangaratta at 9 p.m. Stationmaster John Stanistreet[4] extinguished the lamps in his office and shut up for the evening.[5] The two outlaws rode up along the track for 400 metres to a bend in the line above a 9-metre gully, where they planned to derail the special police locomotive and start a shooting spree. The spot selected for the catastrophe was at a point after the Glenrowan Station where the line, after passing through a deep cutting, suddenly made a sharp curve.[6]

It was Ned Kelly's plan that the gang, in their bulletproof suits, would finish off survivors of the crash, paying special attention to those Aboriginal 'demons' from Queensland.[7] Kelly would later claim that his plan was only to make the police hostages for the release of his mother, Skilling and Williamson,[8] but no one believed him.

The bushrangers had tools that they thought would destroy the tracks, but they couldn't do any damage. So, they rode back to Glenrowan and forced seven railway navvies out of their tents. Ned was worried that the noise late at night might have raised suspicion at the Glenrowan Inn, and he went over to rouse Ann Jones.

She had borne 14 children and buried five,[9] and was on friendly terms with both the Hart family and with the widowed Bridget Kennedy.[10] She kept a photo of the murdered policeman among her things,[11] and Ned suspected she was granted a liquor licence only with help from Detective Ward. Ann was in bed with neuralgia[12] when Ned started banging on her door late at night. He looked twice as big as usual with the armour around his chest and a hump on his back.[13] He shook the flimsy shack to its foundations and almost punched a hole through the front entrance. 'Open this door,' the most wanted man in Australia commanded. Ann was trying to sleep off her pain and called out from the back of her house: 'Who is it?'

Ned ran around to the back door and smashed into it, too.

'If you are a policeman,' Ann called out, 'go to the men's tents to look for whom you want.'

'If I was a policeman, ye'd like me better,' Ned snarled.[14]

Ann now guessed the identity of the midnight caller and asked 14-year-old Jane to unlock the door. Ned stormed into Ann's bedroom.

'Where are your police now to mind you?' he roared. Ann said she had to serve everyone who came to her pub, even police, but Ned responded that he was making her family his prisoners. Even though Ann pleaded that she was 'staggering with sickness',[15] he took her and Jane down to the navvies, leaving Ann's four young sons locked in the hotel kitchen.

Ned wanted the train tracks torn up immediately and was furious that the railway workers didn't have tools handy. He charged down to the stationmaster's house and kicked in his door while a stunned Stanistreet was getting dressed.

Stanistreet was in his little place with his wife, Emily, two young children and baby John.[16] They screamed in terror at the bearded giant holding a gun. Ned ordered the stationmaster to supervise the tearing up of the tracks, but Stanistreet said he would need platelayers to do that. So, Ned rode off to bring back two of them, James Reardon[17] and Dennis Sullivan, as well as Reardon's wife, Margaret, their eight children and their lodger, a Benalla labourer named John Larkins.

Ned told Reardon that he expected a train from Benalla 'with a lot of police and black fellas' and 'I'm going to kill all them buggers'. Reardon pleaded to be left out of any massacre but Ned replied with a menacing growl, 'Do it or I will shoot you.'[18]

ON THE NIGHT OF Sherritt's murder, Stanhope O'Connor had bedded down with his wife, Louise, at the home of her late father, John Thomas Smith, in Mount Alexander Road, Flemington. O'Connor's five surviving trackers were staying with him as their 15 months of service in Victoria were finally over. He had booked berths on a steamer leaving for Queensland on the 29th.

At the same time, in her cold, lonely cell in Melbourne Gaol a few kilometres away, Mrs Kelly tossed and turned during a nightmare in which 'there had been a collision between the police and the gang, and the "Bobbies" had been victorious'.[19]

The real collision between the 'Bobbies' and the gang, though, had been delayed.

Ned Kelly's plan of 'wholesale slaughter' of the police depended on news of Sherritt's murder spreading fast and the police immediately sending the trackers north on the railway line to their doom.

Kelly didn't count on the police inside Sherritt's home lying on their bellies for 12 full hours after the killing, afraid they would be gunned down, too. Despite them all being armed, the police refused even to peer[20] around the corner of the hut until after daylight, and only ventured outside when they were certain Joe and Dan had gone.[21]

A Royal Commission later found 'the conduct of those constables throughout the night was characterized by shameful poltroonery'.[22] The four frightened men saw it, instead, as sensible self-preservation.

BYRNE AND DAN KELLY galloped into Glenrowan and told Ned that Sherritt would tell no more tales. Ned then sent Steve Hart off with the workmen and frail little Jane Jones to the bend in the railway line, where the gang expected to create their human slaughterhouse.

As Hart kept a gun trained on the navvies while they worked, he rested his head on the knee of the teenage girl and told her he felt sick.[23]

The labourers wished that he would drop dead. Ned was furious that it took more than an hour to do the work. Reardon was stalling, trying to save police lives, and told Ned that only one rail needed to be removed, but Ned insisted on two.[24]

Ann Jones then sent Jane back to the pub to light a fire and, realising it was better to have the gunman as a friend than a foe, invited Ned back to have 'breakfast and a wash'.[25]

He was planning to use McDonnell's pub as his base, but Ann could see that having the gang eating and drinking at her digs could bring some outlaw glamour to the inn, as well as some of their stolen money.

For Ned it offered the chance to deflect suspicion away from the McDonnells.

Ann's invitation proved to be the biggest mistake of her life.

Inside her inn, fires roared in the dining room and parlour.

Paddy McDonnell came over with his family, pretending to be a prisoner, and was soon joined by other faux inmates on the Kelly team: Tom Lloyd and his 16-year-old brother Jack, Steve Hart's brother Dick, Wild Wright and James Kershaw, who was now married to Jane Graham, a friend of Mrs Kelly and known by police as a 'loose woman'.[26] There were also three Delaney boys, whose father was said to have helped make the armour.

Jim Kelly hovered close by.

Normally there were four special policemen stationed at Glenrowan, specifically to patrol around Maggie's house up the road at Greta. But all four had been brought down by winter chills[27] and the only officer left in town was Constable Hugh Bracken, who was bedridden with gastric flu.

Ned and Joe were awake all night as they rode about on horseback bailing up strangers, with the intention of keeping them prisoner until the train arrived.

Eventually they had 62 inmates.

Just after 11 a.m., on Sunday, 27 June, Glenrowan's young schoolmaster Thomas Curnow[28] decided to take a leisurely buggy ride along the road to Greta with his wife, Jean, his 11-month-old daughter, Muriel, and his delicate sister Catherine, who had just arrived from Ballarat. It was decidedly chilly, and Catherine had a bright red llama-wool scarf around her neck. David Mortimer, Curnow's brother-in-law, rode with them on horseback, his greyhound trotting along beside him.

When they came in sight of Mrs Jones's hotel, they noticed many people milling about.

In a hushed tone, Curnow told the others, 'Mrs Jones must be dead; she has been very ill.'[29] Then he drove to the railway crossing, and, seeing Stanistreet, asked him, 'What's the matter?'

The stationmaster replied, 'The Kellys are here; you can't go through.' Curnow thought he was joking and made a motion to drive through the gates, when he saw a man on horseback, blocking the crossing while talking to John Delaney. The rider wheeled round his horse and Curnow saw that he had revolvers in his belt.

He asked Curnow, 'Who are you?'

'I'm the teacher at Glenrowan,' Curnow replied. 'We are going out for a drive.'

'I am sorry,' the man replied, 'but I must detain you.'

Curnow soon realised it was Ned Kelly giving him the polite orders, with another armed man, Joe Byrne, nearby.

Thomas Curnow, the plucky young Glenrowan
schoolteacher, risked a bullet in the back to save
the lives of police officers hunting the Kelly
Gang. State Library of NSW, PXB 439

The schoolmaster was afflicted with a deformed hip and after
he climbed out of the buggy he limped along as he led his horse
from the crossing and tied it to the railway fence alongside.
He and his party then became prisoners in Stanistreet's house.
Curnow listened as Kelly threated to kill Delaney for 'having
sought admission into the police force', pointing a revolver at
him several times. Kelly declared to everyone listening that he
would have the life of anyone who aided the police in any way,
or who even showed a friendly feeling for them, and declared
that he could and would find them out. The women pleaded with
Kelly to show mercy. Curnow thought Kelly was acting, though
Delaney seemed genuinely terrified.[30]

Byrne then produced a bottle of brandy and offered some in a
tumbler to all the adults. Ned refused to take any. Kelly and Byrne
then went from the railway crossing to Mrs Jones's hotel, preceded

by most of their male prisoners. Curnow's wife, sister and child stayed behind in the Stanistreet home. When Curnow reached Mrs Jones's inn, he saw that there were already more than 50 people inside, all of whom appeared to be prisoners of the gang.

Dan Kelly asked Curnow to have a drink with him. Curnow told the small but cocky teenager that he had heard he had been at Beechworth during the previous night, and that he had shot several policemen.

'Yeah, we did some shooting,' Dan replied, 'and we burned the bastards out.' Byrne came into the bar, and, looking at Dan Kelly's glass, said, 'Be careful, old man.'

So Dan poured water into his brandy.

The two outlaws told Curnow they were all set to send the train and its occupants 'to hell'.[31]

AFTER FINALLY CRAWLING out from under Aaron's bed, Constable Harry Armstrong arrived in Beechworth at 1 p.m. on Sunday, almost 19 hours after the murder. He told a startled Detective Ward what had happened, but the Beechworth telegraph operator couldn't get a message through to Benalla for more than 90 minutes.[32] Constable Patrick Mullane and four other policemen rode out to Sherritt's hut to investigate but the traces of Dan and Byrne were long gone. Police stations throughout Victoria's north-east were warned to watch all the river crossings and bridges.[33]

At the Glenrowan Inn, Dan was continuing to drink freely as Ann Jones moved her dining-room table onto the veranda so the mood could be lightened with music and dancing. Dave Mortimer played Jack Jones's concertina while the greyhound nestled at his feet, and Ann and Jane danced quadrilles with Ned and Dan. Jane sat on the outlaws' knees and helped them by counting the prisoners while waving a revolver and threatening to tell Ned if anyone tried to escape.[34] One of her old schoolmates later wrote that 'six months in gaol would do her no harm'.[35] Dan, who was in a merry mood with all the liquid refreshments he was consuming, asked Curnow to dance with him,[36] too, and while

Curnow went through the motions with his bung hip, he knew he had to do something 'to prevent the outrage which the outlaws had planned'.[37]

AS SOON AS THE BEECHWORTH telegram reached Hare, he wired the news to Standish at his digs inside the swanky Melbourne Club. Hare asked his boss to approach O'Connor with the request to let bygones be bygones and return at once to Beechworth so the trackers could follow the hoofprints of Sherritt's killer. The commissioner had just gone out, though, and didn't get the telegram until 4.30 p.m., 22 hours after the killing.[38]

By that time Ned Kelly had become entertainment director at the Glenrowan Inn, rather than executioner. He organised games and athletic events in the paddock behind the pub for his captive audience and made sure he won the hop, step and jump, using a revolver in each hand as weights.[39]

The gang kept an eye on all the prisoners but Curnow said 'the intention to do something to baffle the murderous designs of the gang grew on me, and I resolved to do my utmost to gain the confidence of the outlaws, and to make them believe me to be a sympathizer with them'.[40]

Curnow went back to Stanistreet's house and saw Hart lying on a sofa. Hart had three loaded guns by his side but seemed more concerned about his swollen and painful feet, caused, he said, by not having had his boots off for several days and nights. Curnow advised him to bathe them in hot water and requested it for him.

In a quiet moment, with no one listening, Stanistreet whispered to Curnow that someone, somehow had to raise the alarm before the planned atrocity took place. Curnow asked the stationmaster and his wife if it would be a sin to break a promise to the outlaws. They said that it would not. Curnow then asked Stanistreet if the outlaws had taken his revolver from him. He said no.[41]

When the chance came Curnow ingratiated himself further into Ned's confidence by telling him that Stanistreet had a loaded revolver from the Railway Department and that Ned should confiscate it. He didn't mention his sister Catherine's red llama-wool scarf, but Curnow was already thinking, 'what a splendid danger signal that would make'.[42]

Throughout Sunday afternoon Hare and Sadleir kept sending telegrams and paper notes by horseback from Benalla, informing other police stations of the murder at Beechworth and warning all officers to be on the alert for the gang.

As soon as he received his message at the Melbourne Club, Standish sent a note by hansom cab to O'Connor at Flemington. There was none of his usual rancour.

My Dear Sir

I have just received telegraphic information that the outlaws stuck up the police party that was watching Mrs. Byrne's house and shot Aaron Sherritt dead. The police, however, appear to have escaped. In the urgent position of affairs, could you return to Beechworth with your trackers by the early train to-morrow, or by a special train, if that can be arranged. If you can oblige us in this way, could you manage to come in at once to see me at the Club by the hansom which I send out with this?

Yours faithfully,
F.C. STANDISH[43]

The hansom cab arrived at Flemington at 7.30 p.m. as O'Connor was dining with his wife and her sister, Kate Webb, the young wife of a prominent barrister.[44] O'Connor's eyes lit up not just at the prospect of a fight with the Kellys but at the delicious satisfaction of having Standish begging for his help.

O'Connor rode in the cab back to the Melbourne Club where he could hardly contain his smirk as Standish asked, 'in the urgent state of the case, can you manage to accede to my request'.[45]

Standish said that O'Connor 'haw-haw'd' for a while, playing the commissioner on a string, but O'Connor was really champing at the bit, 'only too glad to get the opportunity'. He raced back to Flemington and organised his five troopers, and had their guns unpacked and cleaned.

In Benalla, Hare readied horses and provisions for the Queenslanders and organised a team to follow him to Beechworth – Senior Constable John Kelly and Constables Jim Arthur,[46] Daniel Barry, Charlie Gascoigne, William Canny, Tom Kirkham and William Phillips.

John Kelly was breathing rapidly at the thought of revenge 20 months after he'd loaned Michael Kennedy the Spencer rifle. Belfast-born Jim Arthur had been part of the search for the policemen's bodies just three months after he'd joined the force. Now he had the chance to confront those responsible.

SUNDAY NIGHT ROLLED on but the special train did not. It was now almost 24 hours since Byrne murdered his mate and still the gang waited and waited. With so many mouths to feed and supper time approaching, Kelly considered slaughtering a bullock,[47] then joked about bailing up a circus[48] to keep everyone entertained. He started letting his 'hostages' go, 21 of them, but only those he knew were loyal to his cause, including the McDonnells.[49]

Curnow told Ned, 'I'm with you heart and soul, too.'

'I know that,' Kelly replied, 'I can see it.'[50]

At about dusk, Curnow heard Kelly telling Ann Jones that he was going to the police barracks a mile away to capture the unsuspecting Constable Bracken, who was still in his sick bed.

Curnow convinced Ned that he should take him and his family, too, and make Curnow's brother-in-law Dave Mortimer call out to the ailing policeman, 'because Bracken knew his voice well, and by hearing it would suspect nothing'.[51]

The schoolteacher retrieved his wife, child and sister from Stanistreet's house but had to wait a couple of hours before Ned and Joe buckled on their armour, put their helmets onto the front of their saddles and gave the order to get rolling.

Curnow had his family and the postmaster's young son Alex Reynolds in his buggy. They travelled for about a mile to the police station and on the way Ned told Curnow that he planned to fill all the surrounding gullies and ruts with 'the fat carcasses of the police'.[52]

Ned donned his helmet and bailed up the ailing Bracken, who despite his illness burst out laughing at the sight of someone with what looked like a nail can on his head.[53] He soon stopped laughing. Bracken's wife and young son were in bed, but Ned said Bracken had to leave them and come with Ned to Ann Jones's inn. It was a different story for the lame schoolmaster. Ned told Curnow that he had done a good job for him and that he could go home to bed, but 'don't dream too loud'.[54]

THE SPECIAL TRAIN LEFT Spencer Street Station three minutes before 10 p.m. with one carriage, one break van and four journalists hoping to cover the biggest story of their lives.[55] It stopped at Essendon at 10.15 to collect the five trackers along with O'Connor, and the sisters Louise and Kate, who thought the trip north to hunt the Kellys would be a fascinating adventure.

The train rocketed north,[56] accidentally smashing through a railway gate just past Craigieburn, 24 kilometres out of Melbourne,[57] and badly damaging the brake on the locomotive.

In Benalla, Frank Hare grabbed a couple of hours sleep after a frantic day,[58] but no one got any shut eye at the Glenrowan Inn.

Ned bought drinks for everyone. Ann Jones asked her sickly 13-year-old son Jack to sing, and he gave a rendition of 'The Wild Colonial Boy',[59] a cautionary tale of a rebel shot down by police. Although the bushrangers had already killed four men and were planning a massacre, Ned took a shine to Hugh Bracken. He said the gang had just shot one traitor and that Detective Ward was next on their list, followed by 'those six little demons', then O'Connor and Hare.

'If I had them killed,' Ned told Bracken, 'I would feel easy and contented.'[60]

With that, the dancing resumed. Ann Jones, now wearing an alluring red dress, was reinvigorated by the attention of these rough-and-ready young men.[61] She was enjoying the discomfort of some of the other prisoners who had previously treated her 'like a bloody blackfellow',[62] and was seen flirting with Ned Kelly in the moonlight against a fence. She was also spied playfully trying to tug a ring off Byrne's finger[63] – one of the rings he ripped off the dead fingers of Scanlan and Lonigan. Like Dan Kelly, Steve Hart became 'pretty drunk'[64] and Bracken noticed that Byrne was getting careless, too, leaving the key to the hotel beside the chimney. Bracken made certain that no one noticed as he wandered nonchalantly over to the chimney and dropped the key into the cuff of his trousers.[65]

WHEN FRANK HARE rose a little after midnight, the engineer in charge of the Benalla Station suggested that he put a constable in front of the locomotive, as a lookout along the line. Though only 24, stocky, fair-haired Irishman Constable Barry had been plagued by severe rheumatism for months. Immediately after the police murders, he had volunteered to be a Kelly hunter, gaining a transfer from Learmonth to Benalla, and for the last year and a half he had been engaged in what he called 'the hardest work that has been done'. Only the hope of being at the capture of the police killers had made him able to endure his discomfort on all the cold, hard nights at the cave parties and other bush locations. Barry had received commendations for his bravery and diligence and now he put up his hand and volunteered to be securely fastened to the front of the Benalla locomotive like a ship's figurehead.

The special train carrying O'Connor's team from Melbourne arrived in Benalla at 1.30 a.m. but because the brake was damaged it was decided to use it as the pilot engine to go ahead and have the Benalla locomotive tow the carriage and van to Beechworth where this latest Kelly hunt was to start. The Melbourne engine drivers refused to allow Barry to be tied to the front of their machine, though, saying it was too dangerous, so he was given a seat in the carriage with everyone else.

The train pulled out of Benalla at 2 a.m., now with Hare added to the force along with seven policemen and Charles Rawlins, a local cattle dealer who had enlisted as a civilian volunteer.

The Kelly Gang had planned to derail a speeding train and kill any of the lawmen who survived the crash. State Library of Victoria, A/S31/07/80/177

A few minutes later in Glenrowan, with the train still nowhere in sight, Ned decided to let all the civilians leave. The outlaws had been drinking all day and were now in a playful rather than murderous mood, though Ned warned the crowd that he would shoot them down like dogs if they ever gave information about him to the police. Not that all policemen were bad, he said. He told Bracken he didn't mind it when a policeman did his duty, 'so long as he doesn't overdo it'.[66]

THOMAS CURNOW'S MIND and heart were racing as he steered his buggy towards home. He whispered to his wife that he was going to Benalla to sound a warning. Jean Curnow was terrified that Ned's supporters would see him and she bawled her eyes out, telling her husband he was a damn fool and that he would only make her a widow. Curnow told his wife that she was right, as usual, and with help from his sister calmed her and put her to bed.

Then Curnow collected his sister's red scarf, a candle and some matches, and hobbled off to his buggy as fast as he could.

THE TRAIN REACHED 70 kilometres an hour and the drivers expected to hit 100 when they reached the bend past Glenrowan.[67]

But at 2.30 a.m. the police were about 1.6 kilometres south of the town when Archie McPhee, the guard of the pilot locomotive, noticed a faint red glow on the track. He thought it might be the embers of a burning log – then realised it was a man holding a candle behind a red scarf.

With a screech of metal on metal, the locomotive stopped, and a breathless Curnow revealed the danger ahead. The engine driver sounded his whistle in a series of short, sharp blasts. To all those in the Glenrowan Inn it was like the sound of a cock crowing.[68]

Steve Hart rushed up from Stanistreet's, sore feet or not. Byrne also rushed inside the hotel to announce, 'the train's coming'. For all the hostages hoping to go home, it was now too late.

'All stop here,' Ned bellowed before he and Byrne, decked out in their armour, went outside and leapt onto their horses. They galloped down to the tracks, only to see the train halted in the distance and no mangled bodies anywhere.[69]

Their plans were dashed. Ned raced back and ordered Ann Jones to kill the lights. She rushed about, putting out the fires and lamps with jugs of water, as terrified men and women tried to make sense of the movements being made by these iron-clad creatures now lumbering about in the darkness.

Bracken told everyone to lie on the floor.[70]

Everyone did. Except Bracken. Amid the chaos, he took Byrne's key from his trouser cuff and unlocked the back door.

Then, under a moon as bright as a searchlight and fearing a bullet in his back, Bracken bolted towards the railway station. The police train had halted before reaching it, and was safe, several hundred metres from the torn tracks. Bracken jumped the railway fence and found Hare and his men unloading the horses.

The breathless policeman pointed towards the inn.

'Over there,' Bracken gasped. 'The Kellys, quick, quick, all four of them.[71] For God's sake go as quickly as possible, otherwise they will escape.' [72]

Chapter 17

IN THE FROSTY BLACK MORNING, Superintendent Hare charged towards the Glenrowan Inn and called on his men to follow him.

Many of the lawmen were still holding their horses.

'Let the horses go,' Hare bellowed. 'The Kellys are in Jones's hotel.'

Hare had endured months of privations and agony searching the bush for this very moment and he was not about to let the outlaws escape justice. As he charged towards the inn, Hare was closely followed by John Kelly and Constables Gascoigne, Phillips and Canny, and Inspector O'Connor and some of his trackers. Hare charged through a revolving gate on the railway fence towards the ramshackle pub, the thrill of battle propelling his beefy frame to move faster than he had for years.

The pub was silent and dark, but the moon beams coming over the back of the inn made the anxious lawmen plainly visible.

Within about 20 metres of the veranda Hare saw a flash of fire, but could not distinguish any figures. Instantly there were three other blasts from the veranda, which was otherwise in total darkness.

Ned Kelly came out from under the veranda, and Hare called to him and advised him not to be foolhardy.

'I wish to speak a few words to you,' Hare yelled.

In reply, Kelly roared back, 'I don't want to speak to you.'[1]

Hare, a giant for the era, was all target.

Even though the body armour made it hard for Ned to aim, he raised his five-cylinder Colt revolving rifle, fixed Hare in his gunsights and pulled the trigger.[2]

Hare was aiming at the four shadowy figures when a .56 calibre bullet – more than 1.3 centimetres in diameter – roared from the barrel of Ned's rifle through the cold night air and tore through Hare's left wrist.

'Good gracious I am hit,' he cried out. 'The very first shot!'[3] Hare's left arm dropped useless beside him as he saw three more bullet flashes almost within half a second of the first.

O'Connor ordered his men to take cover, and he dropped into a culvert immediately in front of the hotel door, and about 20 metres from it.

The other three gang members kept firing, the muzzle flashes briefly illuminating the ghostly figures. The police fired back but from a distance did not realise they were shooting at men in iron suits. A voice boomed from inside a helmet with a metallic echo. 'Fire away, you buggers, you can't hurt us.'[4]

Charlie Gascoigne, a first-rate shot,[5] called out, 'That is Ned Kelly's voice.'

Bullets crashed through the flimsy walls of the inn as a continuous fire was kept up on both sides for about five minutes. The lawmen, all in a line as if they were on parade, received volley after volley from the bulky figures on the dark veranda, and replied in kind.

Hare kept using his gun with his right hand, but, badly wounded, he had great difficulty loading with one arm.[6]

The captives inside the inn huddled on the floor and were showered with glass and splinters. Men and women screamed and Ann's little son Jack took a police bullet through the hip.

'Oh Mother, I am shot,' he squealed.

Blood bubbled from his mouth and his weeping was piteous. Another bullet creased Jane Jones's forehead but the young girl and her mother dodged more bullets to carry Jack to shelter behind the brick chimney.

The morning was frosty and clouds of smoke hung all around the hotel as Ned Kelly, virtually invisible in the dark except for the flashes from his Colt gun barrel, again appeared in front of the hotel and walked towards the railway fence, firing at the police.

The gun flashes were dead in front of Gascoigne, who was taking shelter behind a post.

Gascoigne fired at Kelly, and he returned the shot quickly. Then they blasted three or four shots at each other. Two of Kelly's bullets sent splinters from the narrow post that gave Gascoigne only partial cover.

Then Gascoigne sent a bullet from his Martini-Henry rifle straight through Kelly's bent left elbow, exploding bone and flesh and rendering the arm almost useless.

The police were unrelenting with their gunfire and Stanhope O'Connor said the incessant shooting drove the outlaws back into the inn. He heard them barricading it.[7]

A bullet grazed Jimmy, one of the trackers, who was lying in the culvert beside O'Connor. Jimmy jumped up and fired five shots in rapid succession into the inn, while crying out, 'Take that, Ned Kelly.'

'It seemed to afford him great relief,' O'Connor said, 'but rather amused me.'[8]

The gang's idea had been to fortify the hotel and fire through the windows. Kelly had not felt the need for armour on his legs.[9] Bad mistake. As the guns blazed for 15 more minutes, another bullet tore through Kelly's right foot, entering beside his big toe and exiting through his heel.[10] Joe Byrne was also shot through his right calf.[11]

Ned's cousin Jack Lloyd set off two Chinese rockets – one faint, the other glowing brilliantly[12] – to alert Kelly sympathisers that the battle had begun and that they were to gather at a prearranged site to provide back-up. Many of the sympathisers had been issued with the gang's best guns, including a Snider-Enfield with the inscription 'NK Son of Red' carved into the wooden butt.[13] Over the next couple of hours there was a noise of constant galloping between Glenrowan and Greta as Kelly's supporters received directions.[14]

Firing from the veranda finally ceased, and the police could hear screams from men, women and children inside the inn.

Hare and Gascoigne called on the police to stop shooting.

There was a brief ceasefire. Gunsmoke wafted through the cold morning air as all of the women and most of the children left the inn.

Margaret Reardon escaped with her baby and seven children but was stopped in her tracks by more police gunfire. In the darkness the police had no idea who was running from the hotel. Three of the Reardon children made it to safety but Margaret and her husband had to run back inside the inn's bullet-riddled walls with their two eldest boys, two girls and baby Bridget.[15]

Jane Jones stumbled out with a head wound behind a lighted candle. Her mother's mind had been tortured by the plight of her son and Ann walked about waving her arms, wailing.[16] Ann called the police 'murdering hounds'.

'You buggers,' she cried hysterically, the tears running down her face, 'you have shot my boy. You might as well shoot the rest of my family now. Go on, shoot us all.' She abused the outlaws, too, and screamed at them to come outside and fight.[17]

A labourer named Neil McHugh emerged from the hotel with Jack Jones in his arms. He tried to pacify Mrs Jones but as sporadic gunfire continued from police, who feared the gang were hiding among the hostages, McHugh dodged the gunfire to carry little Jack through the darkness. Constable Phillips thought it was one of the outlaws escaping and called on Gascoigne to chase him. Gascoigne overtook McHugh on the railway line, but saw that it was a man carrying a badly wounded boy on his back. The boy was bleeding from the mouth. Gascoigne asked McHugh who was in the hotel and in a rush McHugh gasped: 'There are 30 of them, and they have armour on and for God's sake don't go too near the hotel, for they intend to shoot you all in the morning.'[18]

McHugh took the wounded boy to James Reardon's house,[19] and they eventually conveyed him to Wangaratta Hospital by midday. Jack bled to death 12 hours later.[20] McHugh had not distinguished between the outlaws and the prisoners, so that Gascoigne returned to the fight thinking there were 30 armed men inside the hotel wearing armour.

Hare, bleeding profusely from his wrist wound, yelled out to John Kelly, 'I am badly wounded, take all the men and surround the hotel, don't let them get away.' In return, the senior constable asked Hare to organise some more ammunition.

The superintendent headed back towards the railway platform. On the way he saw O'Connor running up a culvert with Hero and some of his trackers. As Hare passed him he called out that he was hit. 'O'Connor, place your boys round the house,' he said, 'and for God's sake don't let them escape.'[21]

For the next three hours, 13 lawmen including O'Connor's five trackers kept up a steady rain of gunfire on the hotel. The gang continued to shoot back as their prisoners huddled on the floor. For some that was not enough protection.

George Metcalf, a 34-year-old quarryman, was hit in the eye by a bullet that bounced off a chimney,[22] and Martin Cherry, a 58-year-old Irish railway worker who came to the inn to have a look at the famous bushrangers, took a bullet through the groin.[23] Metcalf lingered for four months before dying in Melbourne Hospital.[24]

SUPERINTENDENT HARE made it back to the Glenrowan train station after being shot, and one of the journalists, Tom Carrington[25] from the *Australasian Sketcher*, bandaged his wrist with a handkerchief. Charles Rawlins volunteered to take more ammunition to the policemen.

Hare soon trotted back to the fray but was growing faint from blood loss and he staggered back to the rail platform. He flopped onto a bundle of sacks, exclaiming 'catch me please',[26] then sent a locomotive to Benalla to immediately inform Sadleir of what had occurred, requesting him to come as soon as possible with every available man and a big supply of bullets.

A little sherry rallied Hare, but the blood was still flowing down his arm and he soon followed on another engine to Benalla, hoping to have the wound dressed properly before returning to battle. He was so sick and faint that he struggled not to pass out. Hare reached Benalla in ten minutes and had the stationmaster telegraph Wangaratta, directing Sergeant Steele to bring every available man he had.

Crouched in front of the inn, Constable William Phillips was close enough to hear Ned and Byrne, now at the rear of the hotel.

'Is that you, Joe?'

'Yes. Is that you, Ned? Come here.'

'Come here be damned. What are you doing there? Come with me and load my rifle. I'm cooked.'

'So am I,' Byrne said. 'I think my leg is broke.'

'Leg be damned; you got the use of your arms,' Ned snarled. 'Come on; load for me. I'll pink the buggers.'

Byrne told Ned not to talk so loud about his wounds in case it disheartened Steve and Dan, but with both men carrying bullet wounds and surrounded by police Ned admitted things could have gone better.

'It's your fault,' Byrne snapped. 'I always said this bloody armour would bring us to grief.'

'Don't you believe it,' Ned replied. 'Old Hare is cooked, and we will soon finish the rest.'[27]

WHILE THE POLICE KEPT pumping bullets into the hotel, aiming higher now because they knew prisoners were on the floor, Sergeant Steele was at the Wangaratta train station at 4 a.m. listening for the arrival of the special police transport from Melbourne, his ears pricked constantly by the sound of distant gunfire. He asked that a locomotive be readied for his troops. Before Hare's telegram alerting him to the gun battle arrived, Steele heard the sound of horse hoofs on railway sleepers echoing down the line towards him. With shotgun at the ready, Steele bolted down the tracks to investigate and challenged a rider in the distance. It was Constable Bracken racing for his life on the blue metal beside the rails.

Bracken told Steele that Hare was wounded, and the gang were in Glenrowan 'blazing away at the police'.[28] Steele leapt onto Bracken's horse, and rode back to Wangaratta, rousing his men, and he sent two foot constables on the engine to Glenrowan telling the driver to beware of the torn-up tracks.

DESTRUCTION OF THE KELLY GANG.   DRAWN BY MR. T. CARRINGTON DURING THE ENCOUNTER.

1.- GENERAL VIEW OF THE NIGHT ATTACK ON THE GLENROWAN HOTEL.   2.-SCENE WHERE NED KELLY WAS SHOT.   3.-THE SURRENDER OF THE 25 PRISONERS AT 10 O'CLOCK IN THE MORNING.   4.-THE BODIES OF HART AND DAN KELLY IN THE FLAMES.

Artist Tom Carrington recorded his eyewitness account of the Glenrowan gun battle for *The Australasian Sketcher*. State Library of Victoria, A/S03/07/80/153

Carrying his shotgun and dressed like a big-game hunter, with tweed jacket and tweed hat set off by his walrus moustache, Steele jumped back on his horse and led his mounted constables, rugged up in thick coats, on a mad dash 10 miles south to Glenrowan as fast as they could go.

Ned continued to shoot at the police in the darkness, then he left the hotel and hobbled for 100 metres from the inn to where his mare was tethered. The blood from his arm wound had seeped into the bullet chambers of his Colt rifle and had congealed, making it impossible to fire. He left it where it fell along with his skull cap, which he had been using to soak up the blood from his elbow.[29]

As Charlie Gascoigne trained his gunsight on him, Kelly managed to mount the horse and ride to a nearby hill, where some of his family and friends were waiting with rifles.[30]

'I could easily have shot at him,' Gascoigne related, but knowing the Benalla police were mostly posted on that side, he was afraid he might hit some of them. Gascoigne asked one of the Queensland trackers taking cover in the culvert how many of the police had been killed and he was mistakenly told that Constable Canny and the tracker Jimmy were dead.[31]

Sergeant Steele and his men charged into Glenrowan at 5.03 a.m., dismounted from the sweaty, heaving horses and approached Mrs Jones's hotel stealthily on foot. The firing from the hotel had ceased for a while and in the dark Senior Constable Kelly and Constable Arthur, who were lying behind a log, challenged the new arrivals. John Kelly told Steele that he had picked up a Colt rifle 'all covered with blood'.

Steele sent some of his men to cover the back of the inn and then made a series of darting runs to get behind a large tree as his vantage point to start shooting.

Then, at 5.10 a.m., John Sadleir arrived on a train from Benalla with 11 police officers and the trackers Moses and Spider. The gang welcomed the new leader of the hunt with a volley of gunfire from the windows of the hotel.

DURING ANOTHER CEASEFIRE, Margaret Reardon again tried to get out of the inn. Carrying baby Bridget inside a shawl, she escorted her five-year-old daughter Ellen out into the hotel's yard and called on the police to have mercy.

'I am only a woman, allow me to escape with my children,' she hollered. 'The outlaws will not interfere with us – don't you.'

Sergeant Steele's trigger finger was so itchy that it drove him crazy.

He yelled back: 'Put up your hands and come this way, or I will shoot you like bloody dogs.'

Margaret put her baby under her arm and held up her free hand. Her 17-year-old son Michael was holding his little sister by the hand but also put up his free arm in surrender. To Steele, in the half-light, Michael could have been one of the Kellys. Steele pulled the trigger. Other officers followed. Two shots whizzed past Margaret's head and two more nicked the shawl covering the baby.

Michael Reardon retreated towards the inn, pulling his little sister Ellen by the left hand, and with his right hand raised in surrender.[32]

In his frenzy, Steele may have mistaken Margaret for Ann Jones. Constable Jim Arthur claimed the sergeant exclaimed: 'I have shot Mother Jones in the tits.'[33]

Constable Phillips also claimed that he called out sarcastically to the sergeant that such a feat must be a real feather in Steele's cap.[34]

Margaret cried out, 'Oh, you have shot my child.'

Constable Arthur said later that he roared at Steele, 'It's a poor innocent woman and a baby, if you fire at them again I will shoot *you*.'[35]

So, instead, Steele shot Michael Reardon in the back. A shotgun pellet lodged near his breastbone.[36]

Michael collapsed in the doorway of the hotel and his father dragged his other two children inside.

A shotgun pellet also grazed the head of Margaret's baby Bridget, but mother and child were both lifted over the railway fence to safety by plucky Jesse Dowsett, a Benalla railway guard who had just arrived on the scene.

NED KELLY HAD THE CHANCE to flee on horseback from the carnage he had created but after almost two years living rough he had become sick of running. He rode out to the armed sympathisers waiting for him and told them to go home before they were killed.

What he did next would become the stuff of legend, as he wheeled his horse around. Bleeding profusely and struggling under the weight of his armour, he headed back to the fray. His defiance against insurmountable odds made the phrase 'as game as Ned Kelly' one of the highest of compliments in Australian culture.

Kelly would say later that he had grown sick of life on the run, being 'hunted like a dog'. He said that he could get no rest constantly looking over his shoulder and that he had intended to 'paste as many of the traps' as he could before they got him.[37]

Julian Ashton drew this study of a tracker with Joe Byrne's body for the *Illustrated Australian News*. Despite his suit of armour, Ned Kelly's lieutenant was killed with a bullet to his unprotected groin. The drawing was based on Byrne's corpse as it lay in the Benalla lockup after the gun battle. State Library of Victoria, IAN03/07/80/105

Kelly wobbled into the inn's back entrance just as Byrne fired two shots at the police from the bar window. Then, during a brief lull, Byrne took off his helmet to have a glass of whisky and toasted the others with 'many more years in the bush for the Kelly gang'.[38] Just as he said that, a police bullet burst through the hotel wall and through Byrne's groin, severing his femoral artery.[39] Ned Kelly watched with a sense of forlorn resignation as his best friend crashed to the floor, his body armour making a heavy thud. James Reardon, lying on the floor next to Byrne, could not hear a groan, only the river of blood draining out of his emaciated 23-year-old body, taking Byrne's life with it.[40] One of the bullets hit the inn's clock and sent its chime haywire.

Dan Kelly and Hart were standing side by side 'looking cowed and dispirited, without the slightest sign of fight left in them … like two condemned criminals on the drop, waiting for the bolt to be drawn'.[41] James Reardon suspected they had made a suicide pact.[42]

Yet, the two youngsters were still firing sporadically from inside the inn when Ned Kelly declared that he had no faith in their fighting qualities and staggered outside in his suit of armour once more.

Constable Gascoigne saw movement as a grey dawn started to break, and called out that the Kellys were trying to get away. The police shot eight horses in the paddock behind the inn to make sure they didn't.

Ned made it up a slope to meet with Tom Lloyd in the bush but fainted from blood loss. When he came to, he told his cousin to keep his head down as Lloyd loaded three handguns for him. Two of them were percussion loaders – a .31 pocket Colt that Ned probably used to shoot Fitzpatrick, and a .36 Colt Navy he took from Constable Devine in Jerilderie. He also had Lonigan's .45 Webley, the only gun that he could reload with one hand.

Tom took off Ned's oilskin coat to treat his wounds and then draped it back over his shoulders like a cloak,[43] with the helmet holding it in place. The sun rose slowly in a cloudy sky and there was fog all around. Battered and bloodied but dressed like a knight crusader and ready to fight to the death, Ned Kelly prepared for his last stand.

Chapter 18

BY THE TIME THE SUN began rising over the battlefield at Glenrowan, Mrs Jones's inn had been riddled with so many bullet holes that the walls resembled latticework.[1]

The ground was covered with frost, and mist swirled around the wreckage like phantoms.

Constable Arthur, an expert marksman, was 100 metres away from the hotel, worried that the power of his Martini-Henry rifle would send a bullet through its porous walls and kill a policeman on the other side.

He stopped to fill his pipe with tobacco and light it, hoping for a little balm for his taut nerves.

Just then, a monster of 'a tremendous size', much taller than a human,[2] stumbled through the swirling fog from the direction of Morgan's Look-out that towered over the inn.[3] The monster walked straight towards the hotel and when it was within about 20 metres of Constable Arthur, the pipe fell from the policeman's mouth. He stared dumbfounded at this horrifying apparition.

At first he thought it was a 'madman in the horrors who had put some nail keg on his head', and he continued to gaze slack-jawed as the figure approached steadily. Arthur thought it had the notion of storming the hotel on behalf of the police and called out to it, 'Keep back, you damned fool, you will get shot.'

The figure replied with a metallic roar: 'I could shoot you, Sonny', and then fired at Arthur with his revolver. The constable could see that the monster was crippled, that it could not hold its arm steady to take proper aim. Yet it still shuffled forward and fired another shot that tore up the ground a metre or two away from the officer. Arthur lifted his Martini-Henry and squeezed the trigger.[4] The monster didn't budge. Arthur fired again and the next bullet bounced off the helmet. Still the metal monster continued to lumber forward, though behind the helmet Ned Kelly's eyes were becoming blackened and swollen like a boxer's in a brawl.

Arthur took careful aim at the slit in the helmet and fired again but the bullet only staggered the creature. Once again it shot back.

Terrified cries rose up among the police of 'It's the devil', 'It's a bunyip,'[5] and 'It's a ghost.'[6]

It was the first close-up look any of the police had of their assailant in daylight and they couldn't believe their eyes.

Bullets ricocheted off the iron suit. The force of the lead hitting the metal close to Kelly's flesh felt like mighty blows from a fist and the breastplate and helmet were dented all over.[7] But from inside his helmet, Kelly mocked their impotent efforts, 'Good shots, boys. Fire away, you buggers. You cannot hurt me!'

But they could. After no sleep in two days, massive blood loss and bullet strike after bullet strike, which had caused huge welts and cuts on his torso and head, Kelly was now 'more dead than alive'.[8]

Journalist Tom Carrington, watching the gunfight from the train station, said there was no head visible on the armoured monster, no one knew its real identity and:

> … in the dim light of morning, with the steam rising from the ground, it looked for all the world like the ghost of Hamlet's father with no head, only a very long thick neck …
> The figure continued gradually to advance, stopping every now and then, and moving what looked like its headless neck slowly and mechanically round, and then raising one foot on to a log, and aiming and firing a revolver. Shot after shot was fired at it, but without effect, the figure generally replying

Sergeant Steele and his men confront the strange, seemingly bullet-proof apparition that emerged from the mist at Glenrowan firing a revolver. State Library of Victoria, IAN17/07/80/120

by tapping the butt end of his revolver against its neck, the blows ringing out with the clearness and distinctness of a bell in the morning air. It was the most extraordinary sight I ever saw or read of in my life, and I felt fairly spellbound with wonder, and I could not stir or speak.[9]

Two of Steele's constables, James Healy and John Montiford,[10] came up close and fired their shotguns at the creature.[11]

Steele couldn't make out the figure from his position 100 metres away but suspected it was a local Aboriginal man, Tommy Reid, wearing a top hat and with a thick possum coat over his shoulders.[12]

'Steady firing, lads,' Steele called out from behind a tree, 'it's only a blackfellow.' Steele had mistaken the dark strapping on Kelly's light-coloured trousers for thin black legs.[13]

Hart and Dan Kelly emerged from the inn and fired at Steele, who was moving towards the gang leader.

Ned staggered towards a clump of three small trees where he had earlier dropped his bloody Colt rifle and skull cap. He had only gone about 50 metres since the shooting resumed and had another 100 metres to go before he reached the safety of the brick chimney in the hotel. He sank to his knees. From the bush, like a dream swathed in mist and clouds, Byrne's grey mare Music emerged still with her saddle and bridle.

Kelly let her pass rather than try to get away,[14] but Constable William Moore, worried that the horse might still offer an escape, shot her twice.[15]

Steele shivered and felt 'a creepy feeling' in the roots of his hair when he saw the ghostly apparition of Kelly standing behind the lower part of a fallen tree, and quietly taking pot shots at two or three of the lawmen.[16]

A bullet then knocked the Webley revolver out of Kelly's hand[17] and, unable to reload the pocket Colt with one arm, he drew his last gun, Devine's .36 Colt Navy. He had six shots left.

Dan and Steve were still firing sporadically from the inn but the police had only one target now, and he could hardly move.

More than once Kelly had threatened to roast Steele alive; now he levelled his Colt against a tree and fired at the sergeant, who dived to the ground and was temporarily blinded when hit in the eye by dirt kicked up by the bullet.[18]

Steele shot at the slit in the helmet with his revolver but his hand was unsteady.

Kelly took aim and fired at Steele again, and the crusty lawman 'felt the breath of the bullet'. Steele tried another pistol shot, this time at the main bulk of the figure.

He heard the bullet strike the iron armour but that was all.

There were three or four men shooting at the apparition, but with no effect, although it was close to them.

Constable Healy shot Ned in the hand, and another bullet blew away the tip of his finger and scarred the Colt's walnut grip.

'Fire away, you bloody dogs,' Ned bellowed again, 'you can't hurt me. I am bullet-proof.'[19]

Inside the metal suit, though, Kelly was in horrific pain and almost out of ammunition. Briefly he thought about shooting himself so that the police could not take him alive.[20]

Railway guard Jesse Dowsett emptied his revolver at Ned from 20 metres and one of his bullets lodged in Ned's box of cartridges.[21]

Kelly then stumbled towards a fallen ghost gum as Steele circled from the left.

Brave little Dowsett fired again from 15 metres and hit Ned square in the helmet, but it did not have 'the slightest effect'.

Dowsett fired again and called out to the outlaw, 'How do you like that, old man?'

Kelly still had plenty of fight left in his battered body.

'How do you like this?'[22] Kelly answered, shooting straight back at Dowsett, who narrowly avoided a bullet aimed at his head.

At that moment, the wounded Music staggered to her feet and, in the gathering daylight as Ned's gaze shifted towards her, Steele dropped behind a stump.

Kelly had positioned himself behind a fallen log that in parts had a gap of about two feet to the ground through which his legs, unprotected by armour, were clearly visible.

Steele had arrested Kelly's mother two years earlier and now he was about to claim the major prize.

'I win, Ned,' was the fierce thought that gripped Steele as he now aimed his double-barrelled shotgun.[23]

Kelly raised his revolver again and pointed it at the sergeant. But from 15 metres away, Steele blew Kelly's right knee apart with a blast from his gun's right barrel. Kelly cried out in pain, but as Steele waited for him to fall, the outlaw stood firm, leaned against the log for support and took aim again.

Steele then ran towards Kelly and fired the left barrel at point-blank range and it tore apart Kelly's hip and thigh.

Sergeant Arthur Steele (kneeling) with other Kelly hunters; from left Constables Robert Cawsey, John Montiford, James Healey, Patrick Walsh, William Moore, James Dixon and James Dwyer. State Library of Victoria, H96.160/157

The bushranger stumbled and then collapsed, moaning: 'I'm done, I'm done.'

He still had his finger on the trigger, though, and as Dowsett and Steele wrestled for Ned's gun, a .36 bullet shot off Steele's hat and burned the side of his face.

As Steele yanked off Kelly's helmet, the men yelled in triumph at snaring the gang's leader.

'So, I've got you at last, Ned,'[24] Steele shouted as the lawman and the killer locked eyes, and John Kelly and Charles Rawlins leapt in to help restrain the armoured monster.

Steele took the 10-kilogram helmet[25] and, holding it aloft with one hand, he seized Ned by his thick beard with the other and spat: 'You bloody wretch, I swore I would be in at your death, and I am.'

Steele drew his revolver as if to 'blow the outlaw's brains out'[26] but Dowsett pushed the gun away, exclaiming, 'Take the man alive, take him alive.'[27]

Sergeant Steele and railway guard Jesse Dowsett wrestle Ned Kelly's Colt revolver from him after the 'Iron Outlaw' was brought down with shotgun blasts to the legs. State Library of Victoria, IAN03/07/80/105

Charles Rawlins feared Steele would kill Ned but Hugh Bracken, Ned's prisoner only hours before, stepped into the scene with his shotgun.

'Save me,' Ned pleaded, 'I saved you.'[28] Then he begged the officers surrounding him: 'That's enough. I have got my gruel.'[29]

Constable James Dwyer[30] was still as mad as hell, though, and wanted to make sure Kelly suffered more.

With a war whoop he kicked Kelly where it would really hurt and bellowed, 'Why did you kill my mate Lonigan?'[31] As Kelly pleaded for his life, Dwyer snarled: 'When poor Kennedy was begging you shot him like a dog.'[32]

As the police circled Kelly and still seemed 'inclined to pull him to pieces', Bracken stood over him with the shotgun and protected him, declaring to his comrades that he would shoot any man who dared touch him.[33]

Dowsett picked up Kelly's Navy Colt, which had three rounds

left to fire[34] and was covered in blood. Ned Kelly's last stand was over in less than half an hour.

DR JOHN NICHOLSON, who had known the Kelly family for years, arrived upon the badly wounded Ned Kelly 'a most extraordinary and pitiable object … a wild beast brought to bay, and evidently expecting to be roughly used. His face and hands were smeared with blood. He was shivering with cold, ghastly white, and smelt strongly of brandy.'[35]

Inside the inn, Dan had been spooked by the capture of his brother. He screamed with rage and rushed outside in a frenzy shooting at everyone he could see,[36] perhaps even trying to ensure his brother would not be taken alive.

Dan was shot in the left knee[37] and hobbled back inside the hotel.

Steele and Bracken supported Ned as he was half-carried, half-marched towards the railway station. John Kelly and Dr Nicholson followed behind with the armour, which had been painfully ripped from the prisoner. Police and reporters lifted Ned across the railway fence and he was placed in the guard's van.

Despite the animosity of the police towards him, Kelly was made as comfortable as possible. He now had more to fear from Dan and Steve, who peppered the train with bullets, apparently doing their best to end their leader's misery.

The situation became too hot and Kelly was then carried into Stanistreet's office and put on a stretcher.

As the four journalists surrounded him, Kelly complained that his feet were cold (a result of massive blood loss) and said they would never get warm again.

John McWhirter[38] from *The Age* cut off Ned's boots and put a pillow under his head.[39] He was astounded by the man's courage and his sense of loyalty towards his mates.

'Kelly was wounded at the first shot last night,' McWhirter wrote, 'and could have escaped in the darkness, but he stood to his comrades and fought to the last.'[40]

A kerosene tin full of water was heated and put against Kelly's cold feet and cotton was placed around his damaged leg and arm. Dr Nicholson counted 28 wounds and predicted the bedraggled bushranger would soon die.[41]

He souvenired Kelly's green and gold sash.

At 9 a.m. Kelly's old rival, Senior Constable Patrick Mullane arrived from Beechworth with ten more men, including the four who had stayed on the floor in Sherritt's hut after the murder.

Kelly was being interrogated constantly, sometimes by the police, sometimes by the reporters, and sometimes by gawkers crowding the room. He was listless in most of his answers but Carrington noted that he was 'altogether a fine figure of a man, the only bad part about his face being his mouth, which is a wicked and cruel one'.[42] Kelly fainted once or twice but did not complain about the wounds, which must have been excruciating.

Constable Dwyer, who had kicked Kelly earlier for killing Lonigan, now offered the pathetic figure some brandy. Some spilled onto Kelly's beard.

When he murmured that he was very hungry, Superintendent Sadleir sent Dwyer to get scones from McDonnell's pub.

Ned mumbled, 'This is more kindness than I ever thought to get,' and Sadleir told him, 'You shall have every care and attention, Ned; do not irritate yourself; keep yourself quiet.'

Sadleir had a theory that Kelly became insane at any hint of opposition and that this personality disorder was at the root of all his troubles. Sadleir later wrote:

All those who saw Kelly while he lay helpless on a mattress were struck with the gentle expression of his face. It was hard to think that he was a callous and cruel murderer. But the old spirit, half savage, half insane, was there notwithstanding, for while talking to him the same evening as he lay swathed in bandages, there passed suddenly over his face a startling look of wild passion as he called me to send away the black b— who was leaning over him. It was the fireman with his face blackened from his work on the engine, whom Kelly took to be one of the black trackers.[43]

Sadleir asked Kelly, whose hands were lightly tied and who seemed close to death, to call on Hart and Dan to surrender.

Ned told Sadleir that he saw Joe drop dead and that he had no faith in his brother or Steve, because they were 'two great curs … two great cowards'.[44]

AT ABOUT 10 A.M, under dark clouds, Sadleir called a ceasefire. The deep booming voice of Charles Rawlins bellowed through the sudden stillness towards the inn.

'All those inside there had better surrender at once; we will give you 10 minutes to do so, after that time we shall fire volleys into the house.'[45]

Instantly a white handkerchief was waved from the doorway, and about 25 captives rushed out towards the police with their hands held high above their heads.

'Don't fire,' they pleaded. 'For God's sake, don't shoot us'.[46]

With pistols in their hands rather than notebooks, two reporters, McWhirter and Joe Melvin[47] of *The Argus*, kept guard on the prisoners just in case there was a bushranger in disguise among them.

The captives were ordered to lie down on the cold, wet grass, flat on their stomachs, with their hands still in the air. The captives were so scarred by their ordeal that some of them seemed demented. Two of the McAuliffes, 'known as active sympathisers', were handcuffed, but the rest were set free.

Hart and Dan made no attempt to pot-shot the police during the lull, but after ten minutes the shooting started again and 'volley after volley' was fired at the last two bushrangers through the thin walls of the inn.

The railway line was repaired and more reporters, artists and photographers arrived to cover the biggest news story in Australia. They were joined just after midday by Matthew Gibney,[48] the Vicar-General of the Roman Catholic Church in Western Australia.

The 45-year-old Irishman was travelling from Benalla to Albury to raise money for a West Australian orphanage. He regarded the Kellys as 'a wild, reckless lot'[49] and found it astonishing given their crimes that they had so many sympathisers, 'even amongst those who ought to have known better'.[50]

Gibney knelt next to Ned Kelly in the stationmaster's office as Dr Nicholson ushered all the onlookers out.

In a feeble voice, Ned asked Gibney to help him prepare for death. 'Bless me Father, for I have sinned,' he said, in an understatement, beginning his confession.

When Gibney asked him to say, 'Lord Jesus, have mercy on me', Ned repeated it and added, 'It is not today I began to say that.'[51]

Maggie Skilling, dressed as though headed to a victory party in a sweeping Gainsborough hat, black riding habit and red undershirt,[52] galloped up to a fence on the railway reserve. Constable Montiford told her that she could not enter and that he would 'fire on her if she did not retreat'.[53] Maggie replied with 'a very low obscene expression'[54] and rode off towards the McDonnells.

She re-emerged shortly afterwards, crossing the railway line on foot with her sisters Kate and Grace, and Wild Wright.

Senior Constable Kelly asked her if she would help get Dan and Steve to surrender, but she said 'she would sooner see them burned first'[55] than fall into the clutches of the law. She asked to see Ned before he died and the policeman agreed.

Father Gibney suggested to Ned that Dan and Steve might surrender to a priest but Ned warned him against trying anything because the boys might take him for a policeman in disguise, and 'your cloth won't save you'.

More and more police arrived to see the death throes of the Kelly Gang, including Tom Meehan who had been humiliated two years earlier when asked to convey the news of the police murders to Benalla. Some of the men volunteered to rush the hotel, including Constable Harry Armstrong, trying to dodge the tag of 'coward' for not doing more on the night of Sherritt's murder.

Charlie Johnston heard reports that Sadleir had ordered artillerymen and a cannon, but offered a different plan.

A volley of gunfire covered him as Johnston marched coolly to the windowless southern side of the Glenrowan Inn, placed a bundle of straw against it, poured kerosene over the straw and weatherboards and struck a match.

The match was a dud. He struck another. Then he jogged back to the police line, and waited. Gibney asked Kate Kelly if she would make one last effort to bring Dan and Steve out alive and she exclaimed, 'Of course, I'll go and see my brother',[56] but as she ran towards the hotel the police intercepted her. The fire at the inn was slow to take off, and for a while no one was aware of what was happening. But then a cold breeze from the south-west fanned the flames and soon they snaked into the building, devouring the calico ceiling and paper wall linings. The building was quickly engulfed.

The Kelly sisters burst into tears, with Kate screaming: 'Oh, my poor, poor brother!'

Gibney bravely ran towards the flames, determined to prevent the men from being burned alive. Sadleir demanded he stop but Gibney told him there was no time to lose.[57] With a crowd of perhaps 1000 applauding, including the three bawling Kelly sisters, the priest took off his hat, made the sign of the cross, and holding up his hands cried out: 'In the name of God, men, will you let me hear your confession?'

Sadleir rushed up to Gibney and looked like he was about to enter the burning building, too, when a great sheet of flame – the calico ceiling of the dining room – fell between them.[58]

Gibney ran inside, bolting through the flames. He saw Byrne lying on his side across the doorway of the dining room, his eyes open and his limbs bent as though he was just about to get up.[59]

Gibney was afraid the burning ceiling would collapse onto him and he stepped over the body and called out that he was a Catholic priest there to help these troubled young men.

Onlookers screamed and gasped as they saw Gibney in the middle of the blaze as though he had passed through the gates of hell.

One of the burnt bodies retrieved from the Glenrowan Inn where Dan Kelly and Steve Hart were consumed by fire. State Library of Victoria Accession no: H96.160/184

Then Gibney saw the bodies of two 'beardless boys', near the body of Dave Mortimer's greyhound. He ran out of the inferno and told the police that the bushrangers were all dead.

Harry Armstrong and Constable Dwyer braved the flames and dragged out Byrne's singed body. Dwyer saw Hart's 'face all burnt' and his blood 'frizzling like a steak in a pan'.[60] The two policemen tried to retrieve the corpses but more of the burning calico ceiling fell on top of the bodies. The hotel then imploded and live cartridges exploded amid the flames.

Martin Cherry, the old Irish platelayer, was found barely alive in the hotel's kitchen, behind the main building, and was carried out in a blanket. He asked for a drink of water and was laid out on the grass. Gibney administered the last rites just before Cherry died.[61]

Later, as the charred remains of their brother and his mate — along with the armour that had been molten hot in the blaze — were raked into separate piles, the Kelly girls watched from the railway gate in horror, howling 'loudly and lustily over the blackened bones'.[62] Tom Kirkham, who had lost his wife Ada to a fire was aghast. Tom Carrington, though, did not mourn the dead bushrangers.

'At a quarter-past 3 the roof fell in, and the flames whirled up to heaven,' he wrote, 'and myriads of sparks danced through the air as if with delight at the thought that three as cold-blooded murderers as ever walked the earth since the days of Cain had expiated their crime on a fiery altar, and that the fourth was lying waiting for the rope to be put round his neck.'[63]

Not that Ned Kelly had a single pang of remorse.

Journalist George Allen, from Melbourne's *Daily Telegraph*, who had known Kelly's family for 20 years, questioned him about the killing of Michael Kennedy.

Kelly said that the sergeant did not give anything to him for his wife, Bridget, but only asked him to pass on his love. He denied cutting off the sergeant's ear and said that was a story 'spread about to do me harm'.[64]

The police began collecting the gang's weapons and iron suits, and while the Glenrowan Inn was still smouldering, the romantic legends about the four young killers were already starting to burn brightly.

'Bushrangers clad in armour attacking a train, and standing a siege of many hours,' writer James Stanley noted, 'this is more wonderful than the wildest dreams of fancy indulged in by the author of boys' novels.'[65]

The Kelly hunters did not think it quite so wonderful, though, and nor did Bridget Kennedy, Maria Lonigan or Belle Sherritt, who were all now destitute young widows.

Even though the police had shown Kelly some mercy and kindness after his capture, he still couldn't hide his hatred for the law.

Badly wounded and with every breath potentially his last, Kelly whispered to reporters that he had wanted to destroy the train and kill everyone on it.

'If I were once right again,' he mumbled, 'I would go to the barracks and shoot every one of the bloody traps, and not give one a chance.'[66]

Chapter 19

COMMISSIONER STANDISH arrived at Glenrowan at 5 p.m., seven hours after leaving Melbourne, and with smoke still hovering around what had been Ann Jones's livelihood and future.

Standish was accompanied by a team of six special constables tasked with getting Kelly away from his armed and dangerous support base and back to a Melbourne cell.

The commissioner found Maggie and Grace Kelly crying 'in a mournful strain' at the bushranger's side, with Kate 'sitting at his head with her arms around his neck'.[1] Almost dead, Kelly was carried onto a train along with Byrne's body for transport to Benalla, where he was to spend his first night in captivity. The train also carried many of the Kelly hunters including Alf Falkiner, who had only arrived at Glenrowan after the gun battle was over, having been gathering more information from the Chinese community about the gang's movements.

Kelly needed intensive care and doctors immediately began the delicate process to save his life so that Victoria's judicial system could then legally kill him.

The police also wanted to take the charred remains of Dan Kelly and Hart but the 50 officers on the scene faced overwhelming numbers of Kelly sympathisers who, brandishing guns, angrily demanded the bodies for burial.

Though keen to stamp police authority on the situation, Sadleir did not want more bloodshed for the sake of two bodies burned beyond recognition, and he didn't want to spark an attempt to rescue the gang's leader. He handed over the dead.[2]

They were taken on carts to the hut that Maggie now shared with Tom Lloyd and her children, near Mrs Kelly's home on Eleven Mile Creek. Hart and Dan Kelly were buried in ornate coffins in unmarked graves in Greta cemetery.

On the same day, 50 kilometres away at Beechworth, Aaron Sherritt was buried at sunset. His pregnant 16-year-old widow Belle was 'very much affected', and she suffered a miscarriage.[3]

At Benalla, Kelly hovered close to death on a thin mattress in the lock-up, with Byrne's corpse in the next cell. He must have thought that he had seen a ghost as Senior Constable John Kelly arrived with Stringybark survivor Thomas McIntyre, the only eyewitness to the police killings. Ned again initially mistook McIntyre for his sworn enemy Constable Flood.

Police and trackers pose for photographer Oswald Thomas Madeley at the place where Ned Kelly was taken. State Library of Victoria, H96.160/173

The police reported that in his weakened condition Kelly admitted to shooting Fitzpatrick, but he denied that Kennedy had given him a letter for his wife.

In Glenrowan, souvenir hunters descended from all parts, picking up blood-soaked leaves, burned knives and spent cartridge cases. One even found a charred foot.[4] Stanistreet and his children uncovered Kelly's drum of blasting powder behind a log.[5]

Police posed for photographs to celebrate their triumph, and Constable Jim Arthur donned some of the gang's armour and pointed Kelly's Colt rifle at the lens of photographer Oswald Thomas Madeley[6] to recreate the fearsome scene that confronted police.

Speculation immediately mounted in the press over how the £8000 reward for the gang would be divided, but Stanhope O'Connor and his trackers came under fire again, as did the whole police operation at Glenrowan. Columnist James Stanley declared that 'The indiscriminate firing into a house crowded with women and children was a most disgraceful act ... and [the] gallantry of Sub-inspector O'Connor, of the Queensland native police, and his blacktrackers, who "held a creek" all day long, is to be seriously questioned.' Stanley wrote that O'Connor had seen 'lots of bloodshed in his time' and had no qualms about ordering Indigenous people 'to be shot like dogs' but, although the Queenslanders were in at 'the finish,' he argued that 'they and their commander kept out of harm's way'.

'It is to be hoped they will not get any of the reward,' he wrote.[7]

Nicolson was still furious that Hare had replaced him at 'the finish line' and claimed the gang were all but captured when he was usurped. He called for 'a searching enquiry' into the police administration in the North Eastern District and particularly into the circumstances of his withdrawal.[8] Standish wanted an inquiry, too, as a way of proving what he called Nicolson's 'supineness and apathy'.[9]

ON THE MORNING AFTER the gun battle, Tuesday, 29 June, just after 8 a.m., Kelly, deathly pale and covered with a blanket, was carried on a stretcher from the Benalla police barracks to a

After his death at Glenrowan, Joe Byrne's body
was tied to a door at the Benalla police station and
photographed. He was still wearing Michael Scanlan's
ornate topaz ring that he had ripped from the dead
officer's hand. National Archives of Australia, 11453343

cart surrounded by eight armed policemen on foot. Kate Lloyd
cried 'without restraint' as her sweetheart was wheeled to the
train station.[10]

Superintendent Hare, nursing the bullet wound in his wrist,
looked on impassively. As Kelly was lifted into the guard's van,
a six-man security detail climbed in after him along with Hare
and Dr Charles Ryan,[11] Hare's cousin, who had recently returned
from patching up the wounded for the Sultan of Turkey during
the Russo-Turkish War.[12]

Kelly said little and had the appearance of a man in a trance,[13]
but Dr Ryan was astounded by the young bushranger's physical
condition and 'splendid constitution'.

He recorded Kelly's pulse at 125 beats a minute and his
temperature at 102 degrees Fahrenheit.[14]

Byrne's body was dragged out of the lock-up and tied to a door so pictures could be taken for postcards. His corpse resembled a marionette with broken strings. His hands and his dark striped trousers, dark striped shirt and blue sac coat were covered with blood,[15] but there was a look of serenity on his boyishly handsome face, so at odds with the murder he had recently committed and the violent way he had met his own demise.

On one of the fingers of his right hand he still wore the topaz ring that was taken from Constable Scanlan and on the fourth finger of his left hand was another gold ring, with a large white seal on it.[16]

Although family and friends wanted to take Byrne's body for burial, Standish was not prepared to risk a martyr's funeral, so instead the corpse was stripped, wrapped in canvas, placed in a roughly made coffin, taken to the Benalla Cemetery and buried in secret in a far corner of the paupers' section. The only witnesses were the undertaker and a constable.[17] Martin Cherry was buried at the opposite end of the cemetery a few hours earlier.[18]

ON THE JOURNEY TO MELBOURNE Kelly was understandably reticent and sullen, answering any questions gruffly. Two brake-vans had been attached to the Melbourne train and the wounded prisoner was placed in the last one, lying on a pile of mattresses, and surrounded by a dozen armed policemen. Kelly looked terribly emaciated, his ashen face covered by wicked bruises from all the bullets which had struck his helmet.

At each train station there was a great rush of people anxious to obtain a glimpse of the bushranger and when Senior Constable Patrick Walsh asked Kelly if had any objection to people crowding round the carriage and looking in, he said that he had none. Dr Ryan kept ministering to Kelly throughout the journey, checking his wounds and giving him stimulants.

As the train neared Melbourne, thousands gathered at Spencer Street and Essendon stations, choking the streets, climbing atop all stationary vehicles and houses to see the most feared criminal in Australia, but police fooled them by taking Kelly off the train at North Melbourne at 2 p.m.

He was briefly reunited in Melbourne Gaol with his tearful mother, two and a half years into her sentence. Ellen Kelly wept at the news of Dan's death and at the wounds and short life expectancy of her eldest son.

The police were determined to keep Kelly in isolation and under careful watch to ensure that he did not cheat the hangman with a smuggled packet of poison like the one Joe Byrne had carried to Glenrowan.[19]

Knowing that he was doomed, Kelly nevertheless began a remarkable recovery in the stark confines of Melbourne Gaol, fighting off bouts of fever under the care of the government medical officer Andrew Shields[20] and his designated nurse David Henry, a Collins Street money lender doing four years for jury rigging.[21]

'Why is Kelly like bacon?' became a running joke in Victoria. 'Because he is being cured before he is hung!'[22]

Standish, however, would not allow a meeting between Kelly and Bridget Kennedy, who had sent Standish a telegram asking if she could speak to the prisoner in Melbourne about her husband's final moments.[23] Standish felt such a meeting would be too distressing for the widow, whose life was excruciatingly tough even though the Victorian government was now paying her a pension of £115 a year with an extra allowance of £12 every quarter.[24]

Frank Hare recovered from his Glenrowan bullet wound at Rupertswood, the Sunbury mansion owned by Lady Janet Clarke and her husband, William. Hare wrote to his friend, Mrs Emily Josephine Smith, of Laceby, near Glenrowan.

'I told you that the Kellys would be taken within five miles of your house,' he wrote. 'How glad you must be that the ruffians are swept off the face of the Earth ... who thought as little of taking life as we do of shooting a quail.'[25]

A DAY AFTER KELLY WAS brought to Melbourne, Sadleir sent a telegram to Standish from Benalla warning that there was 'a deal of ill blood stirring',[26] with a looming uprising by armed Kelly sympathisers.

Thomas Curnow and Charles Rawlins were forced to flee to safe houses in Melbourne 'after most bitter and horrible threats' from Kelly's supporters. Railway guard Jesse Dowsett was transferred 350 kilometres south to Queenscliff.[27] Sergeant Steele found several of his greyhounds poisoned,[28] and Sadleir sent a telegram to Standish, denying the rapidly circulating rumour that Kate Kelly had murdered the sergeant.[29]

Hugh Bracken needed a bodyguard of extra police in Glenrowan,[30] while Aaron Sherritt's brothers, Jack and Bill, were eventually allowed to join the police force for their protection.

Meanwhile, Elijah Upjohn, a Ballarat chicken thief, had just been appointed as Victoria's official hangman.

'His first client ... will, of course, be the murderer, Kelly,' the Beechworth paper informed readers. 'Such is fame; to defy the whole police force of the colony for twenty long months and be finished by a miserable chicken-stealer.'[31]

STANHOPE O'CONNOR spent two weeks in Melbourne as the wounded trooper Jimmy was treated by a doctor several times after showing signs of the infection erysipelas. O'Connor billed the Victorian police for 4 guineas, but the claim was refused.[32] He and his five troopers finally left for North Queensland aboard the *Katoomba* on 13 July, stopping off in Sydney as guests of Commissioner Fosbery. The trackers were objects of curiosity there, while O'Connor had the New South Wales police spellbound with 'the story of the Glenrowan tragedy and incidents of collisions with the aborigines in the back country of Queensland'.[33] The *Brisbane Courier* opined that, while the trackers were heroes of the Kelly hunt, they deserved a better fate 'than the imminent extinction with which the Australian aboriginal is threatened'.[34]

ALMOST FIVE WEEKS AFTER he had been carried into prison on a stretcher, Kelly was in pyjamas and slippers at a special 5 p.m. court sitting on Saturday 31 July, in the Melbourne Gaol hospital's kitchen. Constable McIntyre formally identified Kelly as the man who shot his three colleagues, and he was remanded to Beechworth for a court appearance in the district where the murders took place.[35]

The next morning, despite his wounds, Kelly donned a stylish new outfit of Bedford cord trousers, a blue serge coat, a checked waistcoat, a white slouch felt hat cocked over one eye and new boots cut to fit his wounds.[36] He limped into a hansom cab beside Sergeant Steele, who looked ready to shoot Kelly again. A wagonette carrying the armed constables McIntyre, Bracken and Falkiner followed the cab to Newmarket Station near the jail. All five men, along with two more officers, then boarded a special train for the journey to Beechworth.

Sergeant Steele was one of the men guarding Kelly on the way to his court appearance in Beechworth. He needled his old foe the whole way. State Library of Victoria, A/S14/08/80/200

Kelly still had a bullet in his foot and Steele's shotgun pellets scattered throughout his body, and he was full of bravado as well, telling the police that his body was impenetrable, that his powerful ribs were a mass of bullet-proof bone, that the Chinese provided him with constant information about police movements, that he could have killed every policeman in the district if he so chose, and that he was one hell of a singer. He gave the officers renditions of some pro-Kelly songs, singing about the 'brave Kelly Gang' during their time in the mountains. The Kelly hunters thought his singing was overrated.

Sergeant Steele needled his prisoner the whole way and Kelly told his old adversary that he should get out of Victoria and hide in India for his own safety. At Glenrowan, Kelly rose to his feet slowly and gingerly to throw his coat into the sergeant's face. He challenged Steele to a fight until the other officers stepped in.[37] Kelly assured the police that he would never hang.[38] Constable Falkiner was impressed with Kelly's defiance and courage, remarking that 'he was a very plucky man and a very good man if he had put it to better use'.[39]

The train arrived at Beechworth at 3.30 p.m. in front of 100 spectators alerted by spies about what was supposed to be a top-secret mission. Sadleir was also waiting to take charge.

Kelly was again guarded by a large group of heavily armed police, prepared for any breakout attempt. Constable Charlie Magor, who had been at the Glenrowan battle, drove Kelly in a police cab to the local prison alongside Senior Constable Mullane and two mounted constables. Kelly was confined at the rear of Beechworth Gaol close to the governor's house and, in a reversal of the situation at Stringybark Creek, Constable McIntyre now had the gun on him as guard,[40] a prison arrangement that also ensured the Crown's star witness was safe from assassination attempts.

Kelly's 34-year-old solicitor, David Gaunson,[41] was a wiry and persuasive Member for Ararat, who had started his legal career working for his brother-in-law James Macpherson Grant,[42] a lawyer who had saved the rebels of the Eureka stockade from the death penalty. Gaunson planned a similar case of self-defence for Kelly, depicting him as a victim who fought to save himself from an oppressive police force.

'All I want is a full and fair trial and a chance to make my side heard,' Kelly told Gaunson. 'Until now, the police have had all the say. If I get a full and fair trial, I don't care how it goes, but I know this – the public will see that I was hunted and hounded on from step to step; they will see that I am not the monster I have been made out. What I have done has been under strong provocation.'[43]

Before an overflowing crowd, many of whom saw Kelly as a hero,[44] the prisoner hobbled into court for the first day of the week-long trial on 6 August. He was flanked by Steele and Senior Constable Kelly, as Commissioner Standish took his seat on the bench next to Police Magistrate William Henry Foster.[45]

McIntyre did not see Kennedy killed, so Kelly was only charged with murdering Lonigan and Scanlan. The grey-bearded, Irish-born Crown Prosecutor Charles Smyth[46] presented a seemingly open-and-shut case, but Gaunson grilled McIntyre about why the policemen were so heavily armed at Stringybark Creek, asking the constable why they didn't go the whole hog and take a cannon with them.[47] He was relentless in his attack, portraying McIntyre as a coward who left Kennedy in the lurch, and a liar who couldn't get his story straight.

McIntyre, who had suffered post-traumatic stress after seeing his comrades killed, became 'nearly hysterical' with 'nervous excitement' in the witness box and had to be treated by Dr Samuel Reynolds during an adjournment.[48] With Ned Kelly glaring at the witness, Gaunson told the distressed constable that worse would come when the case reached Melbourne and that McIntyre would be turned 'inside out in the Supreme Court'.

On the third day of the trial, Kelly blew kisses and flirted from a distance with Kate Lloyd, described in the press as good-looking, elegant in her manner and 'well attired in a modest way'.[49]

Gaunson forced Senior Constable Kelly to confess that, when he stunned the badly wounded prisoner with McIntyre's appearance in Benalla on the night of his arrest, he had not cautioned the bushranger that what he said could be used in evidence.

But no amount of legal argument from Kelly's lawyer could change the fact that the policemen had been shot dead, and Magistrate Foster ordered the prisoner to stand trial for killing Lonigan and Scanlan. Kelly was whisked out of Beechworth Gaol the next morning, loaded into a wagonette, taken past a decoy locomotive at Beechworth[50] and driven under the guard of an armed escort to Wangaratta station.[51] In spite of the clandestine operation there were 600 people at the railway platform.

Kelly admitted to his police guards that he now realised he would probably soon hang, and with what looked to be tears in his eyes[52] he promised to come back and haunt all those lawmen who had persecuted him and his family.[53]

Kelly's left arm remained withered and his right hand crippled because of bullet wounds, but back in Melbourne Gaol Dr Shields extracted 'with difficulty' a bullet 'firmly embedded in the muscles' of the prisoner's right foot. Some of Steele's shotgun pellets remained lodged near Kelly's right knee, though, and continued to cause him great pain.[54]

Two weeks later, on 25 August 1880, the Kelly Gang were said to have claimed another victim when Sarah McGuirk, a 28-year-old mother of six, died because of severe anxiety attacks over fears of what sympathisers might do to her husband, Constable Henry McGuirk, who was gaining evidence against the gang for Ned's trial.[55]

MELBOURNE WAS BUZZING with excitement over the city's first telephone lines,[56] but Crown Prosecutor Smyth and his assistant Arthur Chomley,[57] brother of the police superintendent Hussey Chomley, were determined that Kelly would not live to phone a friend. Smyth feared that potential jurors in Beechworth could be Kelly sympathisers or in fear of them, and he successfully petitioned for the murder case to be held before the Kellys' long-time nemesis Sir Redmond Barry in Melbourne.

David Gaunson protested to no avail, though with his urging, Kelly was at least allowed a long meeting with his mother and sister Maggie inside the prison walls.[58]

The money from the Euroa and Jerilderie robberies had long gone and while Gaunson represented Kelly for free, he could not act as a barrister in the capital case. Gaunson wanted to use Melbourne's foremost defence barrister, Irish-born Hickman Molesworth,[59] but none of the sympathisers were willing to waste 50 guineas for two days of Molesworth's work and 10 guineas a day after that. Everyone knew the case was a foregone conclusion.

So, the most notorious criminal in Australian history finally stood trial for his life in Melbourne on Thursday, 28 October 1880, represented by another Irishman, 36-year-old Henry Bindon,[60] who had been a barrister for just six weeks,[61] and who had never tried a case in the Supreme Court. Since Constable McIntyre could not swear that Kelly had fired the fatal bullet into Scanlan, the prisoner now faced just one charge, the murder of Lonigan.

In his red robes trimmed with white fur and long grey wig, Redmond Barry, 67 and a diabetic, had the appearance of a fat old lion, though still a sartorially splendid one. He had garnered a reputation as the 'Beau Brummel of the antipodes',[62] and, with his life on the line, Kelly wanted to make a fashion statement, too.

Kelly's blue serge coat had become shabby, and his supporters tried in vain to obtain credit for a suit from Melbourne's leading tailors. At the last moment, Gaunson's brother William, also a lawyer with political ambitions, lent Kelly his 25-shilling Chesterfield overcoat.

One observer said Kelly looked like 'a wolf in sheep's clothing'[63] and, before the prisoner was allowed to limp into court, police searched his pockets. Nothing was found beyond a hand mirror, a penny with a hole in it and the rough draft of William Gaunson's next election speech.

As Kelly took his place in the dock, surrounded by powerfully built guards, dark woodwork, rows of pews and a legal system determined to avenge the deaths of three policemen, young journalist J.F. Archibald watched on for the new magazine he had founded, *The Bulletin*. There was nothing 'especially villainous about the outlaw's appearance', Archibald wrote. Instead:

> He is a rather handsome and essentially manly-looking fellow ... His principal characteristics are his height, which is above the average, and the largeness of his eyes, which are ... guarded by remarkably long eyelashes. His eyebrows are heavy and almost straight, and his lips, so far as one could see, are so thin and determined-looking as to seem in some regards out of keeping with his Celtic cheekbones. No one could see in his face evidence of the ferocity with which he is credited.[64]

The jury consisted of four farmers, a bricklayer, carpenter, gardener, decorator, bookbinder, bootmaker, blacksmith and the foreman Samuel Lazarus, a dairyman from Carlton.[65]

Bindon pursued his line of self-defence as 16 witnesses were called. The evidence of guilt was overwhelming, though Robert Scott, the Euroa bank manager, told the court Kelly had been a 'thorough gentleman' who did not use 'a single rude word' in front of his wife. Kelly winked at the jury, but they were unmoved.[66] John Tarleton, the Jerilderie bank manager, told the court that Kelly had said he had no option but to shoot at the police in 'self-defence' and that he had been driven to become an outlaw.

On the second day of the trial, 29 October, Kelly added to his ensemble an elaborately flowered silk handkerchief worn around his neck, as Bindon did his best to make sure the fashion accessory would not soon be replaced by a rope. Bindon made a mockery of McIntyre's eyewitness account of Lonigan's death but could not come up with another explanation for all the policeman's bullet wounds, and Judge Barry shot down any notion of self-defence before it could take root with the jury. Barry asked the jurors, 'What right had four other armed men to stop them [the police] and ask them to surrender?'[67] Crown Prosecutor Smyth declared

Ned to be 'a mean thief, who picked the pockets of the men he murdered'.[68]

Kelly's defence was manifestly inadequate. No witnesses were called on his behalf and he was not given the chance to explain his actions, apart from occasionally raising an arm during some of the evidence and making a motion to spit, as though the prosecution testimony was ridiculous.

The jury filed out at 5.10 p.m. and returned just 20 minutes later.[69]

Kelly stood defiant, with his shattered hand on the rail of the dock, though a slight shudder went through him when Samuel Lazarus uttered the inevitable word: 'Guilty.'

Judge Barry asked Kelly if he had anything to say before sentence was passed, and at long last Kelly had his moment to unload:

Well, it is rather too late for me to speak now. I thought of speaking this morning and all day, but there was little use, and there is little use blaming anyone now. Nobody knew about my case except myself, and I wish I had insisted on being allowed to examine the witnesses myself. If I had examined them, I am confident I would have thrown a different light on the case. It is not that I fear death; I fear it as little as to drink a cup of tea. On the evidence that has been given, no juryman could have given any other verdict. That is my opinion. But as I say, if I had examined the witnesses, I would have shown matters in a different light, because no man understands the case as I do myself … I lay blame on myself that I did not get up yesterday and examine the witnesses, but I thought that if I did so it would look like bravado and flashness.[70]

A black square cloth of doom was placed on top of Judge Barry's wig as he began to pronounce the death sentence.

But Kelly refused to go quietly, arguing with the judge until the grim finale.

He told Barry that he was forced to defend himself against men he believed had come to kill him: 'A day will come at a bigger court than this when we shall see which is right and which is wrong. No matter how long a man lives, he is bound to come to judgment somewhere.'[71]

Barry replied that Kelly was the worst kind of murderer, because 'with a party of men you took up arms against society, organized as it is for mutual protection, and for respect of law'.

'Foolish, inconsiderate, ill-conducted, unprincipled youths unfortunately abound,' Barry lectured, 'and unless they are made to consider the consequences of crime, they are led to imitate notorious felons, whom they regard as self-made heroes.'[72]

Barry reminded Kelly that by his own statements he had killed men, stolen more than 200 horses[73] and cost Victoria £50,000 during his time on the run.

Judge Redmond Barry sentenced Ned Kelly to death, only to meet his fate 12 days later. State Library of Victoria, H5369

Barry cleared his throat and gravely told Kelly: 'You will be taken from here to the place from whence you came, and thence on a day appointed by the Executive Council to a place of execution, and there you will be hanged by the neck until you be dead. May the Lord have mercy on your soul.'

Kelly refused to budge.

'I will go a little further than that,' he told the judge, 'and say I will see you there where I go.'

Kate Lloyd, watching from the public gallery, broke down, but Kelly blew a kiss towards her and, despite the gravity of the situation, his demeanour 'did not change in the slightest' and he 'looked as quiet and cool as at any time during the trial'.[74]

The next afternoon, Saturday, 30 October, Kelly's sister Maggie, Tom and Kate Lloyd, Dinny McAuliffe and his sister as well as Kelly's cousin Joe Ryan all visited the condemned prisoner, speaking to him through an iron grille in a meeting of 'a very touching nature'.[75] Kelly talked of his mother, serving her long sentence in the same jail, and said, 'I hope there's more justice in the next world than we've been shown in this one.' He told the visitors he hoped that his execution would lead to an investigation into the conduct of the police.[76]

Six thousand people attended a public rally to save Kelly at Melbourne's Hippodrome and there was a protest march to the office of Victorian Premier Graham Berry. In an act of sheer desperation, Kate Kelly fell at the feet of Victoria's governor and begged, in vain, for her brother's life.

On Monday, 8 November, three days before the scheduled hanging, William Gaunson claimed there were 32,424 names on petitions to grant Kelly clemency, and that with more time his supporters could obtain half a million.[77] But Victoria's Executive Council decreed that the hanging would proceed as scheduled.

Kelly had the prison photographer Charles Nettleton shoot two portraits of him as keepsakes for his family. He said goodbye to his friends and relatives and finally to his mother, who through her deep sadness told her first-born boy, 'Mind you die like a Kelly, son.'[78]

Despite Kelly's crimes, prison warders could only admire his toughness and courage, the way he fought back from his injuries and bravely faced the end.

On the night of 10 November, with his death just hours away, Kelly had his last meal of roast lamb, green peas and a bottle of claret. He smoked a pipe and joked with his jailers that he wanted a piece of paper to light it and not a candle, because candles were bad for the lungs.

Kelly stretched out on his prison mattress singing his favourite hymn 'In the Sweet By and By', about a better world beyond. He was restless until 2.30 a.m. but slept until five, when he rose and prayed for 20 minutes. As many as 7000 people were outside the prison gates from early morning protesting the execution. Kelly rested again and hummed some tunes, and at 8 o'clock rose to admire his beard and moustache in a mirror, telling warder William Buck that 'they are fine things to go on the drop with'.[79]

He joked that his ghost would appear in the Condemned Cell the following day.

Kelly had no stomach for breakfast and at 9 a.m., the blacksmith removed his leg irons. Several guards then escorted Kelly to the Condemned Cell next to the gallows in a new wing of the prison. On his way, Kelly passed the hospital cart that would carry his body to the mortuary and he commented on the beauty of the flowers in the garden. As he walked up the stairs to the cell where he would spend the final hour of his life, Kelly passed a heavy Oregon pine beam that had a rope hanging from it about as thick as a stout man's thumb.

But Kelly moved with what warders said was 'a jaunty step ... and a smile'.[80]

Dean Charles O'Hea, the Catholic priest who baptised Kelly almost 26 years earlier, and the prison chaplain, Dean Thomas Donaghy, prayed with the condemned prisoner.

Kelly's mother chose to wait with her fellow inmates in the prison laundry, near the gallows, while her son was killed. Her mental anguish was almost unbearable.

Ned Kelly was hanged by a Ballarat chicken thief, Elijah Upjohn, on 11 November 1880. State Library of Victoria, A/S20/11/80/305

At 10 a.m. on 11 November 1880, Kelly finally came face to face with the burly, broad-shouldered hangman Elijah Upjohn, a hideous, hulking creature with heavy lips, bristles of pure white hair sticking up all over his crown, and a bulbous nose with a carbuncle at the end.[81]

Upjohn pinioned the prisoner's crippled arms behind his back with a strap and placed a white calico hood on top of his head. He pushed the hood back off Kelly's forehead so the condemned prisoner could still see as he was led out to the noose behind a priest holding a cross and the two Catholic deans reciting the sacrament of the dying. There were eight journalists watching from below the gallows among the 22 official witnesses. With head held high, Kelly did not hesitate as he hobbled on his injured legs to the trapdoor. He flinched at the first touch of the rope but moved his chin to ease the hangman's task. Upjohn adjusted the heavy knot quickly, positioning it behind the left ear so Kelly's neck would snap instantly and avoid a slow, ghastly death by strangulation. Kelly mumbled something and looked up to a skylight and heaven beyond it as Upjohn yanked the calico hood down over Kelly's face and jerked a lever beside his hip. With an almighty clang the trapdoor opened, and Kelly dropped 2 metres. His hooded, trussed body came to a shuddering halt a metre from the floor. Kelly's unshackled legs drew up and down several times in involuntary spasms. Then his corpse spun slowly round and round.[82]

The noise of the trapdoor was greeted by jeers and howls of anger from the other inmates and, in the prison laundry, Kelly's mother was overcome with shock and grief.

The stunned journalists quizzed each other in whispers about what Kelly might have said with his last desperate breath. Jim Middleton,[83] the star reporter for Melbourne's *Herald*, jotted down an immortal quote for the dead man: 'Such is life.'[84]

Under the requirement of the law, the convicted murderer's body was left to hang for half an hour. It was then placed on the waiting cart and wheeled over to the Dead House of the prison hospital. The white hood was removed, and Kelly's eyes retained a 'bright expression'[85] like a 'smile in death'.[86] The eyes were then stitched shut, and Max Kreitmayer,[87] the German owner of the waxworks in Bourke Street, shaved off Kelly's thick hair and beard and made a mould of his head for a plaster death mask, to be exhibited the following day. Then doctors and medical students began dissecting the body, examining and souveniring organs, sawing off Kelly's head and removing his brain. His skull has never been found.[88]

What was left of the headless, mutilated corpse was tossed into a packing case used for axes, covered with quicklime and buried in the prison yard with no marker the next day.

Almost two weeks after Ned's death, shots were fired into the Greta Police Station,[89] and relatives and friends of the gang talked openly of vengeance. One man who refused to support the petition for Kelly's reprieve was 'savagely beaten'.[90]

Three days after Kelly's brusque burial, his courtroom curse on Redmond Barry appeared to come true when an infection from a carbuncle on the judge's neck took hold of his body. Barry died just 12 days after the hanging.

While Kelly sympathisers portrayed the judge as a heartless ogre, Union Jacks in Victoria were lowered to half-mast as civic-minded people across Australia mourned a man who had been a prime mover behind such important Victorian institutions as its university, state library and public art gallery.[91]

Chapter 20

THE DISSECTION OF NED KELLY'S corpse was quickly followed by the carve-up of the £8000 reward for the gang's demise. There were 92 claimants for a share of the money but many missed out including Constables McIntyre and Falkiner, although they were both recommended for 'special recognition'[1] for their service.

The day after he was sentenced to hang, Kelly had told his family that he hoped his execution might lead to an investigation into the conduct of the police, and a Royal Commission wasted no time putting the force on trial. It began taking evidence on 23 March 1881. Its chairman was Irish-born politician Francis Longmore, a long-time critic of Standish. One of the other six commissioners was George Wilson Hall, a fellow Member of the Legislative Assembly, who owned newspapers in Mansfield and Benalla and had been scathing of what he regarded as police bullying of the Kelly family.

Sadleir later wrote that 'Mr. Longmore was eminently honest and conscientious, but he went relentlessly for scalps'.[2] One of them was Sadleir's. Over six months the Royal Commission exposed the clash of egos between senior officers, the frequent mishandling of the police pursuit and the brutal treatment of suspects. Its public identification of informers and police spies sparked a new wave of terror and reprisals. In prison, Brickey Williamson had backed up every word of Constable Fitzpatrick's evidence against the Kelly family and provided officers with vital information on the gang. He was told he would die like a dog if he showed his face in Kelly Country again. Kelly sympathisers scoured the countryside looking for other informers and some of the police agents dropped everything and fled the district.[3]

Between March and September 1881, the Royal Commission interrogated 62 witnesses with more than 18,000 questions and even visited Ellen Kelly at Greta after the model prisoner was released from jail to re-join her surviving children on 7 February 1881, four months after Ned swung.

On 14 May 1881, the commissioners drove out in three wagonettes from Benalla to Mrs Kelly's shack at Greta. She and her children were understandably wary about this posse of lawmen, one of them being commissioner James Graves.[4] Ned had wanted to kill Graves for threatening to poison the water around Greta to drive the gang out of hiding.[5]

Mrs Kelly told the commissioners that the police had treated her children very badly while she was in jail.

Inspector Brooke Smith was the worst, she said, and 'had less sense than any of them. He used to throw things out of the house, and he came in once to the lock-up staggering drunk ... I wonder they allowed a man to behave as he did to an unfortunate woman.'[6]

Ned's sister Grace, now 15, told Longmore that Detective Ward threatened to shoot her if she did not tell him where her brothers were and that Brooke Smith would 'chuck our milk, flour, and honey, on the floor. Once they pulled us in our night clothes out of bed. Sergeant Steele was one of that party.'[7] Mrs Kelly hinted that the police had also taken liberties with her daughters, but when Longmore asked her to make a formal complaint she said that she had no such charge to make.

The Royal Commission finally brought down its findings in October 1881. Standish had already resigned as head of the police to become chairman of the Victorian Racing Club, and the commission declared that his evidence was not trustworthy and his conduct in charge of the force 'was not characterized either by good judgment, or by that zeal for the interests of the public service which should have distinguished an officer in his position'. They attributed 'much of the bad feeling which existed amongst the officers' hunting the Kelly Gang to Standish's 'want of impartiality, temper, tact, and judgment'.[8]

The 'strained relations' between Hare and Nicolson – likened in the press to schoolboy squabbling[9] – were found to have had a 'damaging influence on the effectiveness of the service'.

The press labelled Standish a 'discourteous, insolent and ungentlemanly ... twaddler without energy'.[10] Less than a year and a half after Kelly's death, Standish's mind was addled from booze, shame and stress. He died of cirrhosis of the liver and fatty degeneration of the heart aged just 58 at his residence inside the Melbourne Club. He left his two horses and his pictures to his servant. The Standish Handicap run over 1200 metres at Flemington on New Year's Day remains his memorial.

The Kelly Reward Board handed down its findings not long after the Royal Commission opened, having taken evidence from Charles Rawlins and the journalists at the Glenrowan siege.

Frank Hare received the largest portion of the reward, £800, largely through the support of Colonial Chief Secretary Robert Ramsay.[11]

But the Royal Commission branded Hare a windbag, and Longmore noted that the government paid £607 of Hare's medical bills for his wrist wound, 'about £480' of it to his cousin, Dr Ryan. 'While this officer was being petted and coddled on all sides, and a special surgeon despatched almost daily some 30 miles by train to attend him,' Longmore said, 'the Government questioned the payment of four guineas for the treatment of one of the black trackers who had received a wound in the head at Glenrowan.'[12]

The commission recommended that the warring Hare and Nicolson be removed from active duty and become police magistrates. Nicolson, it said, had 'shown himself in many respects a capable and zealous officer' but had laboured under great difficulties because of Standish's interference.[13]

Hare penned his account of the Kelly hunt in *The Last of the*

Bushrangers, but Nicolson had one parting shot, scoffing that Hare borrowed 'his facts from his imagination'.[14]

Hare and his wife, Janet, lived in Hotham Street, St Kilda, until he became bedridden with diabetes in 1892. He died at the Rupertswood Mansion soon after.

Nicolson, who received none of the reward money, eventually became District Court Magistrate in Melbourne and lived in Anderson Street, South Yarra, until his death in 1898. He and his wife, Helen, had eight children and his football-playing sons were said to be 'as dashing and athletic as their father in his cadet days'.[15]

Schoolteacher Thomas Curnow received £550 of the reward but a year later the payment was boosted to £1000 after the Victorian government decided that, while most of the prisoners at Glenrowan 'were standing aloof, in a cautious, if not a cowardly, spirit', Curnow had risked his life to save the police on the special train.[16] After fleeing the north-east of Victoria in fear of his life, Curnow settled in Ballarat and over the next 35 years taught at the Central, Humffray Street and Urquhart Street schools.

His son Thomas junior was killed fighting in France in 1918 three months before the Armistice. Another son, Leonard, was severely wounded, while Curnow's daughter Isobel served as a nurse on the Greek island of Lemnos just across the water from Gallipoli.

Senior Constable John Kelly received £377, but told the Royal Commission that with all the animosity towards the law in Greta it was now 'the worst place in the colony', and that 'ill-disposed people' were likely to assassinate him.[17] Despite pressure from Sadleir, Kelly refused a posting to the little town. He later served at Hamilton, Terang and Koroit and retired as a sergeant in 1898. Kelly died at his home in Havelock Street, St Kilda, in 1905.

The job of patrolling Greta, the toughest job in Australian law enforcement, instead went to 36-year-old Senior Constable Robert Graham, a tall, straight-talking cop known as 'Honest Bob'. He was the man who had dropped the Martini-Henry rifle while on lookout near Mrs Kelly's. Graham had also been part of

Sadleir's team that arrived at the Glenrowan shootout as dawn was breaking. After gaining the trust and support of Kelly's mother in Greta, Graham was able to talk around many of the local hotheads, convincing them to put away their guns and prevent more violence.

Graham was awarded £115 of the Kelly reward. Following the death of his first wife in childbirth, he married Mary Kirk six weeks after Kelly's execution and they had seven children, including Robert junior, who died at Gallipoli a week after the ANZACs' first landing. After three years at Greta, Graham was moved to Shepparton, where he became a prominent freemason. In 1887 he was presented with an award from the Royal Humane Society for helping to rescue survivors in the flood of the Goulburn River. He also served at Warrnambool and Bairnsdale before retiring to Hawthorn in Melbourne. Graham died in 1931.

One of Graham's constables in Greta was William Wallace, who was among the search parties sent to find the bodies at Stringybark Creek and who fought the gang at Glenrowan. Wallace married Bridget O'Brien in 1882 and they took over the Broken River Hotel in Benalla. More than a decade later, Wallace heard that a family in the area had Sergeant Kennedy's gold watch. He used his influence – and the promise of a £10 reward – to retrieve it. A girl of 14 or 15, said to be one of Ned Kelly's cousins,[18] left it for him in a parcel. Wallace sent a telegram to Bridget Kennedy telling her that after 15 years her husband's keepsake had been returned and had not received 'much ill-usage'.[19] The watch is still with the Kennedy family.

Sergeant Arthur Steele received £290 from the reward and his supporters gave him an elaborate sword engraved by the Melbourne gunsmith Rosier with the words: 'Presented to Sergeant Steele, Victoria Police by the Moyhu Stock Protection Society as a testimony of the high esteem they entertain of his public services during the recent outbreak. Wangaratta 1880.'[20]

Steele endured an intense grilling at the Royal Commission, though, and was forced to vehemently deny claims by Constables Jim Arthur and William Phillips that he shot at Margaret

Reardon. The commission still recommended that he be demoted 'to the lowest position in the police force'.[21]

However, after 310 citizens from Wangaratta, 23 from Yackandandah and 12 from Chiltern signed a petition supporting Steele and a public meeting in Wangaratta on 29 October 1881 gave him a ringing endorsement, a separate inquiry in 1882 acquitted him and declared that he had 'showed himself to be a courageous man and an excellent officer'.[22]

Steele retired in 1896. It was claimed that he was hissed and booed when spotted at a screening of the world's first feature film *The Story of the Kelly Gang*, made in 1906, and that he protested over a scene showing him being shot in the back.[23] In later years Steele devoted himself to his local Anglican church, and to his garden in Faithfull Street, Wangaratta, which produced many prize-winning flowers. He died of heart failure in his sleep at home in 1914, leaving behind Ruth, his wife of 49 years, and their eight children.[24]

Inspector Alexander Brooke Smith did not fare so well. He was posted to Horsham after his bungling of the Kelly hunt, and was lambasted by the Royal Commission for his lethargic pursuit.[25] It was recommended he be retired on a pension of £100 a year.[26] He left the force on 7 March 1882 and died just 15 days later with what was termed 'diseased liver, jaundice'. He was buried close to Redmond Barry in the Melbourne General Cemetery.

Constable Hugh Bracken ambitiously applied for the full £8000 of the reward money and was devastated to receive a £275 share he regarded as insulting. An appeal for more was rejected with the press reporting that, while his escape from the Glenrowan Inn showed courage and skill, Bracken 'vanished into darkness' after telling Hare the outlaws were in the hotel, and had seriously erred by galloping to Wangaratta to warn Steele, who was already alarmed by the lateness of the train and the sound of gunshots in the distance. The newspapers said Bracken should have told Hare that the outlaws had armour on and that the hotel was crowded with people. If Bracken had stayed at Glenrowan, one paper declared, it would have prevented 'the disastrous rush' and the death of innocents.[27] The admonition was galling. Bracken was transferred to Melbourne but left the force a broken man in 1883. The death of two wives contributed to a sad man killing himself with a gunshot on 22 February 1900. He was buried in an unmarked grave at Wallan Cemetery.

Superintendent John Sadleir received £240 of the reward, but by the time of the Royal Commission he was 48 and the father of 11 children. The commissioners felt it was time he moved on.

They said Sadleir was 'guilty of several errors of judgment' in the Kelly hunt following the police murders, and at Glenrowan with the constant firing on the hotel and the hostages. It recommended that he be 'placed at the bottom of the list of superintendents'.[28] Sadleir replied that the commission allowed 'foolish or disaffected witnesses' to make any statements they chose.[29]

He was placed in charge of the Ballarat District, but in 1883 given command of Melbourne's Metropolitan District, filling in many times for the new commissioner Hussey Chomley. Sadleir retired in 1896 and lived on Kooyong Road, Elsternwick. When he died in 1919 aged 86 he was lauded as 'an efficient and exemplary officer of police, with a high sense of duty'.[30]

THE ROYAL COMMISSION had opened with fiery blasts between Standish and Stanhope O'Connor.

O'Connor appeared at the hearings after having resigned from the Queensland police force three weeks after Kelly was hanged. He had taken steps in North Queensland to be discharged from his bankruptcy and was back in Melbourne living with Louise in Robe Street, St Kilda. He told the Royal Commission he was now 'a gentleman living on my means'.[31]

O'Connor was awarded £237 of the reward but the commission could not recommend his wish for a position as an inspector in the Victorian police, given his belligerence during the Kelly hunt.

While the Royal Commission was sitting, O'Connor was forced to issue 'a most emphatic denial' against the continued accusations that he had led a massacre against the First Peoples near Cape Bedford just after the Kellys raided Jerilderie.

In O'Connor's version, his trackers came upon the Guugu Yimithirr people who panicked, jumped into the ocean and swam away 'towards a distant headland'. End of story.[32]

O'Connor worked as a wool-broker in Melbourne but by February 1883 he was a partner in a stockbroking business in Collins Street. By the time he became a father to Stanhope junior in 1884, O'Connor and his wife had moved into a newly built house, 'Charnworth', in Puckle Street, Moonee Ponds, where they raised four children. O'Connor also dabbled in property development, building five two-storey shops on part of his estate.[33]

When he died at his home 'Bolac' in Queens Road, St Kilda, in 1908, aged 59, the Melbourne Stock Exchange took the afternoon off out of respect.[34]

The eventual cost of Queensland's involvement in the Kelly hunt was £2039 5s 9d, almost 40 per cent of which was O'Connor salary.[35]

All five of his trackers as well as Moses Bulla and Tommy Spider were each granted £50 after Glenrowan but the Kelly Reward Board declared: 'In dealing with the claims of the Queensland and Victorian native trackers, the Board … feel that it would not be desirable to place any considerable sum of money in the hands of persons unable to use it.' The money was handed to the Queensland and Victorian governments 'to be dealt with at their discretion'.[36]

Most of the trackers, it seems, never saw their reward.

Just six weeks after Ned Kelly was hanged, one of them, Trooper Johnny, was accused of the 'cruel and deliberate murder by chopping and spearing' of his wife during what police said was a Christmas feast near Cooktown that had degenerated into a 'drunken orgy'. Johnny had been riding with the Palmer River gold escort at the time. Sub-inspector Hervey Fitzgerald told the court in Cooktown that he had known Johnny for seven years and 'first recruited him on the Burdekin [River]. His character is bad, and I was about to have him removed, and was even arranging for his passage south. He has been drunk and mutinous, and I have every reason to believe that he is of unsound mind. There is a charge recorded against him of having killed a [woman] three years ago at Charters Towers.'[37]

Corporal Hero also worked on the Cooktown gold escort and as a tracker at Bowen, where he was said to be 'the saviour of many persons who had lost their way in the bush'. He died on the Burdekin in 1920.[38]

In an 1898 letter to the Queensland police commissioner, the then Aboriginals Protector Archibald Meston said Gary Owens, aka Trooper Barney, whom he regarded as 'thoroughly reliable', had told him that, in response to repeated requests, he was assured his £50 reward was on its way. Meston believed Owens had been done 'serious wrong'.[39]

After years of legal wrangling, claims by descendants of Owens and Jack Noble for a share of the reward – plus interest – were rejected by Queensland's Supreme Court in 2000 on the grounds that neither man left a will and that the descendants, Kurt Noble and May McBride, of Fraser Island, could not prove that they were the rightful heirs[40] to a fortune they estimated had grown to $42 million through the magic of compound interest.

Stanhope O'Connor's second in command, Tommy King, redeemed himself after the senior constable was sent back to Queensland following his drunken rampage in Victoria. At Tewantin near Noosa, King ran down the Aboriginal bushranger Kagariu, better known as Johnny Campbell, who was hanged for rape at Brisbane's Boggo Road jail a few weeks after the Kellys' battle at Glenrowan. Campbell's execution was brought forward because the eminent Scots-Russian scientist Baron Nikolai Miklouho-Maclay wanted to pickle the corpse and send it back to Berlin for study.[41]

Thirteen years later, King and his brother Nat, along with Jack Noble and other trackers, scoured hundreds of miles of bush from northern New South Wales to Mackay to arrest two Fraser Island men known as the 'Dora Dora Blacks'. The pair had absconded from their positions as Victorian trackers and killed a man. When King retired from the police force, he built the Urangan Hotel. He died in 1917 aged 65 after a heart attack on Fraser Island.[42]

Jack Noble died at Pialba, near Hervey Bay, on 15 January 1935 aged 80.[43] He was buried in the Polson Cemetery.

Tommy Spider's services were dispensed with after Hussey Chomley arrived back from Queensland with his new trackers or what he called his 'five smart boys'. Spider arranged for Frank Hare to put his £50 share of the Kelly reward into a trust fund and returned to the Coranderrk reserve. He married Bella Lee from the Loddon River area in 1882 and they had a daughter, Cath. Sadly Cath died aged two and her mother soon after. Spider moved to the Framlingham Mission near Warrnambool and died there aged just 26.[44]

Moses Bulla stayed in Victoria for five years after the Kelly Gang's capture and occasionally appeared as a witness in court cases. In 1884 a defence lawyer objected to him appearing in an arson case saying that he looked more like a 'native of Madras' than of Australia. Moses replied that he was indeed an Australian, born in Queensland and proud of it.[45] The following year, Moses was accused of inciting the other trackers to purchase beer, a tactic Sergeant Whelan and Tom Kirkham believed was deliberate so that he would be sacked and sent home. The tactic worked and Moses and two other Aboriginal trackers happily headed north. Moses had to pay his own way back to Maryborough, though, with Kirkham telling superiors that the Queensland Police Commissioner David Seymour 'had a very strong dislike to see these Victorian boys return with money'.[46]

Kirkham was given charge of Hussey Chomley's new team of Queensland trackers,[47] and declared them 'superior to Mr O'Connor's "boys," as far as tracking goes'.[48] But Kirkham's time in the force was short. He was blamed for the Moses Bulla trouble and was replaced as the officer in charge of the trackers, with a transfer to Wodonga for good measure. Kirkham applied for leave from the police to travel to Melbourne and Tasmania, saying he wanted to buy property to sustain him in his retirement. But

Kirkham had theatre in his blood and instead of travelling south, he was spotted performing with a theatrical troupe in Myrtleford. He faced a disciplinary hearing for taking leave under false pretences and quit before he was sacked.

He remarried and continued to appear on stage as an amateur thespian and also opened a bakery in Melbourne. By the time he died from a stroke in 1911 at his home in Spring Street, Prahran, aged just 55, he had earned a reputation for his 'extremely charitable disposition'.[49]

The gallant railway guard Jesse Dowsett, who helped Margaret Reardon and her baby to safety and then helped the police overpower the wounded Kelly, received £175 of the reward. He also souvenired Kelly's revolver and a boot with a bullet hole in it. Dowsett fathered eight children and died at his daughter's house at Dandenong aged 86.

James Whelan, who had spent a decade battling Ned Kelly, collected £165 as his share of the reward after arriving in

As an old man Jesse Dowsett proudly displays Ned Kelly's boot with a bullet hole in it and the Colt revolver he took from the wounded bushranger. State Library of Victoria, H2010.76/48

Glenrowan with John Sadleir's team just before dawn. Whelan retired in 1892 and died at his home in Hawthorn, Melbourne, in 1914. Another veteran Kelly hunter, Patrick Mullane, received £47. After he retired from the force, Mullane farmed at Ballan where he died in 1910. Constable Anthony Strahan, another of Kelly's sworn enemies, became a farmer in Rutherglen. He died in 1898, his widow, Marion, surviving him by 40 years.

Ernest Flood, who Kelly wanted to roast alive, died in 1899 aged 56 while living in North Fitzroy.

THE SIX MOUNTED CONSTABLES From Benalla – Gascoigne, Canny, Phillips, Arthur, Barry and Kirkham – who were first on the scene at Glenrowan with Frank Hare, received a £137 reward as did Charles Rawlins.

Charlie Gascoigne also grabbed a shoulder piece from Ned Kelly's armour that had been shot off in the gunfight. He threw it into a creek to keep it hidden from other lawmen who were also collecting pieces of history for their private collections. The shoulder piece remained with Gascoigne's descendants until 1970 and in 2001 was bought by the State Library of Victoria for $202,725.[50]

Three months after Kelly's capture, Gascoigne was posted to Glenrowan and stayed there until 14 December 1881 before moving to Cheshunt, a village in the King Valley below Harry Power's lookout. He continued his hobby of fossicking in the area and in 1888 found a large outcrop of grey rock with blue veins near the King River.[51]

Gascoigne opened the first turquoise mines in Australia, the Hedi and New Discovery, and the gems from there, cut in Germany, were sold at high-end jewellery stores in Melbourne,[52] with some eventually fetching 'very high prices' in London.[53]

The first man to shoot Ned Kelly died suddenly in Wangaratta in 1927 aged 73.[54]

William Canny left the police force to run hotels in Benalla, Richmond and central Melbourne. He was also vice-president of the Richmond Football Club in 1903. He died on 26 July 1935.[55]

Daniel Barry, who had volunteered to be tied to the front of the police locomotive roaring towards Glenrowan, was praised in police reports as a man who 'behaved bravely' and was 'a zealous well-conducted constable'.[56] But Barry complained of terrible rheumatism from his time watching the Byrne house and his devotion to duty lagged. Owing to misconduct, he was repeatedly fined, reprimanded, cautioned and transferred. By 1891 his police record said he could not perform his duty because of alcoholism and the following year he was charged with wife desertion, before reconciling.[57]

He lived a lonely life beside the Eildon Weir in his later years and died from heart disease at Alexandria Hospital, midway between Glenrowan and Melbourne, on 20 June 1939.[58]

Jim Arthur, who posed for photographs in the gang's armour at Glenrowan, was a deaf widower when he died suddenly at the Port Melbourne home of his sister-in-law in 1924 aged 70.[59] A few months earlier, the father of two had been hospitalised with a fractured arm and abrasions to his head and body after being hit by a train he didn't hear coming.[60]

James Allwood, who helped recover the bodies of Lonigan and Scanlan, was awarded the police badge for bravery for saving a party of surveyors from drowning in the Mitta Mitta flood of 1887.[61] He spent 21 years as a sergeant in charge of the Rutherglen station on the Murray and died there in 1924 aged 68.

FRANK HARE ALWAYS said his three best horsemen, Alf Falkiner, Tommy Lawless and Charlie Johnston, could have run down the Kellys if given half a chance.

Lawless's hard riding came to an end, though, at just 32 when he was killed at the annual Melbourne Show at Flemington on 30 August 1886. Witnesses said there were large crowds at a showjumping event in which he was competing, making it dangerous for the riders as the horses were distracted. Lawless's mount jumped right into the last hurdle, and the one-time Kelly hunter crashed onto his head. He was admitted to the Alfred Hospital unconscious and died soon after.[62]

Falkiner missed out on a share of the Kelly reward despite Hare saying he did as much work as anyone in bringing the gang down. Two years after the money was allocated, he was given £25 for his efforts. Falkiner was in charge of the police horse stud in Dandenong for 32 years, and when he retired in 1915 a grateful district hosted an emotional function for him and his wife, Hester, for their long history of public service.[63]

Charlie Johnston, who set fire to the Glenrowan Inn, received £97 of the reward money and, although Sadleir tried to force him to stay, he immediately asked to be transferred out of Kelly Country to the safer surrounds of Melbourne. He retired in 1885 aged 45 and spent the rest of his life farming around Ballarat, where the energetic Irishman died in 1936, four years short of his century.

The Royal Commission declared that Detective Mick Ward had 'rendered active and efficient service during the pursuit of the gang' but was also 'guilty of misleading his superior officers upon several occasions'. It recommended that he be censured and reduced one grade. Ward received £100 of the reward money because of his 'connection with the employment of Aaron Sherritt', which ultimately led to the young husband being killed.

The day before Ned was hanged, Ward and Joseph Eason arrested Ann Jones among Kelly sympathisers drowning their sorrows at Melbourne's Robert Burns Hotel.[64] She faced a charge of helping the gang at Glenrowan, but six months later was acquitted in Beechworth Court.[65] She strenuously denied that she ever put her arms around Ned in an affectionate way, and said she only played friendly with the gang to placate them.[66] Mrs Jones received £306 compensation for the destruction of her hotel, an amount she declared was 'ridiculously low' given the death of her son, the ruin of her home and livelihood, and the shooting of her daughter, Jane. Every change of weather made Jane suffer[67] until she died in her mother's arms on 16 April 1882, another victim of the Kelly outbreak.[68]

In 1885 Mick Ward was promoted to detective first class and five years later to sub-inspector. He retired from the force in 1905 and became a prosperous private detective in Melbourne, forming the agency Cawsey and Ward with Henry Cawsey, a detective who in 1892 had tracked down the Melbourne murderer Frederick Deeming, a British immigrant also suspected of the Jack the Ripper killings in London.

Ward married Ellen McDonald a year after the Royal Commission and following her death at the age of just 30 he married Margaret Aiken 12 years later. He died at his Melbourne home in Airdrie Road, Caulfield, in 1921 aged 75. Jerilderie policeman George Devine became a racecourse detective in Perth and died there in 1926, his widow, Mary, six years later.

The constables who were inside Aaron Sherritt's hut on the night of his murder – Henry Armstrong, William Duross, Thomas Patrick Dowling and Robert Alexander – all received £42 from the Kelly reward for their actions at Glenrowan but the Royal Commission ruled that they were guilty of 'gross cowardice' on the night of Sherritt's death, and that, Armstrong having already resigned, the other three should be sacked, too.[69]

FOR NED KELLY'S BROTHER JIM, old habits died hard. Just as the Royal Commission was handing down its findings in Melbourne, he and Ned's old sparring partner Wild Wright were arrested for stealing horses in Cootamundra, New South Wales. Wright was acquitted, but a year after his brother was hanged, Jim Kelly was sentenced to another five years' hard labour.[70]

On his release from Parramatta Gaol in January 1886 Jim set up a boot-making shop at Winton, near Benalla. He sometimes travelled as a drover and shearer, but spent more than a quarter of a century looking after his mother, who died in 1923, aged 91, having outlived seven of her 12 children, including her daughters Maggie and Kate.

Despite the Kelly family's war with the police, Ned's half-brother Jack became Probationary Constable No. 880 in Western Australia on 12 March 1906 and a second-class constable on 1 August. He went on to become a world-renowned trick rider whose name went up in lights on Broadway.

Ned Kelly's half-brother Jack King became a respected policeman and world famous showman. State Library of Victoria, H2003.25/27

Another man with close ties to the Kelly Gang, Tom Lloyd junior,[71] also joined the police force as a horse trainer in 1934. Lloyd's father was Ned Kelly's cousin and right-hand man, and his mother was Steve Hart's sister, Rachel. Lloyd served with the police until 1963 and worked closely with the Aboriginal trackers, mostly to rescue people lost in the bush.

THE KELLY FAMILY ALWAYS claimed that Constable Alexander Fitzpatrick was a liar who ruined their lives with false testimony.

Following the attempted arrest of Dan Kelly that started the Kelly outbreak, Fitzpatrick was sent to Sydney early in 1879 to identify Jim Kelly, who was then in Darlinghurst Gaol after the brutal beating of a policeman who was trying to arrest him on a horse-stealing charge in the Snowy Mountains. Jim was using the alias of James Wilson but authorities were sure he was Ned Kelly's brother and Fitzpatrick went there to prove it.

A few weeks later, Fitzpatrick was seconded to watch for signs of Ned or his supporters at Sydney's Central Railway Station, but was habitually late for duty. Soon after, Fitzpatrick was accused of being involved in the robbery of Polish-born Kazimerz Thomas Pogonowski, an aging hairdresser and tobacconist living near Central. Pogonowski claimed his maid Edith Jones robbed him of £70 worth of jewellery, apparel and cash and that Fitzpatrick had been a frequent visitor at Pogonowski's store at 723 George Street South and knew Edith well. He suspected the young policeman kept him in conversation while Edith robbed him.

When alerted to this, Standish replied that he feared Fitzpatrick was 'a useless and worthless young man.'[72] Fitzpatrick was sent back to Melbourne's police depot in Richmond in disgrace on 20 May 1879, and then transferred to another country posting at Lancefield.

Superintendent Hare said he would put Fitzpatrick 'under a hard man' who would watch him 'night and day'[73] and Fitzpatrick was soon offside with his boss, Senior Constable Joseph Ladd Mayes, who until recently had been watching Joe Byrne's house. Fitzpatrick found that with many Kelly sympathisers he now had 'a great many enemies in the working class' and many even 'swore vengeance … as the cause of driving the Kellys out'.[74] He received no sympathy from Mayes, though, and after nine months of friction between them Mayes sent a telegram to the police depot, saying Fitzpatrick should be sacked. Still, Fitzpatrick must have been doing something right: Standish was soon hit with petitions featuring signatures from '200 respectable citizens of Lancefield and Romsey'. One petition said: Mounted Constable Fitzpatrick was discharged on a report from a superior officer that he did not do his duty, could not be trusted out of sight, and associated with low persons. We felt constrained to give our free testimony to the fact that during the time Mounted Constable Fitzpatrick was in this district he was as far as we could see, and we came in contact with him every day, zealous, diligent, obliging and universally liked, while we never saw him in the company of any but the best citizens … He made several clever captures and appeared to us as one of the most efficient and obliging men in the Force …'[75] Fitzpatrick made an appeal to Standish that the signatures of the 200 petitioners 'and nine justices of the peace' ought to count more than the word of Constable Mayes.[76]

'I might have erred in small things,' Fitzpatrick argued, '[but] there are many constables in the force who have done more serious things than I did, and have remained in the force and got promotion.'[77] Standish, though, believed that Fitzpatrick's attempt at a solo arrest at the Kelly house two years earlier allowed no chance for corroborating evidence from other constables, and provided the outlaws with ammunition against the police forever. He told the petitioners on 10 May 1880 that 'the ex-constable's conduct ... was generally bad and discreditable', and that he would not be reinstated. Fitzpatrick was left unemployed, with a mother, wife and child to support. He battled on though for more than four decades.

Fitzpatrick died at his home in Liddiard Street, Glenferrie, Melbourne, in 1924 aged 67. His grieving family remembered him as a 'dearly beloved husband', a 'loving father' and a 'darling papa' to his grandchildren.[78]

For more than 140 years Fitzpatrick has been portrayed as the arch villain in the Kelly story and the men who hunted Kelly down have largely been forgotten. In 2018, however, Victoria's Chief Commissioner Graham Ashton and Leo Kennedy, the great-grandson of the brave Sergeant Michael Kennedy, formally opened a new memorial to the slain officers at Stringybark Creek.

Thomas McIntyre, the only man who was still alive of the eight involved in the ambush there, left the police force in 1881 still suffering post-traumatic shock. He took a job handling explosives for a Ballarat mining company. It was safer than police work.

He had married Eliza Ann Fowler in 1879 and they had eight children. In 1912 his daughter Florence married Basson Rowlands Humffray, the grandson of J.B. Humffray, the pacifist voice of the Eureka Stockade rebellion. McIntyre died in 1918.

The destruction of the Kelly Gang in 1880 was greeted with joy by newspapers around Australia as the press likened them to 'a horde of hyenas, wolves and tigers, thirsting for human blood'.[79]

In the 20th century, though, Ned Kelly was transformed into an Australian folk hero due largely to sympathetic books, the iconic artwork of Sidney Nolan and a variety of motion pictures, one even curiously casting the slightly-built rock star Mick Jagger of the Rolling Stones as the iron outlaw.

Kelly and his family always complained that the police treated them with a heavy hand, and, while it acknowledged the brave efforts of so many officers, the resulting Royal Commission swept a broom through the force.

But it also put into perspective the actions of a young, heavily armed hothead with a propensity for violence and a disregard for the sanctity of human life.

'There seems no reason to suppose that the [police] murders were the result of premeditation,' the Royal Commission found.

'The [police] were shot down when, with an instinctive sense of duty, they endeavoured to repel the attack of their assailants. The cold-blooded despatch of the brave but ill-fated Kennedy when, wounded and hopeless of surviving, he pleaded to be allowed to live to bid farewell to his wife and children, is one of the darkest stains upon the career of the outlaws.

'It was cruel, wanton, and inhuman, and should of itself, apart from other crimes, brand the name of his murderer, the leader of the gang, with infamy.'[80]

Appendix I

Police Force At Ned Kelly's Last Stand At Glenrowan

ARRIVED 2 a.m. ON THE SPECIAL TRAIN
Superintendent Frank Hare
Senior-constable John Kelly
Mounted-constable Daniel Barry
Mounted-constable William Phillips
Mounted-constable Jim Arthur
Mounted-constable Tom Kirkham
Mounted-constable Charlie Gascoigne
Mounted-constable William Canny
Sub-Inspector Stanhope O'Connor
Tracker Hero
Tracker Gary 'Barney' Owens
Tracker Johnny
Tracker Jack Noble
Tracker Jimmy

ARRIVED AT 5.03 a.m. ON HORSEBACK FROM WANGARATTA
Sergeant Arthur Steele
Mounted-constable John Montiford
Mounted-constable William Moore
Mounted-constable Patrick Healy

ARRIVED ON TRAIN FROM BENALLA AT 5.10 a.m.
Superintendent John Sadleir
Sergeant James Whelan
Senior-constable Robert Smyth
Mounted-constable Robert Graham

Mounted-constable Cornelius Ryan
Mounted-constable William Wallace
Mounted-constable P. P. Wilson
Mounted-constable John Stillard
Foot-constable Patrick Kelly
Foot-constable Thomas Reilly
Foot-constable John Milne
Foot-constable John Hewitt
Tracker Moses Bulla
Tracker Tommy Spider

ARRIVED 5.20 a.m. ON TRAIN FROM WANGARATTA
Foot-constable Patrick Walsh
Foot-constable James Dwyer

ARRIVED 9 a.m. FROM BEECHWORTH
Senior-constable Patrick Mullane
Mounted-constable Anthony Alexander
Foot-constable Richard Wickham
Foot-constable Robert Armstrong
Foot-constable John McHugh
Foot-constable William Duross
Foot-constable Richard Glenny
Mounted-constable Robert Alexander
Foot-constable Tom Dowling
Mounted-constable Charlie Magor
Mounted-constable Robert McColl

ARRIVED AT 10 a.m. FROM BENALLA
Mounted-constable Jim Dixon

ARRIVED AT NOON FROM VIOLET TOWN
Senior-constable Charles Johnston
Mounted-constable Thomas Meehan
Mounted-constable Michael Dwyer
Foot-constable John Stone

ARRIVED 1 p.m. FROM VIOLET TOWN
Foot-constable Peter McDonald

Appendix 2

The Kelly Reward

1	Superintendent Frank Hare	£800 0s 0d
2	Thomas Curnow, schoolteacher	£550 0 0
3	Senior-Constable John Kelly	£337 11 8
4	Sergeant Arthur Steele	£290 13 9
5	Constable Hugh Bracken	£275 13 9
6	Superintendent John Sadleir	£240 17 3
7	Sub-inspector Stanhope O'Connor	£237 15 0
8	Jesse Dowsett, railway guard	£175 13 9
9	Sergeant James Whelan	£165 13 9
10	Constable William Canny	£137 11 8
11	Constable Charlie Gascoigne	£137 11 8
12	Constable William Phillips	£137 11 8
13	Constable Daniel Barry	£137 11 8
14	Constable Jim Arthur	£137 11 8
15	Charlie Rawlins	£137 11 8
16	Constable Tom Kirkham	£137 11 8
17	Senior-Constable Robert Smyth	£137 11 8
18	Constable Patrick Kelly	£137 11 8
19	Constable James Dixon	£115 13 9
20	Constable James Dwyer	£115 13 9
21	Constable P. P. Wilson	£115 13 9

22	Constable John Milne	£115 13 9
23	Constable John Stillard	£115 13 9
24	Constable Cornelius Ryan	£115 13 9
25	Constable Tom Reilly	£115 13 9
26	Constable Robert Graham	£115 13 9
27	Constable John Hewitt	£115 13 9
28	Constable William Wallace	£115 13 9
29	Constable Patrick Walsh	£115 13 9
30	Constable John Montiford	£115 13 9
31	Constable Robert Cawsey	£115 13 9
32	Constable James Healy	£115 13 9
33	Constable William Moore	£115 13 9
34	Archie McPhee, guard on pilot engine	£104 4 6
35	Henry Alder, driver, pilot engine	£104 4 6
36	Hugh Burch, fireman, pilot engine	£104 4 6
37	Detective-Constable Michael Ward	£100 0 0
38	Senior-Constable Charlie Johnston	£97 15 9
39	John Bowman, engine driver	£84 4 6
40	Herbert Hollows, train fireman	£84 4 6
41	Frank Bell, train guard	£84 4 6
42	Richard Coleman, engine driver	£68 3 4
43	John Stewart, fireman	£68 3 4
44	Senior-Constable Patrick Mullane	£47 15 9
45	Constable Richard Glenny	£42 15 9
46	Constable Robert Armstrong	£42 15 9
47	Constable Charlie Magor	£42 15 9
48	Constable Robert McColl	£42 15 9
49	Constable Tom Dowling	£42 15 9
50	Constable William Duross	£42 15 9
51	Constable Anthony Alexander	£42 15 9

52	Constable John McHugh	£42 15 9
53	Constable Richard Wickham	£42 15 9
54	John Sherritt	£42 15 9
55	Constable Michael Dwyer	£42 15 9
55	Constable John Stone	£42 15 9
57	Constable Peter McDonald	£42 15 9
58	Hero, blacktracker	£50 0 0
59	Johnny, blacktracker	£50 0 0
60	Jimmy, blacktracker	£50 0 0
61	Jack Noble, blacktracker	£50 0 0
62	Gary 'Barney' Owens, blacktracker	£50 0 0
63	Moses Bulla, blacktracker	£50 0 0
64	Tommy Spider, blacktracker	£50 0 0
65	Harry Cheshire, telegraph operator	£25 0 0
66	William Osborne, telegraphic assistant	£25 0 0
	Total	£8000 0 0

Bibliography

Noelene Allen, *Ellen: A Woman of Spirit*, Network Creative Services, 2012.

Robyn Annear, *A City Lost & Found: Whelan the Wrecker's Melbourne*, Black Inc, 2014.

Joseph William Ashmead, 'The Thorns and the Briars: The True Story of the Kelly Gang', unpublished manuscript, 1922.

Dagmar Balcarek and Gary Dean, *Ellen Kelly*, Glen Rowen Cobb & Co, 1984.

Dagmar Balcarek and Gary Dean, *Ned and the Others*, Glen Rowen Cobb & Co, 1995.

Dagmar Balcarek and Gary Dean, *To Crack a Whip*, Yesteryears Publishers, 1990.

Edwin Barnard, *Capturing Time: Panoramas of Old Australia*, National Library of Australia, 2012.

A.N. Baron, *Blood in the Dust*, Network Creative Services, 2004.

Susan Campbell Bartoletti, *Black Potatoes: The Story of the Great Irish Famine, 1845–1850*, Houghton Mifflin Harcourt, 2001.

Jill Blee, *Gold: Greed, Innovation, Daring and Wealth*, Exisle Publishing, 2007.

Beverley Boissery, *A Deep Sense of Wrong: The Treason, Trials and Transportation to New South Wales of Lower Canadian Rebels*, Dundurn, 1995.

Max Brown, *Ned Kelly: Australian Son*, Angus & Robertson, 1948.

Amelia Jane Burgoyne, *Memories of Avenel*, Halstead Press, 1954.

Alex C. Castles, *Ned Kelly's Last Days*, Allen & Unwin, 2005.

Florence Cathcart, *Pictures on My Screen: Growing Up in Kelly Country*, Spectrum Publications, 1989.

Charles Henry Chomley, *The True Story of the Kelly Gang of Bushrangers*, Fraser & Jenkinson, 1920.

Ellen Clacy, *A Lady's Visit to the Gold Diggings of Australia in 1852–53*, Hurst & Blackett, 1853.

Charles Manning Hope Clark (abridged by Michael Cathcart), *Manning Clark's History of Australia*, Melbourne University Press, 1993.

Frank Clune, *The Kelly Hunters*, Angus & Robertson, 1954.

Justin Corfield, *The Ned Kelly Encyclopaedia*, Lothian Books, 2003.

Craig Cormick, *Ned Kelly: Under the Microscope*, CSIRO Publishing, 2014.

Paul De Serville, *Port Phillip Gentlemen and Good Society in Melbourne Before the Gold Rushes*, Oxford University Press, 1980.

Paul De Serville, *Pounds and Pedigrees: The Upper Class in Victoria 1850–80*, Oxford University Press, 1991.

Richard Everist, *The Traveller's Guide to the Goldfields: History & Natural Heritage Trails Through Central & Western Victoria*, BestShot, 2009.

Edmund Finn (writing as Garryowen), *The Chronicles of Early Melbourne, 1835 to 1852*, Vols 1–3, centennial edition, Heritage Publications, 1976.

Mark Finnane, ed., *The Difficulties of My Position: The Diaries of Prison Governor John Buckley Castieau 1855–1884*, National Library of Australia, 2004.

Ann Galbally, *Redmond Barry: An Anglo-Irish Australian*, Melbourne University Press, 1995.

Joan Gillison, *Colonial Doctor and his Town*, Cypress Books, 1974.

Anna Haebich and Baden Offord (eds), *Landscapes of Exile: Once Perilous, Now Safe*, Peter Lang, 2008.

George Wilson Hall, *The Book of Keli, or, The Chronicles of the Kelly Pursuers*, Charquin Hill, 1985.

George Wilson Hall, *The Kelly Gang, or, The Outlaws of the Wombat Ranges*, Australian History Promotions, 2004 (a reprint of the first book ever published on Ned Kelly, 1879).

Francis Augustus Hare, *The Last of the Bushrangers: An Account of the Capture of the Kelly Gang*, Hurst & Blackett, 1895.

Neil Hegarty, *The Story of Ireland*, Random House, 2011.

David Hill, *The Gold Rush*, William Heinemann, 2010.

Joan Hoff and Marian Yeates, *The Cooper's Wife Is Missing: The Trials of Bridget Cleary*, Basic Books, 2008.

William Howitt, *Land, Labour, and Gold: Two Years in Victoria: with Visits to Sydney and Van Diemen's Land*, Vol. 1, Ticknor and Fields, 1855.

Brian Igoe, *The Story of Ireland*, Aidan Kelly, 2009.

Ian Jones, *Ned Kelly: A Short Life*, Hachette UK, 2010.

Ned Kelly, *The Jerilderie Letter*, Text Publishing, 2012.

Brendon Kelson and John McQuilton, *Kelly Country: A Photographic Journey*, University of Queensland Press, 2001.

J. J. Kenneally, *The Complete Inner History of the Kelly Gang and Their Pursuers*, Ruskin Press, 1929.

Leo Kennedy, *Black Snake*, Affirm Press, 2018.

Susan Kingsley Kent, *Gender and Power in Britain, 1640–1990*, Routledge, 1999.

Marilyn Lake and Farley Kelly, *Double Time: Women in Victoria, 150 Years*, Penguin, 1985.

Ian MacFarlane, *The Kelly Gang Unmasked*, Oxford University Press, 2012.

T.N. McIntyre, 'A True Narrative of the Kelly Gang', unpublished manuscript, *c.* 1902.

Keith McMenomy, *Ned Kelly: The Authentic Illustrated Story*, C.O. Ross, 1984.

John McQuilton, *The Kelly Outbreak 1878–1880*, Melbourne University Press, 1987.

John Molony, *I am Ned Kelly*, Allen Lane, 1980.

George Morris, *Devil's River Country: Selections from the History of the Mansfield District*, Shepparton Advertiser, 1952.

Kevin J. Passey, *In Search of Ned: A Travelogue of Kelly Country*, Lachlan Publishing, 1988.

J.W. Payne, *The History of Beveridge*, Lowden Publishing, 1974.

Cyril Pearl, *Australia's Yesterdays: A Look at Our Recent Past*, Readers Digest Services, 1974.

Cyril Pearl, *Rebel Down Under*, Heinemann, 1970.

Gary Presland, *For God's Sake Send the Trackers: A History of Queensland Trackers and Victoria Police*, Victoria Press, 1998.

Tom Prior, Bill Wannan and H. Nunn, *A Pictorial History of Bushrangers*, Paul Hamlyn, 1968.

Bob Reece, 'Ned Kelly and the Irish Connection: a Re-appraisal', *Tipperary Historical Journal*, 1990.

Edith C. Rickards, *Bishop Moorhouse of Melbourne and Manchester*, John Murray, 1920.

Peter Ryan, *Redmond Barry*, Oxford University Press, 1972.

John Sadleir, *Recollections of a Victorian Police Officer*, George Robertson & Co, 1913.

Ian W. Shaw, *Glenrowan*, Macmillan Publishers, 2012.

Jeremy Stoljar, *The Australian Book of Great Trials: The Cases That Shaped a Nation*, Murdoch Books, 2011.

Alexander Sutherland, *Victoria and Its Metropolis: Past and Present*, Vol. 2, Today's Heritage, 1888.

Glenn Wahlert and Russell Linwood, *One Shot Kills: A History of Australian Army Sniping*, Big Sky Publishing, 2014.

William Bramwell Withers, *The History of Ballarat, from the First Pastoral Settlement to the Present Time*, F.W. Niven and Co., 1887.

INTERNET RESOURCES

academia.edu

aguidetoaustralianbushranging.com

ancestry.com.au

anzacportal.dva.gov.au

archaeologyonthefrontier.com

aussietowns.com.au

australia.gov.au

australianculture.org

beechworth.com

benhallaustralianbushranger.com

bordermail.com.au

canterburyphotography.blogspot

catholic-hierarchy.org

collections.museumsvictoria.com.au

cv.vic.gov.au

database.frontierconflict.org

denheldid.com

elevenmilecreek.blogspot.com

emelbourne.net.au

fethard.com

fordsofkatandra.com

freesettlerorfelon.com

heritageinschools.ie

historyaustralia.org.au

irishdemocrat.co.uk

irishtimes.com

ironicon.com.au

ironoutlaw.com

jerilderie.nsw.gov.au

julianburnside.com.au

justice.vic.gov.au

kellygang.asn.au

kellygang0.tripod.com

kellylegend.blogspot.com

kilmorehistory.info

libraries.tas.gov.au

merchantnetworks.com.au

monumentaustralia.org.au

naa.gov.au

nationalarchives.gov.uk
nationalunitygovernment.org
nedkellysworld.com.au
nedkellyunmasked.com
nedkellytouringroute.com.au
offalyhistory.com
parliament.vic.gov.au
policewahistory.org.au
ports.com
prov.vic.gov.au
slv.vic.gov.au
smh.com.au
sydneylivingmuseums.com.au
theaustralian.com.au
thevictoriantrooper.home.blog
tipperarylibraries.ie
trove.nla.gov.au
vhd.heritagecouncil.vic.gov.au
victoriancollections.net.au
victorianplaces.com.au
vsv.vic.edu.au
wikipedia.com

Endnotes

Prologue

1 Edward Kelly, born December 1854, Beveridge, Victoria; executed by hanging, 11 November 1880, Melbourne Gaol. His exact birth date was never record but school records indicate it was in the last month of 1854.

2 'The Kelly raid on Jerilderie', *Jerilderie Herald and Urana Advertiser*, 18 July 1913, p. 1.

3 'The drought in Victoria', *Adelaide Observer*, 12 April 1879, p. 9.

4 Evidence of Alfred John Falkiner, 'Minutes of Evidence Taken Before Royal Commission on the Police Force of Victoria, Together with Appendices', Victorian Parliamentary Paper No. 31, 1881, question 5162, p. 214.

5 Michael Kennedy, born 20 October 1842, Tonaghmore, near Collinstown in Westmeath, Ireland; died 26 October 1878, Stringybark Creek, Victoria.

6 Thomas Lonigan, born 1 November 1844, Sligo, Ireland; arrived in Victoria 1867; died 26 October 1878, Stringybark Creek.

7 Michael Scanlan, born 25 December 1843, Fossa, Ireland; died 26 October 1878, Stringybark Creek. Sometimes referred to as Scanlon.

8 Daniel Kelly, born 1 June 1861, Beveridge; baptised 28 August 1861, St Paul's, Coburg; died 28 June 1880, Glenrowan.

9 Joseph Byrne, born November 1856, Woolshed Valley, Victoria; died 28 June 1880, Glenrowan.

10 Stephen Hart, born 4 October 1859, Wangaratta; died 28 June 1880, Glenrowan.

11 'The Kelly raid on Jerilderie', *Jerilderie Herald and Urana Advertiser*, 18 July 1913, p. 1.

12 'The bushrangers', *Riverine Herald* (Echuca), 12 February 1879, p. 2.

13 'Spearing of Hartley and Sykes', *Brisbane Courier*, 5 January 1924, p. 18.

14 *Ibid.*

15 Stanhope Edward Dunn (also Dunne) O'Connor, born 1848, Westmeath, Ireland; died 1 September 1908, St Kilda, Melbourne.

16 Joanne Scott, Ross Laurie, Bronwyn Stevens and Patrick Moray Weller, *The Engine Room of Government: The Queensland Premier's Department 1859–2001*, University of Queensland Press, 2001, p. 36.

17 Georgia Moodie, Coming to terms with the brutal history of Queensland's Native Mounted Police, abc.net.au, 24 July 2019.

18 'Queensland', *Adelaide Observer*, 22 March 1879, p. 19.

Chapter 1

1   'Ballarat diggings', *Geelong Advertiser*, 1 October 1851, p. 1.

2   Peter Turbet, *First Frontier: the Occupation of the Sydney Region 1788–1816*, Rosenberg Publishing, 2011, pp. 163, 268.

3   aboriginalhistoryofyarra.com.au

4   John 'Red' Kelly, baptised 20 February 1820 in the Catholic Church in Moyglass, the first child of Thomas Kelly and Mary Cody; died 27 December 1866, Avenel, Victoria.

5   Ellen Kelly, née Quinn, born 1832, Antrim, Ireland; died 27 March 1923, Greta West, Victoria.

6   'The Jerilderie Letter', penned by Ned Kelly and his lieutenant Joe Byrne in 1879, National Museum of Australia transcription, p. 31.

7   John O'Connell Bligh, born 3 March 1834, Buckinghamshire, England; died 12 October 1880, Gympie, Queensland.

8   'Maryborough', *Moreton Bay Courier* (Brisbane), 21 February 1860, p. 4.

9   *Ibid.*

10 Inquest into Death of Darkey at Maryborough, JUS/N1/60/6a, State Coroner's Office/Coroner's Court of Queensland.

11 'Lieutenant Bligh's sword', *Moreton Bay Courier*, 25 April 1861, p. 2.

12 'Maryborough', *Moreton Bay Courier*, 21 February 1860, p. 4.

13 'Lieutenant Bligh's Sword', *Moreton Bay Courier*, 25 April 1861, p. 2.

14 'Local intelligence', *Moreton Bay Courier*, 24 January 1861, p. 2.

15 'The "Sword" presented to John O'Connell Bligh, Esq.', *Maryborough Chronicle, Wide Bay and Burnett Advertiser*, 28 February 1861, p. 3.

16 Ian Jones, *Ned Kelly: A Short Life*, Hachette UK, 2010, p. 18.

17 Richard John Shelton, born c. 1860; died 10 September 1931.

18 The sash is on display at Benalla's Costume and Pioneer Museum.

19 *Victoria Police Gazette*, 6 June 1867, pp. 221, 224.

20 Sir Redmond Barry, born 7 June 1813, Ballyclough, County Cork, Ireland; died 23 November 1880, East Melbourne.

21 'Commutation of sentence', *Ovens and Murray Advertiser*, 20 June 1868, p. 2.

22 'About the Kellys', *Ovens and Murray Advertiser*, 11 January 1879, p. 8.

23 Item 177, Unit 4, Part 2, VPRS 4965, Public Record Office Victoria.

24 'About the Kellys', *Ovens and Murray Advertiser*, 11 January 1879, p. 8.

25 I – The Kelly Family, 'Second Progress Report of the Royal Commission of Enquiry into the Circumstances of the Kelly Outbreak, the Present State and Organisation of the Police Force, etc.', Victorian Parliamentary Paper No. 22, 1881, p. vii.

26 'A juvenile bushranger', *Ovens and Murray Advertiser*, 19 October 1869, p. 2.

27 Henry (Harry) Power, also known as Johnson, born Waterford, Ireland, 1820; drowned in the Murray River, 11 October 1891, Swan Hill, Victoria.

28 'The country', *Leader* (Melbourne), 19 June 1869, p. 19.

29 James Whelan, born 24 July 1829, Queen's County, Ireland; died 9 May 1914, 49 Melville Street, Hawthorn, Melbourne.

30 David McEnerney, sometimes written as McInerney (1843–1876).

31 *Sydney Morning Herald*, 27 October 1869, p.6.

32 'A juvenile bushranger', *Ovens and Murray Advertiser*, 19 October 1869, p. 2.

33 'A juvenile bushranger', *Argus* (Melbourne), 22 October 1869, p. 2 (supplement).

34 'Current topics', *Geelong Advertiser*, 11 May 1870, p. 2.

35 John Sadleir, *Recollections of a Victorian Police Officer*, George Robertson & Co, 1913, pp. 281–282.

36   *Benalla Ensign and Farmer's and Squatter's Journal*, 6 May 1870, p. 2.

37   William Keigwin Nicolas (1830–1885).

38   Patrick Mullane, born 17 November 1845, Melbourne; died 14 December 1910, Ballan, Victoria.

39   William Arthur, born 16 March 1853; died 17 January 1924, Melbourne.

40   Charles Hope Nicolson, born 7 October 1829, Orkney Islands, Scotland; died 30 July 1898, Melbourne.

41   Francis Augustus Hare, born 4 October 1830 in the village of Wynberg, 13km from Cape Town; died 9 July 1892, Rupertswood, Victoria.

42   Frederick Charles Standish, born 1824, in his ancestral home, Standish Hall, Wigan, Lancashire; died 1883 at the Melbourne Club, where he had lived for 11 years.

43   Paul Williams, *The Last Confederate Ship at Sea: The Wayward Voyage of the CSS Shenandoah*, McFarland, 2015, p. 94.

44   Curtis Candler (1827–1911), 'Addenda to Diary', 1867, MS 9502, La Trobe Australian Manuscripts Collection, State Library Victoria.

45   Paul de Serville, *Pounds and Pedigrees: The Upper Class in Victoria 1850–80*, Oxford University Press, 1991, p. 69.

46   Cyril Pearl, *Rebel Down Under*, Heinemann, 1970, p. 87.

47   Sadleir, *Recollections*, p. 267.

48   Alexander Brooke Smith (1834–1882).

49   Evidence of C.H. Nicolson, Royal Commission, question 1028, p. 47.

50   Francis Augustus Hare, *The Last of the Bushrangers: An Account of the Capture of the Kelly Gang*, Hurst & Blackett, 1895. p. 93.

51   'The police murders', *Argus* (Melbourne), 2 November 1878, p. 8.

52   F.C. Standish, Diary, 15 May 1870, State Library of Victoria, MS Box 4346/5.

53   *Benalla Ensign and Farmer's and Squatter's Journal*, 6 May 1870, p. 2.

54   Benjamin Gould (1830–1920).

55   *Ovens and Murray Advertiser*, 21 December 1878, p. 4.

56   'A juvenile bushranger', *Argus* (Melbourne), 22 October 1869, p. 2 (supplement).

57   Hall to Superintendent Barclay, 22 April 1871, Unit 413, VPRS 937, Public Record Office Victoria.

58   Isaiah Wright (1849–1911).

59   'Beechworth general sessions', *Ovens and Murray Advertiser*, 5 August 1871, p. 3.

60   Ernest Flood (1843–1899).

61   Charles Nettleton (1826–1902).

62   Item 1, Unit 1, Consignment P0, VPRS 4966, Public Record Office Victoria.

Chapter 2

1   'Edward Kelly and David Gaunson', *Ovens and Murray Advertiser*, 13 November 1880, p. 4.

2   Kelly, 'The Jerilderie Letter', p. 14.

3   *Ovens and Murray Advertiser*, 21 December 1878, p. 4.

4   *Ibid.*

5   'The Kelly scare at Kerang', *Argus* (Melbourne), 10 March 1879, p. 3 (reprinted from *Kerang Times*, 7 March 1879). Sometimes referred to as Gnawarra Station (*Gippsland Times*, 12 March 1879, p. 3).

6   'Edward Kelly and David Gaunson', *Ovens and Murray Advertiser*, 13 November 1880, p. 4.

7   Detective Michael Ward to Brian Cookson, 'The Kelly Gang', *Advertiser* (Adelaide), 30 September 1911, p. 7.

8   'Evidence of James Gloster, from trial of Edward Kelly', *Argus* (Melbourne), 29 October 1880, p. 6.

9   Kelly, 'The Jerilderie Letter', p. 55.

10   Evidence of A.L.M. Steele, Royal Commission, question 8855, p. 320.

11   'Wangaratta Police Court', *Ovens and Murray Advertiser*, 22 December 1877, p. 1.

12   Aaron Sherritt, born 1854, Prahran, Melbourne; shot dead by Joe Byrne, 1880, Woolshed Valley.

13   William 'Brickey' Williamson (1847–1932), born Newcastle upon Tyne to a ship's carpenter; came to Australia aged 14.

14   Reference: 940 / 1874, Births, Deaths and Marriages Victoria.

15   Alexander Wilson Fitzpatrick, born 18 February 1856, Mount Egerton, Victoria; died 6 May 1924, 68 Liddiard Street, Hawthorn, Melbourne.

16   Alexander Fitzpatrick 2867, Record of Conduct and Service, Police Muster Rolls, VPM 10018, Unit 7 (1877, Ovens), VPRS 55, Public Record Office Victoria.

17   'The Kelly Gang', *Advertiser* (Adelaide), 4 November 1911, p. 8.

18   Catherine Ada Kelly, born 12 July 1863, Beveridge; died October 1898, Forbes, New South Wales.

19   Ned Kelly to Governor of Victoria, 3 November 1880, Condemned Cell Correspondence, Record 11, Item 4, Unit 2, Consignment P0, VPRS 4966, Public Record Office Victoria.

20   Kelly, 'The Jerilderie Letter', p. 23.

21   Patrick Day, born 1833; married Alice O'Brien, 1865; died suddenly, 19 July 1900, at his home in Thomas Street, Benalla West.

22   Thomas Lonigan, born 1 November 1844, Sligo, Ireland; arrived in Victoria 1867; died 26 October 1878, Stringybark Creek

23   'Interview with Ned Kelly', *Age* (Melbourne), 9 August 1880, p. 3.

24   Kelly, 'The Jerilderie Letter', p. 27.

25   'Interview with Ned Kelly', *Age*, 9 August 1880, p. 3.

26   J.J. Kenneally, *The Complete Inner History of the Kelly Gang and Their Pursuers*, Ruskin Press, 1929, p. 18.

27   Cause List Book, Benalla Petty Sessions, 18 September 1877, Public Record Office Victoria.

28   'Family notices', *Australasian* (Melbourne), 12 September 1908, p. 64.

29   Inward Overseas Passenger Lists (British Ports) [Microfiche Copy of VPRS 947]; Series: VPRS 7666, Public Record Office Victoria.

30   'New South Wales', *Express and Telegraph* (Adelaide), 4 March 1879, p. 2.

31   'On the track', *Townsville Daily Bulletin*, 24 April 1937, p. 12.

32   Evidence of Stanhope O'Connor, Royal Commission, question 11432, p. 405.

33   *Ibid.*, question 11985, p. 426.

34   'Black and white in Queensland', *Sydney Morning Herald*, 2 February 1874, p. 3.

35   Robert Logan Jack, *Northmost Australia: Three Centuries of Exploration, Discovery and Adventure in and around the Cape, Vol II*, p. 422.

36   J.J. Hogg, 'The Palmer goldfield: narrative of a pioneer miner', John Oxley Library OM91-100/1-206.

37   Arthur Laurie, 'The black war in Queensland', *The Royal Historical Society of Queensland*, Vol 6, Issue 1, September 1959, p. 169.

38   *Ibid.*

39   Arthur C. Ashwin and Peter J Bridge, *Gold to Grass*, Hesperian Press, 2002.

40   'Cooktown and the Palmer', *Capricornian* (Rockhampton), 8 January 1876, p. 18.

41 'Seeing the wood and the trees: culturally modified Cooktown ironwood trees at Lower Laura (Boralga) Native Mounted Police Camp, Cape York Peninsula', archaeologyonthefrontier.com/2020/05/18/seeing-the-wood-and-the-trees.

42 'Cooktown', *Brisbane Courier*, 10 January 1876, p. 3.

43 *Mackay Mercury and South Kennedy Advertiser*, 18 March 1876, p. 2.

44 *Brisbane Courier*, 20 December 1880, p. 3.

45 *Maryborough Chronicle, Wide Bay and Burnett Advertiser*, 10 October 1876, p. 2.

46 'On the track', *Townsville Daily Bulletin*, 24 April 1937, p. 12.

47 O'Connor 1/12/1877, Queensland State Archives (QSA) A/40117 File 1449, 4072/77.

48 William Henry Corfield (1843–1927).

49 William Henry Corfield, *Reminiscences of North Queensland 1862–1878*, A.H. Frater, 1921, pp. 62–64.

50 *The Cooktown Courier*, 21 February 1877, p. 2.

51 William Skilling (aka Skillion), born 1840, Donnybrook, Victoria.

52 'The Kellys are out', *Daily Advertiser* (Wagga Wagga), 24 December 1930, p. 3.

53 Kenneally, *Complete Inner History*, p. 28.

54 Frank Clune, *The Kelly Hunters*, Angus & Robertson, 1954, p. 349.

55 *Victoria Police Gazette*, 20 March 1878, p. 7.

56 Item 4, Unit 1, VPRS 4966, Public Record Office Victoria.

57 'Bushranging and burglary', *Ovens and Murray Advertiser*, 2 October 1877, p. 2.

58 'Bendigo', *Argus* (Melbourne), 8 September 1853, p. 4.

59 Evidence of A. Fitzpatrick, Royal Commission, questions 12841 and 12848, p. 464.

60 Police Offences Statute 1865 (Victoria), ss 19, 61; Dr Stuart E. Dawson, 'Redeeming Fitzpatrick: Ned Kelly and the Fitzpatrick incident', *Eras Journal*, Vol. 17, No. 1, p. 64, artsonline.monash.edu.au/eras.

61 Evidence of James Whelan, Royal Commission, question 5951, p. 236.

62 Evidence of A. Fitzpatrick, *Ibid.*, questions 12817–12818, p. 463.

63 *Ibid.*, question 12873, p. 465.

64 'Beechworth sessions', *Age*, 5 March 1878, p. 3.

65 'Kelly Gang echo', *Northern Star* (Lismore), 30 December 1930, p. 7.

66 Evidence of A. Fitzpatrick, Royal Commission, question 12825, p. 464.

67 *Ibid.*, question 12825, p. 464.

68 William Williamson to Inspector Green, 29 October 1878, Item 353, Unit 5, VPRS 4965, Public Record Office Victoria.

69 Margaret Mildred Skilling, née Kelly, born 15 June 1857, Beveridge; died 22 January 1896, Greta.

70 Fitzpatrick deposition, 17 May 1878, Item 4, Unit 1, VPRS 4966, Public Record Office Victoria.

71 Fitzpatrick to Crown Solicitor, 20 September 1878, Item 4 Unit 1, VPRS 4966, Public Record Office Victoria.

Chapter 3

1 Evidence of James Whelan, Royal Commission, question 5947, p. 236.

2 Dr Stuart E. Dawson, 'Redeeming Fitzpatrick: Ned Kelly and the Fitzpatrick incident', *Eras Journal*, Vol. 17, No. 1, p. 76, artsonline.monash.edu.au/eras.

3 'Reappearance of the bushrangers', *Argus* (Melbourne), 12 December 1878, p. 5.

4 Kelly, 'The Jerilderie Letter', p. 23.

5 *Ovens and Murray Advertiser*, 10 October 1878, p. 5.

6   'The Mansfield murderers: the outlaws' explanations', *Maitland Mercury and Hunter River General Advertiser*, 12 November 1878, p. 3.

7   'Interview with Ned Kelly', *Age*, 9 August 1880.

8   Arthur Loftus Maule Steele, born 26 August 1837, Tours, France; died 9 February 1914, at his home in Faithful Street, Wangaratta.

9   Evidence of A.L.M. Steele, Royal Commission, questions 8817–8821, p. 319.

10   Anthony Strahan, born 1841, Kildare, Ireland; died 1898, Rutherglen, Victoria.

11   Ned Kelly to Governor of Victoria, 3 November 1880, Condemned Cell Correspondence, Record 11, Item 4, Unit 2, Consignment P0, VPRS 4966, Public Record Office Victoria.

12   James Quinn, born 1840, County Antrim, Ireland.

13   Evidence of A.L.M. Steele, Royal Commission, question 8822, p. 319.

14   'Mrs Kelly', *Ovens and Murray Advertiser*, 6 June 1878, p. 2.

15   Max Brown, *Ned Kelly: Australian Son*, Angus & Robertson, 1948, p. 130.

16   Douglas Smith Kennedy (1831–1902).

17   Evidence of A. Fitzpatrick, Royal Commission, question 12925, p. 467.

18   Andrew George Scott, also known as Captain Moonlite; baptised 5 July 1842, Rathfriland, Ireland; executed Darlinghurst Gaol, 20 January 1880.

19   Michael Edward Ward, born 5 December 1845, Galway, Ireland; died 27 August 1921, Caulfield, Melbourne.

20   'Wangaratta Police Court', *Ovens and Murray Advertiser*, 25 January 1872, p. 3.

21   Evidence of Michael Ward, Royal Commission, question 3026, p. 160.

22   *Ibid.*, questions 3039–3040, p. 160.

23   *Ibid.*, question 3042, p. 160.

24   James Joseph Hayes, born March 1854, Cork, Ireland; died 13 April 1892, West Melbourne.

25   Evidence of Michael Ward, Royal Commission, questions 3121–3122, p. 163.

26   *Victorian Government Gazette*, 3 May 1878, p. 963.

27   Visit of the 1881 Royal Commission on the Police Force in Victoria to Mrs Kelly, 14 May 1881. 'The police commission', *Argus* (Melbourne), 16 May 1881, p. 6.

28   John Sadleir, born 26 May 1833, County Tipperary, Ireland; died 21 September 1919, at his home in Kooyong Road, Elsternwick.

29   Justin Corfield, *The Ned Kelly Encyclopaedia*, Lothian Books, 2003, p. 420.

30   'Death of Mr John Sadleir', *Australasian* (Melbourne), 27 September 1919, p. 40.

31   Sadleir, *Recollections*, pp. 105–106.

32   Kenneally, *Complete Inner History*, p. 51.

33   *Ibid.*

34   Corfield, *Ned Kelly Encyclopaedia*, p. 424.

35   *Victoria Police Gazette*, 2 December 1873.

36   Evidence of John Sadleir, Royal Commission, question 1742, p. 106.

37   Henry Pewtress, born 1827, Huntingdon, England; died 6 May 1915, Carlton, Melbourne.

38   Sadleir, *Recollections*, p. 184.

39   'Lost in the bush', *Courier* (Ballarat), 25 September 1878, p. 4.

40   T.N. McIntyre, 'A True Narrative of the Kelly Gang', unpublished manuscript, *c.* 1902, Victoria Police Museum.

41   Information supplied by Michael Kennedy's great-grandson Leo Kennedy.

42   On the ship *Reliance* in March 1850.

43   Information supplied by Leo Kennedy.

44 'Victorian police murderers', *Sydney Morning Herald*, 12 November 1878, p. 7.
45 Robert Haldane, *The people's force: a history of the Victoria Police*, Melbourne University Press, 1995, pp. 82, 87.
46 Evidence of Michael Ward, Royal Commission, questions 3115–3117, p. 163.
47 *Ibid.*, question 3109, p. 162.
48 *Ibid.*, question 3125, p. 162.
49 'The Greta shooting case', *Ovens and Murray Advertiser*, 10 October 1878, p. 4.
50 Ellen Kelly: No. 3520, Central Register of Female Prisoners, VPRS 516/P0002/7, Public Record Office Victoria, p. 197.
51 Kelly, 'The Jerilderie Letter', p. 23.
52 III – Causes of the Outbreak, 'Second Progress Report of the Royal Commission of Enquiry into the Circumstances of the Kelly Outbreak', p. x.
53 William Williamson to Inspector Green, 29 October 1878, Appendix 13: Miscellaneous, Royal Commission, p. 702.
54 'Bushranging in Victoria', *Kerang Times and Swan Hill Gazette*, 1 November 1878, p. 4.
55 *Ovens and Murray Advertiser*, 30 October 1880, p. 4.
56 Evidence of Police Magistrate Alfred Wyatt, Royal Commission, question 2275, p. 131.
57 *Ibid.*, question 2327, p. 133.
58 William Williamson to Inspector Green, 29 October 1878, Appendix 13: Miscellaneous, Royal Commission, p. 702.
59 *Ibid.*, p. 701.
60 Margret Byrne, née White, born 1834, Galway, Ireland; died 21 May 1921, Albury, New South Wales.
61 William Williamson to Inspector Green, 29 October 1878, Appendix 13: Miscellaneous, Royal Commission, p. 702.
62 Ned Kelly to Governor of Victoria, 10 November 1880, Condemned Cell Correspondence, Record 11, Item 4, Unit 2, Consignment P0, VPRS 4966, Public Record Office Victoria.
63 'Stephen Hart's boyhood', *Mercury* (Hobart), 16 July 1880, p. 3.
64 *Ibid.*
65 Rachel Hart, born 1870, Wangaratta; died 13 September 1958, Henty, New South Wales.
66 Jones, *Ned Kelly*, p. 104.
67 Hart, Stephen: No. 14823, Central Register of Male Prisoners, VPRS 515, P0001, Public Record Office Victoria, p. 106.
68 Evidence of A.L.M. Steele, Royal Commission, question 9133, p. 331.
69 *Ibid.*, questions 3111–3114, p. 331.
70 Evidence of John Sadleir, *Ibid.*, question 1742, p. 106.
71 Edward Batten Shoebridge (1827–1907).
72 Hugh Thom (1847–1920).
73 Cornelius Ryan (1838–1899).
74 Ned Kelly to Governor of Victoria, 10 November 1880, Condemned Cell Correspondence, Record 11, Item 4, Unit 2, Consignment P0, VPRS 4966, Public Record Office Victoria.
75 Kelly, 'The Jerilderie Letter', p. 26.
76 John McQuilton, *The Kelly Outbreak 1878–1880*, Melbourne University Press, 1987, p. 99, citing James to Sadleir, 24 June 1898, Sadleir Papers, La Trobe Library, Melbourne.
77 *Ibid.*
78 'The Kellys', *Week* (Brisbane), 4 December 1880, p. 18.
79 Sadleir, *Recollections*, p. 193.

80 'The Kelly haunts', *Argus* (Melbourne), 13 November 1880, p. 9.

81 McIntyre, 'A True Narrative of the Kelly Gang'.

82 'The Baumgarten cases', *Ovens and Murray Advertiser*, 30 May 1878, p. 2.

83 Thomas Newman McIntyre, born 24 May 1846, Downpatrick, County Down, Ireland; died Ballarat, 13 September 1918.

84 Kenneally, *Complete Inner History*, p. 52.

Chapter 4

1 Sir Graham Berry, born 28 August 1822, Twickenham, England; died 25 January 1904, St Kilda, Melbourne.

2 Sadleir, *Recollections*, pp. 179–180.

3 IV – The Wombat Murders, 'Second Progress Report of the Royal Commission of Enquiry into the Circumstances of the Kelly Outbreak', p. xi.

4 McIntyre, 'A True Narrative of the Kelly Gang'.

5 John Kelly, born 1837, Loughtane, County Limerick; died 6 March 1905, at his home, 35 Havelock St, St Kilda, Melbourne.

6 Evidence of C.H. Nicolson, Royal Commission, question 436, p. 19.

7 Leo Kennedy interviewed by author.

8 McIntyre, 'A True Narrative of the Kelly Gang'.

9 Evidence of John Kelly, Royal Commission, question 7978, p. 299.

10 Rev. Samuel Sandiford, born 1845, Cork, Ireland; died 1 May 1926, Ashfield, Sydney.

11 Evidence of John Sadleir, Royal Commission, question 1742, p. 106.

12 McIntyre, 'A True Narrative of the Kelly Gang'.

13 *Kilmore Free Press*, 7 November 1878, p. 2.

14 McIntyre, 'A True Narrative of the Kelly Gang'.

15 Née Charlotte (Maria) Siggins (1852–1891).

16 Emily, ten; Catherine (Ann), seven; Ernest (Henry), five; and Violet Jane, two.

17 Evidence of Captain F.C. Standish, Royal Commission, question 6, p. 1.

18 *Ibid.*

19 *Kilmore Free Press*, 7 November 1878, p. 2.

20 *Australasian Sketcher with Pen and Pencil* (Melbourne), 23 November 1878, p. 135.

21 McIntyre, 'A True Narrative of the Kelly Gang'.

22 Archibald McKenzie to Sub-inspector Pewtress, 6 December 1878, Victoria Police Museum.

23 Kelly, 'The Jerilderie Letter', p. 28.

24 Jones, *Ned Kelly*, p. 132.

25 McIntyre, 'A True Narrative of the Kelly Gang'.

26 *Ibid.*

27 *Ibid.*

28 Evidence of J.H. Graves, MLA, Royal Commission, questions 15518–15523, p. 564.

29 Kelly, 'The Jerilderie Letter', p. 24.

30 McIntyre, 'A True Narrative of the Kelly Gang'.

31 Kelly, 'The Jerilderie Letter', p. 25.

32 Evidence of Stanhope O'Connor, Royal Commission, question 11432, p. 405.

33 On 20 February 1878.

34 *Brisbane Courier*, 20 December 1880, p. 3.

35 'Cooktown', *Week* (Brisbane), 13 April 1878, p. 17.

36 Kelly, 'The Jerilderie Letter', p. 25.

37 *Ibid.*

38   Ned Kelly, Euroa letter, Record 1, Item 3, Unit 1, Consignment P0, VPRS 4966, Public Record Office Victoria, p. 10.

39   McIntyre, 'A True Narrative of the Kelly Gang'.

40   'Constable McIntyre's evidence', *Evening News* (Sydney), 7 August 1880, p. 5.

41   *Ibid.*

42   McIntyre, 'A True Narrative of the Kelly Gang'.

43   'The bushranging tragedy', *Australasian Sketcher with Pen and Pencil* (Melbourne), 23 November 1878, p. 129.

44   McIntyre, 'A True Narrative of the Kelly Gang'.

45   *Ibid.*

46   Ned Kelly, Euroa letter, Record 1, Item 3, Unit 1, Consignment P0, VPRS 4966, Public Record Office Victoria, p. 11.

47   McIntyre, 'A True Narrative of the Kelly Gang'.

48   'Constable McIntyre's evidence', *Evening News* (Sydney), 7 August 1880, p. 5.

49   McIntyre, 'A True Narrative of the Kelly Gang'.

50   *Ibid.*

51   'The Kelly Gang', *Argus* (Melbourne), 9 August 1880, p. 6.

52   McIntyre, 'A True Narrative of the Kelly Gang'.

53   George Wilson Hall, born 1836, Brighton, England; died 21 September 1916, Melbourne.

54   'Sergeant Kennedy's last moments', *Argus* (Melbourne), 13 December 1878, p. 5.

55   George Wilson Hall, *The Kelly Gang, or, The Outlaws of the Wombat Ranges,* Australian History Promotions, 2004 (a reprint of the first book ever published on Ned Kelly in 1879), p. 54.

56   *Ibid.*

57   Kenneally, *Complete Inner History*, p. 63.

58   Wilson Hall, *The Kelly Gang*, p. 54.

Chapter 5

1   'How Constable McIntyre escaped', *Tribune* (Hobart), 11 November 1878, p. 3.

2   The horse was found some months later about 16 kilometres closer to Greta.

3   Charles Henry Chomley, *The True Story of the Kelly Gang of Bushrangers*, Fraser & Jenkinson, 1920, pp. 11–12.

4   McIntyre, 'A True Narrative of the Kelly Gang'.

5   *Ibid.*

6   The knife was later discovered at the Mansfield morgue. Wilson Hall, *The Kelly Gang*, p. 54.

7   Ned Kelly, Euroa letter, Record 1, Item 3, Unit 1, Consignment P0, VPRS 4966, Public Record Office Victoria, p. 11.

8   McIntyre, 'A True Narrative of the Kelly Gang'.

9   He was still wearing them when killed at Glenrowan 20 months later.

10   Sadleir, *Recollections*, p. 193.

11   Kelly, 'The Jerilderie Letter', p. 37.

12   Sadleir, *Recollections*, p. 193.

13   *Ibid.*

14   'A noted police officer', *Leader* (Melbourne), 8 May 1915, p. 40.

15   Sadleir, *Recollections*, p. 186.

16   Chomley, *True Story of the Kelly Gang*, p. 13.

17   Thomas Meehan, born 1853, County Cork, Ireland; died 11 June 1920, Sunbury, Victoria.

18   Evidence of Thomas Meehan, Royal Commission, question 17647, pp. 667–668.

19 *Ibid.*, question 17649, p. 668.
20 *Victoria Police Gazette*, 30 December 1885, p. 368.
21 McIntyre, 'A True Narrative of the Kelly Gang'.
22 Evidence of John Kelly, Royal Commission, question 7978, p. 299.
23 *Ibid.*
24 Appendix 7: District Strength and Distribution, North-Eastern District, from July 1878 to June 1880, Royal Commission, p. 697.
25 Sadleir, *Recollections*, p. 186.
26 *Ibid.*
27 McIntyre, 'A True Narrative of the Kelly Gang'.
28 Thomas Hewitt Kirkham, born 4 January 1856, Sydney; died 15 July 1911, 23 Spring Street, Prahran, Melbourne.
29 James Allwood, born 3 March 1855, Warrnambool, Victoria; died 22 June 1924, Rutherglen, Victoria.
30 Chomley, *True Story of the Kelly Gang*, p. 6.
31 Edward William Monk (1844–1928).
32 McIntyre, 'A True Narrative of the Kelly Gang'.
33 Chomley, *True Story of the Kelly Gang*, p. 14.
34 Joan Gillison, *Colonial Doctor and his Town*, Cypress Books, 1974, p. 71.
35 McIntyre, 'A True Narrative of the Kelly Gang'.
36 *Ibid.*
37 Kenneally, *Complete Inner History*, p. 73.
38 Corfield, *Ned Kelly Encyclopaedia*, p. 465.
39 'The Mansfield tragedy', *Age*, 8 November 1878, p. 3.
40 Evidence of Michael Ward, Royal Commission, question 3149, p. 164.
41 'The Mansfield tragedy', *Age*, 8 November 1878, p. 3.
42 *Ibid.*
43 Constable Bracken telegram, 4 November 1878, Kelly Papers, Public Record Office Victoria.
44 Hugh Bracken, born 12 July 1840, Drumgague, County Fermanagh, Ireland; died 22 February 1900, Beveridge, Victoria.
45 Edward Coulson, born 1844, Newcastle upon Tyne; died 1936, Clifton Hill, Melbourne.
46 'The Mansfield tragedy', *Age*, 8 November 1878, p. 3.
47 'The police murders', *Argus* (Melbourne), 30 October 1878, p. 6.
48 McIntyre, 'A True Narrative of the Kelly Gang'.
49 'The police tragedy', *Geelong Advertiser*, 31 October 1878, p. 2.
50 Evidence of Thomas Meehan, Royal Commission, question 17651, p. 668.
51 *Ibid.*, question 17654, p. 668.
52 Sadleir, *Recollections*, p. 173.
53 'Trial of Kelly at Beechworth', *Age*, 9 August 1880, p. 3.
54 Item 23, Unit 1, VPRS 4969, Public Record Office Victoria.
55 'The police murders', *Argus* (Melbourne), 30 October 1878, p. 6.
56 'The police tragedy', *Geelong Advertiser*, 30 October 1878, p. 4.
57 John Lawrence Scanlon (1846–1880).
58 'The Mansfield murders', *Gippsland Times*, 6 November 1878, p. 3.
59 *Leader* (Melbourne), 2 November 1878, p. 16.
60 McIntyre, 'A True Narrative of the Kelly Gang'.
61 *Ibid.*
62 Sadleir, *Recollections*, p. 189.

Chapter 6

1   'Murder of constables', *Kerang Times and Swan Hill Gazette*, 8 November 1878, p. 4.

2   Gideon James Margery (1831–1895).

3   Evidence of C.H. Nicolson, Royal Commission, question 354, p. 15.

4   'The murders by bushrangers', *Star* (Ballarat), 4 November 1878, p. 3.

5   *Ibid.*

6   'The Mansfield outrage', *Camperdown Chronicle*, 5 November 1878, p. 3.

7   Born Niels Christian in Denmark, 1829.

8   'The Felons Apprehension Bill', *Argus* (Melbourne), 31 October 1878, p. 10.

9   *Ibid.*

10   'The Mansfield tragedy', *Age*, 8 November 1878, p. 3.

11   'Victorian police murderers', *Sydney Morning Herald*, 12 November 1878, p. 7.

12   Florence Cathcart, *Pictures on My Screen: Growing Up in Kelly Country*, Spectrum Publications, 1989, p. 25.

13   'Mrs. Kennedy's grief', *Herald* (Melbourne), 2 November 1878, p. 3.

14   Samuel Reynolds deposition, 1 November 1878, VPRS 4966: Kelly Historical Collection – Part 2: Crown Law Department: Unit 1: item 6, Public Record Office Victoria.

15   James Moorhouse, born 19 November 1826; died 9 April 1915.

16   Edith C. Rickards, *Bishop Moorhouse of Melbourne and Manchester*, John Murray, 1920, pp. 127–130.

17   'The Mansfield murders', *Gippsland Times*, 6 November 1878, p. 3.

18   *Ibid.*

19   'The Mansfield tragedy', *Age*, 2 November 1878, p. 5.

20   McIntyre, 'A True Narrative of the Kelly Gang'.

21   Rickards, *Bishop Moorhouse*, pp. 127–130.

22   *Ibid.*

23   On 14 March 1877.

24   Frank James (1838–1905).

25   Sadleir, *Recollections*, p. 170.

26   Evidence of John Kelly, Royal Commission, question 7983, p. 299.

27   *Ibid.*, 7986, p. 299.

28   Sadleir, *Recollections*, p. 194.

29   Henry Harkin (1834–1917). He joined the force in 1857.

30   'The police tragedy', *Geelong Advertiser*, 31 October 1878, p. 2.

31   Sadleir, *Recollections*, p. 194.

32   *Ibid.*

33   Hare, *Last of the Bushrangers*, p. 108.

34   Evidence of John Sadleir, Royal Commission, question 1865, p. 111.

35   Sadleir, *Recollections*, p. 195.

36   Frederick Alfred Winch, born 21 November 1827, Maidstone, Kent; died 25 December 1892, Hawthorn, Melbourne.

37   Appendix 13: Miscellaneous, Royal Commission, p. 702.

38   James Morton and Susanna Lobez, *Gangland Australia*, Victory Books, 2010, p. 352.

39   Winch to Standish, Item 34, Unit 1, Part 2, VPRS 4965, Public Record Office Victoria.

40   *Ibid.*, Item 155, Unit 3, VPRS 4695, Public Record Office Victoria.

41   *Ibid.*

42   Michael Woodyard; (Michael Robinson); (Albert Laxon): No. 15374, Central Register of Male Prisoners, VPRS 515, Public Record Office Victoria.

43   Hare, *Last of the Bushrangers*, p. 108.

44   Evidence of A.L.M. Steele, Royal Commission, question 8856, p. 321.
45   Hare, *Last of the Bushrangers*, p. 108.
46   Evidence of Michael Twomey, Royal Commission, question 17415, p. 656.
47   *Ibid.*
48   Evidence of Henry Laing, Royal Commission, question 13960, p. 508.
49   Evidence of A.L.M. Steele, *ibid.*, question 8856, p. 321.
50   Evidence of C.H. Nicolson, *ibid.*, question 412, p. 18.
51   'Victorian police murderers', *Sydney Morning Herald*, 12 November 1878, p. 7.
52   Hare, *Last of the Bushrangers*, p. 108.
53   'The police murders', *Argus* (Melbourne), 2 November 1878, p. 8.
54   McIntyre, 'A True Narrative of the Kelly Gang'.
55   'Murder of constables', *Kerang Times and Swan Hill Gazette*, 8 November 1878, p. 4.
56   Hare, *Last of the Bushrangers*, p. 136.

Chapter 7
1   Michael Twomey (1848–1923).
2   VII – Inspector Brook[e] Smith in Pursuit, 'Second Progress Report of the Royal
     Commission of Enquiry into the Circumstances of the Kelly Outbreak', p. xiii.
3   Evidence of A.L.M. Steele, Royal Commission, questions 8862–8865, p. 321.
4   Henry Handel Richardson, *The Fortunes of Richard Mahony*, William Heinemann, 1917.
5   Kelly, 'The Jerilderie Letter', p. 33.
6   James Joseph Hayes, born March 1854, Cork, Ireland; died 13 April 1892, West
     Melbourne.
7   Kelly, 'The Jerilderie Letter', pp. 23–24.
8   Evidence of Michael Twomey, Royal Commission, question 17418, p. 656.
9   *Ibid.*, question 17443, p. 657.
10   VII – Inspector Brook[e] Smith in Pursuit, 'Second Progress Report of the Royal
     Commission of Enquiry into the Circumstances of the Kelly Outbreak', p. xii.
11   Evidence of Brooke Smith, Royal Commission, question 17363, p. 655.
12   Evidence of Charles Johnston, *ibid.*, question 12509, p. 448.
13   Evidence of Brooke Smith, *ibid.*, question 17583, p. 662.
14   VII – Inspector Brook[e] Smith in Pursuit, 'Second Progress Report of the Royal
     Commission of Enquiry into the Circumstances of the Kelly Outbreak', p. xiii.
15   Charles Johnston, born 1840, Edenreagh, County Tyrone, Ireland; died 3 June 1936,
     Ballarat.
16   Hare, *Last of the Bushrangers*, p. 179.
17   Evidence of Charles Johnston, Royal Commission, question 12362, p. 444.
18   *Ibid.*, question 12365, p. 444.
19   James Brien (1829–1919).
20   Evidence of Brooke Smith, Royal Commission, question 17578, p. 662.
21   Evidence of Charles Johnston, *ibid.*, question 12412, p. 446.
22   Evidence of C.H. Nicolson, *ibid.*, question 16894, p. 629.
23   Gary Dean and Dagmar Balcarek, 'Maggie Kelly', Ned Kelly's World (members.iinet.net.
     au/~gdean1).
24   Sadleir, *Recollections*, p. 195.
25   'History of the Kelly family', *Age*, 13 November 1878, p. 3.
26   *Ibid.*, p. 196.
27   Robert Vincent Keating (1852–1918).
28   Evidence of F.C. Standish, Royal Commission, question 11, p. 2.

29   'The police murders', *Argus* (Melbourne), 8 November 1878, p. 6.

30   Evidence of C.H. Nicolson, Royal Commission, question 403, p. 17.

31   Sadleir, *Recollections*, p. 197.

32   *Ibid.*

33   'The police murders', *Argus* (Melbourne), 8 November 1878, p. 6.

34   *Ibid.*

35   Chomley, *True Story of the Kelly Gang*, p. 48.

36   *Ibid.*

37   Catherine Byrne, born 1860, Sebastopol, Victoria; died 1934.

38   Evidence of John Sadleir, Royal Commission, question 1801, p. 109.

39   Chomley, *True Story of the Kelly Gang*, p. 49.

40   Evidence of C.H. Nicolson, Royal Commission, question 407, p. 18.

41   *Ibid.*, question 16896, p. 631.

42   Chomley, *True Story of the Kelly Gang*, p. 52. Nicolson called him Jimmy in his Royal Commission evidence.

43   Evidence of C.H. Nicolson, Royal Commission, question 16899, p. 631.

44   Evidence of John Sadleir, *ibid.*, questions 1875–1880, p. 112.

45   *Ibid.*

46   *Ibid.*

47   *Ibid.*

48   Sadleir, *Recollections*, p. 199.

49   Chomley, *True Story of the Kelly Gang*, p. 52.

50   Evidence of C.H. Nicolson, Royal Commission, question 16899, p. 632.

51   Evidence of Captain F.C. Standish, *ibid.*, question 16233, p. 591.

52   Chomley, *True Story of the Kelly Gang*, p. 54.

53   Evidence of C.H. Nicolson, Royal Commission, question 440, p. 19.

54   Sadleir, *Recollections*, p. 200.

55   Chomley, *True Story of the Kelly Gang*, p. 55.

56   'The police murders', *Herald*, 2 December 1878, p. 3.

57   Unit 364, Bundle 2, VPRS 937, Public Record Office Victoria.

58   VIII – Provisioning the Outlaws, 'Second Progress Report of the Royal Commission of Enquiry into the Circumstances of the Kelly Outbreak', p. xiii.

59   Sadleir, *Recollections*, p. 24.

60   Appendix 13: Miscellaneous, Royal Commission, p. 702.

Chapter 8

1   Edward Batten Shoebridge, born 21 May 1827, London; died 13 November 1907, Bright, Victoria.

2   VIII – Provisioning the Outlaws, 'Second Progress Report of the Royal Commission of Enquiry into the Circumstances of the Kelly Outbreak', p. xiii.

3   Evidence of Ernest Flood, Royal Commission, question 12655, p. 456.

4   VIII – Provisioning the Outlaws, 'Second Progress Report of the Royal Commission of Enquiry into the Circumstances of the Kelly Outbreak', p. xiii.

5   Evidence of John Sadleir, Royal Commission, question 1890, p. 112.

6   *Ibid.*, question 1915, p. 113.

7   VIII – Provisioning the Outlaws, 'Second Progress Report of the Royal Commission of Enquiry into the Circumstances of the Kelly Outbreak', p. xiii.

8   Appendix 13: Miscellaneous, Royal Commission, p. 702.

9   Chomley, *True Story of the Kelly Gang*, p. 58.

10 Evidence of John Sadleir, Royal Commission, question 1893, p. 112.

11 Chomley, *True Story of the Kelly Gang*, p. 56.

12 Appendix 13: Miscellaneous, Royal Commission, p. 701.

13 *Ibid.*, p. 702.

14 *Ibid.*

15 Evidence of John Sadleir, Royal Commission, question 2058, p. 120.

16 'Kelly, the outlaw, bushranger, and murderer', *Sydney Mail and New South Wales Advertiser*, 9 November 1878, p. 732.

17 Isaac Younghusband (1833–1892).

18 Andrew Lyell (1836–1897).

19 Donald Cameron (1841–1888).

20 *Australasian* (Melbourne), 16 November 1878, p. 2.

21 *West Australian* (Perth), 13 August 1888, p. 3.

22 'The Mansfield murderers', *Argus* (Melbourne), 18 December 1878, p. 6.

23 Ned Kelly, Euroa letter, Record 1, Item 3, Unit 1, Consignment P0, VPRS 4966, Public Record Office Victoria, p. 16.

24 Evidence of J.H. Graves, MLA, Royal Commission, question 15545, p. 566.

25 Evidence of Police Magistrate Alfred Wyatt, *ibid.*, question 2246, p. 130.

26 Telegram, Euroa Bank robbery, Record 1, Item 60, Unit 1, Consignment P0, VPRS 4969, Public Record Office Victoria.

27 'Re-appearance of the bushrangers', *Argus* (Melbourne), 12 December 1878, p. 5.

28 *Ibid.*

29 *Ibid.*

30 William McCauley, born 1846. He could still recall the Kelly raid in vivid detail while living on an irrigation block at Nanneella, Victoria, in 1923. His name is often reported as Macaulay.

31 'Re-appearance of the bushrangers', *Argus* (Melbourne), 12 December 1878, p. 5.

32 'Kelly Gang at Euroa', *Argus* (Melbourne), 20 February 1923, p. 7.

33 'The Kelly Gang at Euroa', *Argus* (Melbourne), 13 December 1878, p. 5.

34 Sadleir, *Recollections*, p. 203.

35 James Gloster (1838–1907).

36 'The Kelly investigation', *Ovens and Murray Advertiser*, 10 August 1880, p. 3.

37 'The Kelly Gang', *Bendigo Advertiser*, 13 December 1878, p. 2.

38 'Re-appearance of the bushrangers', *Argus* (Melbourne), 12 December 1878, p. 5.

39 *Ibid.*

40 'The bushrangers', *Argus* (Melbourne), 14 December 1878, p. 8.

41 *Courier* (Ballarat), 14 December 1878, p. 4.

42 'Kelly Gang at Euroa', *Argus* (Melbourne), 20 February 1923, p. 7.

43 'Re-appearance of the bushrangers', *Argus* (Melbourne), 12 December 1878, p. 5.

44 'The Kelly outrages', *Brisbane Courier*, 19 December 1878, p. 3.

45 John Carson (1856–1918).

46 'Kelly incidents retold', *Bendigo Independent*, 8 March 1918, p. 6.

47 Robert MacDougall (1855–1940). Born near Adelaide, he spoke with a strong Scottish accent.

48 Glenn Wahlert and Russell Linwood, *One Shot Kills: A History of Australian Army Sniping*, Big Sky Publishing, 2014, p. 6.

49 Cormick, *Ned Kelly: Under the Microscope*, CSIRO Publishing, 2014, p. 146.

50 William Henry Bradly, born 1855, Richmond, Victoria; died 9 September 1924, Caulfield.

51 Robert David Booth (1859–1929).
52 Frances Mary Shaw (1863–1939).
53 'The raid on the Euroa Bank', *Evening News* (Sydney), 14 December 1878, p. 5.
54 Robert Scott, born 20 December 1833, St Vigeans, Forfarshire; died 10 February 1884, Kew, Melbourne.
55 Susannah Anne Scott, née Calvert, born 28 November 1846, Montrose, Angus, Scotland; died 3 June 1926, Karrakatta, Perth.
56 Chomley, *True Story of the Kelly Gang*, p. 77.
57 Anne Calvert, née Brown, born 13 March 1815, Montrose, Angus, Scotland; died 26 July 1892, Rochester, Victoria.
58 Max Brown, *Ned Kelly: Australian Son*, p. 79.
59 Hare, *Last of the Bushrangers*, pp. 127–128.
60 Susy Scott, *The Kelly Gang at Euroa*, State Library of NSW, A 4143.
61 'The bushrangers', *Argus* (Melbourne), 14 December 1878, p. 8.
62 'The Kelly Gang at Euroa', *Argus* (Melbourne), 13 December 1878, p. 5.
63 'The raid on the Euroa Bank', *Evening News* (Sydney), 14 December 1878, p. 5.
64 Chomley, *True Story of the Kelly Gang*, p. 78.
65 Evidence of Police Magistrate Alfred Wyatt, Royal Commission, question 2363, p. 135.
66 *Ibid.*, question 2137, p. 123.
67 *Age*, 13 December 1878, p. 3.
68 Booth's daughter Alexa Snellgrove eventually donated both items to the archives of the National Australia Bank.
69 'Witness in bushranger's trial', *Camperdown Chronicle*, 7 April 1927, p. 6.
70 'Description of the outlaws', *Weekly Times* (Melbourne), 14 December 1878, p. 16. The watch was later given to the police.
71 'The Kelly Gang', *Argus* (Melbourne), 10 August 1880, p. 7.
72 'Re-appearance of the bushrangers', *Argus* (Melbourne), 12 December 1878, p. 5.
73 'The raid on the Euroa Bank', *Evening News* (Sydney), 14 December 1878, p. 5.
74 *Ibid.*
75 'Statements of Robert McDougall [sic] and Henry Smith Dudley', *Advocate* (Melbourne), 14 December 1878, p. 14.
76 Sadleir, *Recollections*, p. 197.

Chapter 9
1   Evidence of Captain F.C. Standish, Royal Commission, question 28, p. 3.
2   Evidence of C.H. Nicolson, *ibid.*, question 553, p. 24.
3   *Ibid.*, question 548, p. 23.
4   *Age*, 16 December 1878, p. 3.
5   Kelly Historical Collection – Part 1, VPRS 4965/P0000, 351, Public Record Office Victoria.
6   Evidence of C.H. Nicolson, Royal Commission, question 551, p. 23.
7   *Ibid.*
8   Sadleir, *Recollections*, p. 206.
9   Evidence of C.H. Nicolson, Royal Commission, question 584, p. 24.
10 Evidence of Captain F.C. Standish, question 41, p. 3.
11 *Ibid.*, question 25, p. 2.
12 *Ibid.*, questions 15–16, p. 2.
13 *Ibid.*, question 43, p. 3.
14 Evidence of Francis A. Hare, *ibid.*, question 16321, p. 597.

15 'The Kelly outrages at Euroa', *Illustrated Australian News* (Melbourne), 27 December 1878, p. 219.

16 'The raid on the Euroa Bank', *Evening News* (Sydney), 14 December 1878, p. 5.

17 *Express and Telegraph* (Adelaide), 13 December 1878, p. 2.

18 'Re-appearance of the bushrangers', *Argus* (Melbourne), 12 December 1878, p. 5.

19 'The bushrangers', *Australasian* (Melbourne), 14 December 1878, p. 20.

20 *Age*, 16 December 1878, p. 3.

21 Appendix 7: District Strength and Distribution, North-Eastern District, from July 1878 to June 1880, Royal Commission, p. 697.

22 *Ibid.*

23 'The bushrangers', *Argus* (Melbourne), 14 December 1878, p. 8.

24 Evidence of Captain F.C. Standish, Royal Commission, question 47, p. 4.

25 'The bushrangers', *Argus* (Melbourne), 14 December 1878, p. 8.

26 Evidence of C.H. Nicolson, Royal Commission, question 17196, p. 648.

27 Evidence of Francis A. Hare, *ibid.*, question 16460, p. 603.

28 'Country news', *Australasian*, 4 January 1879, p. 15.

29 'The Kelly Gang', *Mount Alexander Mail*, 21 December 1878, p. 2.

30 'The bushrangers', *Argus* (Melbourne), 14 December 1878, p. 8.

31 *Ovens and Murray Advertiser*, 18 January 1879, p. 4.

32 'The Mansfield murderers', *Argus* (Melbourne), 16 December 1878, p. 6.

33 *Ibid.*

34 Report by Senior Constable James Gill, Kelly Historical Collection, Part 1 Police Branch 256, 161/79, Public Record Office Victoria.

35 Frank Clune, 'The life of Ned Kelly', *Truth* (Brisbane), 14 November 1954, p. 22.

36 *Ibid.*

37 *Age*, 16 December 1878, p. 3.

38 Evidence of Francis A. Hare, Royal Commission, questions 1369–1372, p. 74.

39 *Ibid.*

40 *Ibid.*, question 1581, p. 92.

41 Sadleir, *Recollections*, p. 206–7.

42 Chomley, *True Story of the Kelly Gang*, p. 89.

43 Evidence of F.C. Standish, Royal Commission, question 11, p. 2.

44 Evidence of Francis A. Hare, *ibid.*, questions 1266–1269, p. 63.

45 Evidence of John Sadleir, *ibid.*, question 2065, p. 120.

46 *Ibid.*, question 2029, p. 118.

47 Evidence of Francis A. Hare, *ibid.*, question 1269, p. 63.

48 Beechworth Record of the Court of Petty Sessions, Burke Museum, quoted in McQuilton, *The Kelly Outbreak*, p. 114.

49 Evidence of Francis A. Hare, Royal Commission, question 1522, p. 90.

50 *Riverine Herald* (Echuca), 13 June 1879, p. 3.

51 'The Accident at the Academy', *Herald*, 23 January 1879, p. 3.

52 'History of the Kelly family', *Age*, 13 November 1878, p. 3.

53 Evidence of Francis A. Hare, Royal Commission, question 1270, p. 63.

54 Evidence of M.E. Ward, *ibid.*, question 13847, p. 500.

55 *Ibid.*

56 Hare, *Last of the Bushrangers*, p. 140.

57 Evidence of Francis A. Hare, Royal Commission, question 1270, p. 63.

58 'The bushrangers', *Riverine Herald*, 12 February 1879, p. 2.

59 'The Kelly raid on Jerilderie', *Jerilderie Herald and Urana Advertiser*, 25 July 1913, p. 1.

60　'The outlaws at Jerilderie', *ibid.*, 1 August 1913, p. 1.

61　Mary Devine (1844–1932).

62　George Denis Devine (1847–1926).

63　'Dream that came true', *Daily News* (Perth), 20 May 1926, p. 1.

64　*Ibid.*

65　'The outlaws at Jerilderie', *Jerilderie Herald and Urana Advertiser*, 1 August 1913, p. 1.

66　*Ibid.*, 18 July 1913, p. 1. The Woolshed Inn was sometimes also called the Woolpack Inn.

67　'The Kelly raid on Jerilderie', *Jerilderie Herald and Urana Advertiser*, 25 July 1913, p. 1.

68　*Ibid.*

69　*Ibid.*, 1 August 1913, p. 1.

70　*Ibid.*

71　*Ibid., 8 August* 1913, p. 1

72　*Ibid.*, 1 August 1913, p. 1.

Chapter 10

1　*Ibid.*, 8 August 1913, p. 1.

2　'Dream that came true', *Daily News* (Perth), 20 May 1926, p. 1.

3　'The bushrangers', *Riverine Herald*, 12 February 1879, p. 2.

4　'The Kelly raid on Jerilderie', *Jerilderie Herald and Urana Advertiser*, 8 August 1913, p. 1.

5　*Ibid.*

6　Harc, *Last of the Bushrangers*, p. 5.

7　'The Kelly Gang in New South Wales', *Queanbeyan Age*, 15 February 1879, p. 2.

8　*Ibid.*

9　*Ibid.*

10　'The Kelly raid on Jerilderie', *Jerilderie Herald and Urana Advertiser*, 8 August 1913, p. 1.

11　*Ibid.*, 15 August 1913, p. 1.

12　*Ibid.*, 22 August 1913, p. 1.

13　Kelly, 'The Jerilderie Letter', p. 31.

14　*Ibid.*, pp. 29–30.

15　*Herald*, 18 February 1879.

16　'Dream that came true', *Daily News* (Perth), 20 May 1926, p. 1.

17　'The Kelly raid on Jerilderie', *Jerilderie Herald and Urana Advertiser*, 15 August 1913, p. 1.

18　*Ibid.*

19　*Ibid.*, 29 August 1913, p. 1.

20　Sadleir, *Recollections*, p. 208.

21　'The Jerilderie Bank robbery', *Sydney Mail and New South Wales Advertiser*, 10 July 1880, p. 65.

22　Edwin Richard Living, born 1856, Castlemaine; died 1936, at his home, 'Wareena', in Swan Street, Wangaratta.

23　James Thomson Mackie, born 1861, St Kilda, Melbourne; died 24 January 1942, Jerilderie Hospital.

24　William Elliott, born 30 June 1851, County Fermanagh, Ireland; died 13 February 1934, Jerilderie.

25　John Brown Gribble, born 1 September 1847, Redruth, Cornwall, England; died 1893, Sydney.

26　'The Kelly raid on Jerilderie', *Jerilderie Herald and Urana Advertiser*, 29 August 1913, p. 1.

27　*Ibid.*, 5 September 1913, p. 1.

28　Samuel Gill (1849–1928).

29　'The Kelly raid on Jerilderie', *Jerilderie Herald and Urana Advertiser*, 12 September 1913, p. 1.

30   James Denny Rankin, born 1834, Craignish, Argyllshire, Scotland; died 7 April 1896, Jerilderie, from peritonitis.

31   Hugh Duffin Harkin, born 1842; died 1928, Elsternwick, Melbourne.

32   'The Kelly raid on Jerilderie', *Jerilderie Herald and Urana Advertiser*, 12 September 1913, p. 1.

33   'The Kelly Gang at Jerilderie', *Argus* (Melbourne), 12 February 1879, p. 6.

34   *Weekly Times* (Melbourne), 22 February 1879, p. 14.

35   'The Kelly raid on Jerilderie', *Jerilderie Herald and Urana Advertiser*, 26 September 1913, p. 1.

36   Henry H. Neary, *The Kellys*, C. Merritt, 1930, p. 29.

37   'The Kelly raid on Jerilderie', *Jerilderie Herald and Urana Advertiser*, 19 December 1913, p. 1.

38   'The Kelly Gang', *Burrowa News*, 21 February 1879, p. 3.

39   Henry Betteley Jefferson (1856–1926).

40   'The Kelly raid on Jerilderie', *Jerilderie Herald and Urana Advertiser*, 26 September 1913, p. 1.

41   'The Kelly Gang at Jerilderie', *Argus* (Melbourne), 12 February 1879, p. 6.

42   Thomas McDougall, born 6 August 1832, Windsor, New South Wales; buried 20 March 1903 after death at Jerilderie Hospital.

43   Later known as the Albion Hotel. *Jerilderie Herald*, 25 October 1912, p. 2.

44   'Gribble, John Brown (1847–1893)', *Australian Dictionary of Biography*, National Centre of Biography, Australian National University, https://adb.anu.edu.au/biography/gribble-john-brown-3668/text5727, published first in hardcopy 1972.

45   'The Kelly raid on Jerilderie', *Jerilderie Herald and Urana Advertiser*, 7 November 1913, p. 1.

46   'The Kelly Gang in New South Wales,' *Queanbeyan Age*, 15 February 1879, p. 2.

47   'The Kelly Gang of bushrangers', *Advertiser* (Adelaide), 19 August 1911, p. 23.

48   'The Kelly raid on Jerilderie', *Jerilderie Herald and Urana Advertiser*, 10 October 1913, p. 1.

49   *Ibid.*, 17 October 1913, p. 4.

50   *Ibid.*, 24 October 1913, p. 1.

51   *Ibid.*, 28 November 1913, p.1.

52   *Ibid.*, 14 November 1913, p. 1.

53   *Ibid.*

54   *Ibid.*, 21 November 1913, p. 1.

55   *Ibid.*, 31 October 1913, p. 1.

56   *Ibid.*, 7 November 1913, p. 1.

57   *Ibid.*, 21 November 1913, p. 1.

58   'The Kelly Gang', *Gippsland Times*, 19 February 1879, p. 3.

59   Kelly Historical Collection, Item 11, Unit 1, Consignment P0, VPRS 4967, Public Record Office Victoria.

60   *Ibid.*

61   *Ibid.*

62   *Ibid.*, item 14.

63   *Ibid.*

64   *Ibid.*

65   'The unemployed', *Toowoomba Chronicle and Queensland Advertiser*, 15 September 1866, p. 4.

Chapter 11

1   Archibald Meston (1851–1924).

2   Mike Colman and Ken Edwards, *Eddie Gilbert: The True Story of an Aboriginal Cricketing Legend*, ABC Books, 2002, p. 6.

3   'The Queensland Native Police', *Herald*, 13 March 1879, p. 3.

4   *Ibid.*

5   'A new way with the northern blacks', *Queenslander*, 15 February 1879, p. 208.

6   'General epitome', *Week* (Brisbane), 8 March 1879, p. 15.

7   *Brisbane Courier*, 19 February 1879, p. 2.

8   'A battle among the blacks at Cooktown', *Morning Bulletin* (Rockhampton), 24 February 1879, p. 2.

9   *Ibid.*

10 Kelly's original letter was returned to Living and remained in private hands until it was donated to Victoria's State Library in 2000.

11 'The Kelly raid on Jerilderie', *Jerilderie Herald and Urana Advertiser*, 31 October 1913, p. 1.

12 *Ibid.*, 2 January 1914, p. 1.

13 The letter, with grammar and spelling corrected and with the reference to the calf's testicles deleted, was included in *The Kellys Are Out* by J.M.S. Davies, which was serialised in the Adelaide newspaper *Register News-Pictorial* in September and October 1930.

14 Corfield, *Ned Kelly Encyclopedia*, p. 320.

15 Captain Standish and Superintendent Hare in Charge of the Pursuit, 'Second Progress Report of the Royal Commission of Enquiry into the Circumstances of the Kelly Outbreak', p. xv.

16 'Sydney echoes', *Newcastle Morning Herald and Miners' Advocate*, 15 March 1879, p. 2.

17 Evidence of Stanhope O'Connor, Royal Commission, questions 11451–11452, p. 406.

18 Louise Mary Farewell Smith, born 1859, Melbourne; died 18 June 1930 at her home in Tennyson Street, St Kilda.

19 John Thomas Smith, born 28 May 1816, Sydney; died 30 January 1879, Flemington, Melbourne.

20 Jill Eastwood, 'Smith, John Thomas (1816–1879)', *Australian Dictionary of Biography*, National Centre of Biography, Australian National University, https://adb.anu.edu.au/biography/smith-john-thomas-4609/text7583, published first in hardcopy 1976.

21 *Morning Bulletin* (Rockhampton), 27 February 1879, p. 2.

22 Kelly Historical Collection, Item 14, Unit 1, Consignment P0, VPRS 4965, Public Record Office Victoria.

23 Thomas Orpen Irvine King, born 13 August 1851, Kerry, Ireland; died 28 January 1917, Fraser Island, Queensland.

24 *Telegraph* (Brisbane), 18 March 1879, p. 3.

25 Noble & McBride v State of Vic & State of Qld, In the Court of Appeal Supreme Court of Queensland, Appeal No 9023 of 1997.

26 Evidence of S. O'Connor, Royal Commission, question 11995, p. 427.

27 Georgia Moodie, 'Coming to terms with the brutal history of Queensland's Native Mounted Police', abc.net.au, 24 Jul 2019.

28 Noble & McBride v State of Vic & State of Qld, In the Court of Appeal Supreme Court of Queensland, Appeal No 9023 of 1997.

29 'Maryborough', *Telegraph*, (Brisbane), 26 March 1879, p. 3.

30 'Christmas festivities by Queensland black troopers', *Evening News* (Sydney), 12 January 1881, p. 4.

31 Evidence of S. O'Connor, Royal Commission, question 11994, p. 427.

32 *Ibid.*, question 11988, p. 426.

33 *Ibid.*, question 11982, *ibid.*

34 *Maryborough Chronicle, Wide Bay and Burnett Advertiser*, 30 January 1917, p. 5.

35 *Brisbane Courier*, 13 March 1879, p. 3.

36 *Ibid.*
37 Evidence of S. O'Connor, Royal Commission, question 11993, p. 426.
38 'The Kelly Gang', *Bendigo Advertiser*, 5 March 1879, p. 2.
39 'Destruction of the Kelly Gang', *Argus* (Melbourne), 2 July 1880, p. 7.
40 *Argus* (Melbourne), 30 June 1880, p. 6.
41 'The Mansfield murderers', *Geelong Advertiser*, 12 March 1879, p. 3.
42 'Black trackers for the border', *Evening News* (Sydney), 4 March 1879, p. 2.
43 *Brisbane Courier*, 3 March 1879, p. 2.
44 *Maryborough Chronicle, Wide Bay and Burnett Advertiser*, 1 March 1879, p. 2.
45 'Sydney echoes', *Newcastle Morning Herald and Miners' Advocate*, 15 March 1879, p. 2.
46 'Queensland', *Sydney Morning Herald*, 6 March 1879, p. 5.
47 *Telegraph*, 6 March 1879, p. 2.
48 Raymond Evans, Kay Saunders and Kathryn Cronin, *Race Relations In Colonial Queensland*, Australia and New Zealand Book Company, 1975, p. 63.
49 George William Rusden, *History of Australia*, Chapman and Hall, 1883, p. 246.
50 Evidence of Stanhope O'Connor, Royal Commission, question 1073, p. 49.
51 Memo, Police Department, Superintendent's Office, Benalla 25-3-79, Item 142, Unit 3, Consignment P2, VPRS 4965, Public Record Office Victoria.
52 'The Mansfield murderers', *Geelong Advertiser*, 12 March 1879, p. 3.
53 *Ibid.*

Chapter 12

1 Detective report, 17 September 1879, Kelly Papers, Public Record Office Victoria.
2 Hare, *Last of the Bushrangers*, p. 231.
3 *Ibid.*, p. 159.
4 *Ibid.*, p. 161.
5 *Ibid.*, p. 168.
6 Joseph Ladd Mayes, born 20 January 1833, Headford, Ireland; died 11 July 1902, at his home, 'Toronto', in Union Street, Brighton, Melbourne.
7 Hare, *Last of the Bushrangers*, p. 168.
8 Item 74, Unit 2, VPRS 4969, Public Record Office Victoria.
9 Evidence of S. O'Connor, Royal Commission, questions 11791–11792, p. 417.
10 Evidence of John Sadleir, *ibid.*, question 2040, p. 119.
11 Sadleir, *Recollections*, p. 214.
12 Evidence of John Sadleir, Royal Commission, question 2039, p. 119.
13 Sadleir, *Recollections*, p. 211.
14 Evidence of S. O'Connor, Royal Commission, question 1078, p. 49.
15 'Death of a black tracker', *Evening News* (Sydney), 27 March 1879, p. 3.
16 *Morning Bulletin* (Rockhampton), 2 April 1879, p. 2.
17 Item 130, Unit 2, Consignment P0, VPRS 4965, Public Record Office Victoria.
18 *Ibid.*
19 Evidence of W.B. Montford, Royal Commission, question 11026, p. 394.
20 Evidence of S. O'Connor, *ibid.*, question 11506, p. 408.
21 'Fighting in Australia, forty years' happenings. William Maher's reminiscences', *Australasian* (Melbourne), 19 December 1908, p. 16.
22 'The Hicken and Foley prize fight', *Tribune* (Hobart), 29 March 1879, p. 3.
23 O'Connor to Seymour, 29 March 1879, Royal Commission, p. 451.
24 Sadleir, *Recollections* p. 171.
25 *Ibid.*, pp. 215–216.

26   Daniel Barry, born 1 August 1855, County Kerry, Ireland; died 20 June 1939, District Hospital Alexandria, Victoria.

27   Evidence of Daniel Barry, Royal Commission, question 7300, p. 281.

28   Evidence of S. O'Connor, *ibid.*, question 1096, p. 50.

29   Thomas Lawless, born 1853, County Kilkenny, Ireland; died 27 August 1886, Prince Alfred Hospital, Melbourne.

30   Alfred John Falkiner, born 13 October 1854, Eltham, Melbourne; died 17 December 1921, Dandenong, Victoria.

31   Hare, *Last of the Bushrangers*, p. 180.

32   *Ibid.*, p. 217.

33   *Ibid.*, p. 181.

34   Patrick Byrne, born 1862, Chiltern; buried 15 July 1922, Albury Cemetery.

35   Hare, *Last of the Bushrangers*, p. 140.

36   Evidence of F.A. Hare, Royal Commission, question 1281, p. 65.

37   *Ibid.*, question 1282, p. 65.

38   Hare, *Last of the Bushrangers*, pp. 191–192.

39   Standish to Attorney General O'Loghlen, 9 January 1879, Kelly Papers, Public Record Office Victoria.

40   James Wallace, born 1854, Collingwood, Melbourne; died 20 November 1910, Perth, Western Australia.

41   Item 74, Unit 2, VPRS 4969, Public Record Office Victoria.

42   Hare, *Last of the Bushrangers*, p. 209.

43   Luke Mills, born 1836, County Clare, Ireland; died 21 December 1892, at his home at the Melbourne Police Depot.

44   Evidence of F.A. Hare, Royal Commission, question 1284, p. 66.

45   *Ibid.*

46   *Ibid.*

47   Hare, *Last of the Bushrangers*, p. 187.

Chapter 13

1   *Ibid.*, p. 227.

2   Evidence of John Sadleir, Royal Commission, question 11898, p. 422; Kelson & McQuilton, *Kelly Country*, University of Queensland Press, 2001. p. 56. The horses were eventually returned to New South Wales.

3   Evidence of F.C. Standish, Royal Commission, question 312, p. 13.

4   Evidence of S. O'Connor, *ibid.*, question 1091. p. 50.

5   Evidence of F.C. Standish, *ibid.*, question 318, p. 13.

6   Evidence of S. O'Connor, *ibid.*, question 1092, p. 50.

7   Evidence of F.C. Standish, *ibid.*, question 316, p. 13.

8   Evidence of S. O'Connor, *ibid.*, question 1104, p. 51.

9   Hare, *Last of the Bushrangers*, p. 210.

10   William Canny, born 12 June 1854, County Clare, Ireland; died 26 July 1935, at his home in Johnston St, Collingwood, Melbourne.

11   Hare, *Last of the Bushrangers*, p. 224.

12   *Ibid.*

13   Evidence of S. O'Connor, Royal Commission, question 1099, p. 51.

14   *Ibid.*

15   Hare, *Last of the Bushrangers*, p. 205.

16 Private Correspondence Between Mr O'Connor and His Government, Royal Commission, p. 451.

17 *Gympie Times and Mary River Mining Gazette*, 21 June 1879, p. 3.

18 'The fatal occurrence at Greta', *Ovens and Murray Advertiser*, 1 May 1879, p. 3.

19 'A fatal freak', *Adelaide Observer*, 17 May 1879, p. 19.

20 'Committal of Lloyd for manslaughter', *Ovens and Murray Advertiser*, 3 May 1879, p. 5.

21 *Ibid.*

22 *Ibid.*

23 *Ibid.*

24 'A fatal freak', *Adelaide Observer*, 17 May 1879, p. 19.

25 'The execution of Thomas Hogan, the fratricide', *Ovens and Murray Advertiser*, 10 June 1879, p. 3.

26 Joe Byrne to Aaron Sherritt, asking him to join the Kelly Gang, Record 14, Item 18, Unit 1, Consignment P0, VPRS 4969, Public Record Office Victoria.

27 'The Kelly Gang', *Geelong Advertiser*, 23 July 1879, p. 3.

28 *Ovens and Murray Advertiser*, 29 July 1879, p. 2.

29 Patrick (Charles) Gascoigne, born 1854, Beechworth; died 27 September 1927, Wangaratta.

30 Evidence of Charles Gascoigne, Royal Commission, questions 9628 and 9652, p. 348.

31 Sergeant Whelan to Sadleir, 8 October 1879, Kelly Papers, Public Record Office Victoria.

32 'The Kelly Gang', *Herald*, 4 June 1879, p. 3.

33 Evidence of F.C. Standish, Royal Commission, question 321, p. 14.

34 In November 1879.

35 Evidence of S. O'Connor, Royal Commission, question 322, p. 14.

36 *Maryborough Chronicle, Wide Bay and Burnett Advertiser*, 1 May 1879, p. 2.

37 Hare, *Last of the Bushrangers*, p. 210–11.

38 *Ibid.*, p. 212.

39 Evidence of Charles Gascoigne, Royal Commission, question 9614, p. 347.

40 Hare, *Last of the Bushrangers*, p. 216.

41 Evidence of A.J. Falkiner, Royal Commission, question 5234, p. 216.

42 Hare, *Last of the Bushrangers*, p. 219.

43 John Bellis, born 1850, Liverpool, England; died 12 April 1893, Yarrawonga, Victoria.

44 Hare, *Last of the Bushrangers*, p. 220.

45 *Ibid.*, p. 224–5.

46 Evidence of S. O'Connor, Royal Commission, question 1106, p. 51.

47 Hare, *Last of the Bushrangers*, p. 226.

Chapter 14

1 Evidence of Captain F.C. Standish, Royal Commission, question 16164, p. 588.

2 Evidence of S. O'Connor, *ibid.*, question 1105, p. 51.

3 *Ibid.*, question 1092, p. 50.

4 *Ibid.*

5 *Ovens and Murray Advertiser*, 23 October 1879, p. 2.

6 *Gympie Times and Mary River Mining Gazette*, 21 June 1879, p. 3.

7 *Mackay Mercury and South Kennedy Advertiser*, 21 May 1879, p. 3.

8 Evidence of Captain F.C. Standish, Royal Commission, question 57, p. 4.

9 *Herald*, 18 July 1879, p. 3.

10 Evidence of C.H. Nicolson, Royal Commission, question 16901, pp. 622–623.

11 Evidence of Captain F.C. Standish, *ibid.*, question 52, p. 4.

12 The robbers were Samuel Lowe and Christopher Bray.

13 'The Kelly Gang supposed to have re-appeared', *Herald*, 15 August 1879, p. 3.

14 Evidence of A.J. Falkiner, Royal Commission, question 5240, p. 216.

15 Evidence of James Whelan, *ibid.*, question 6494, p. 251.

16 Evidence of F.A. Hare, *ibid.*, question 1594, p. 94.

17 *Ibid.*

18 *Ibid.*

19 O'Connor to Seymour, 22 August 1879, Royal Commission, pp. 451–452.

20 Item 244, Unit 5, Consignment P2, VPRS 4965, Public Record Office Victoria.

21 *Ibid.*, Item 249.

22 *Ibid.*

23 Bundle 1, Unit 368, VPRS 937, Public Record Office Victoria.

24 *Age*, 21 August 1879, p. 3.

25 XI – The Queensland Trackers, 'Second Progress Report of the Royal Commission of Enquiry into the Circumstances of the Kelly Outbreak'.

26 *Ibid.*

27 Evidence of C.H. Nicolson, Royal Commission, question 1024, p. 47.

28 'Breaking up of the Kelly Gang', *South Bourke and Mornington Journal* (Melbourne), 30 June 1880, p. 3.

29 *Gympie Times and Mary River Mining Gazette*, 21 June 1879, p. 3.

30 *Ibid.*

31 Evidence of Francis A. Hare, Royal Commission, question 1544, p. 91.

32 James Watson Rosier, born 22 December 1834, Langham, Suffolk; died 30 June 1920, South Yarra, Melbourne.

33 It was later moved to Bourke Street.

34 collections.museumvictoria.com.au.

35 Kenneally, *The Complete Inner History*, p. 161.

36 Evidence of John Kelly, Royal Commission, question 8461, p. 310.

37 *Star* (Ballarat), 7 October 1874, p. 2. Laurence O'Brien was thrown from a horse in 1874 after riding back from an Oxley Shire Council meeting.

38 Corfield, *Ned Kelly Encyclopaedia*, p. 104.

39 Ward to Nicolson re alleged assistance by Chinese towards the outlaws, 1 September 1879, Record 1, Item 75, Unit 5, Consignment P0, VPRS 4965, Public Record Office Victoria.

40 Evidence of A.J. Falkiner, Royal Commission, question 5331, p. 220.

41 Item 393, Unit 5, VPRS 4965, Public Record Office Victoria.

42 Evidence of Mrs Sherritt senior, Royal Commission, questions 13166–13170, p. 475.

43 XI – The Queensland Trackers, 'Second Progress Report of the Royal Commission of Enquiry into the Circumstances of the Kelly Outbreak', p. xvii.

44 Appendix 5: Reported Appearances of the Kelly Outlaws, Royal Commission, p. 694.

45 *Ibid.*, p. 693.

46 *Ibid.*

47 Steve Meacham, 'Childhood sweetheart Ned's secret love', smh.com.au, 3 March 2012.

48 Catherine 'Kate' Lloyd, born 1863; died 1934, Shepparton, Victoria.

49 Evidence of M.E. Ward, Royal Commission, question 13854, p. 501.

50 Appendix 5: Reported Appearances of the Kelly Outlaws, *ibid.*, p. 694.

51 *Ibid.*, p. 693.

52 Evidence of M.E. Ward, Royal Commission, question 15624, p. 569.

53 Sadleir, *Recollections*, p. 191.

54 'The Wantabadgery bushrangers', *Sydney Morning Herald*, 21 November 1879, p. 5.

55 Jeff Sparrow, 'A queer bushranger: The tale of Captain Moonlite', *The Monthly*, November 2015.

56 *New South Wales Police Gazette*, 21 January 1880.

57 Evidence of H. Armstrong, Royal Commission, question 12167, p. 435.

58 Unit 169, VPRS 937, Public Record Office Victoria.

59 'Family Notices', *Argus*, 18 February 1880, p. 1.

60 Evidence of Mrs Sherritt junior, Royal Commission, question 13291, p. 479.

61 'Moyhu Races', *Ovens and Murray Advertiser*, 9 March 1880, p. 3.

62 *Avoca Mail*, 19 March 1880, p. 3.

63 Daniel Keith Kennedy, born 1843, Seymour, Victoria; died 8 February 1921; buried Williamstown Cemetery, Melbourne.

64 Appendix 5: Reported Appearances of the Kelly Outlaws, Royal Commission, p. 694.

65 R.D. Blackmore, *Lorna Doone*, Sampson, Low, Son & Marston, 1869, p. 35.

66 Statement of Constable Phillips tendered by Superintendent Hare, Royal Commission, p. 674.

67 Ward and Constable Considine to Inspector Secretan, 22 December 1881, Kelly Papers, Public Record Office Victoria.

68 Evidence of F.A. Hare, Royal Commission, question 1597, p. 95.

69 Item 22, Unit 1, VPRS 4969, Public Record Office Victoria.

70 Appendix 5: Reported Appearances of the Kelly Outlaws, Royal Commission, p. 694.

71 Evidence of John Sadleir, Royal Commission, question 2979, p. 158.

72 Item 51, Unit 1, VPRS 4969, Public Record Office Victoria.

73 Evidence of H. Armstrong, Royal Commission, questions 12184–12187, p. 435.

74 'Arrest of Mrs Byrne and her son', *Newcastle Morning Herald and Miners' Advocate*, 6 December 1880, p. 2.

75 Jones, *Ned Kelly*, p. 217.

76 Evidence of H. Armstrong, Royal Commission, question 12214, p. 437.

77 Evidence of Mrs Sherritt senior, *ibid.*, question 13179, p. 476.

78 *Ibid.*, question 13184, p. 476.

79 *Ibid.*

Chapter 15

1 'The warning by Mr Curnow', *Age*, 29 June 1880, p. 3.

2 Evidence of C.H. Nicolson, Royal Commission, question 753, p. 33.

3 *Ibid.*, question 751, p. 33.

4 Robert Graham, born 10 June 1844, Victoria; died 11 September 1931; buried Box Hill Cemetery, Melbourne.

5 Evidence of C.H. Nicolson, Royal Commission, question 755, p. 33.

6 Montfort to Inspector Secretan, 8 July 1880; Mead to Secretan, 31 May 1881. Kelly Papers, Public Record Office Victoria; *Argus* (Melbourne), 26 November 1880.

7 Ashmead, 'The Thorns and the Briars', pp. 42–43.

8 'Unveiling the monument to the police at Mansfield', *Illustrated Australian News* (Melbourne), 8 May 1880, p. 74.

9 'The murdered police memorial', *Leader*, 24 April 1880, p. 22.

10 'Unveiling the monument to the police at Mansfield', *Illustrated Australian News* (Melbourne), 8 May 1880, p. 74.

11 'The Kelly Gang', *Camperdown Chronicle*, 27 April 1880, p. 3.

12 Appendix 5: Reported Appearances of the Kelly Outlaws, Royal Commission, p. 695.

13 *Ibid.*

14 Evidence of C.H. Nicolson, Royal Commission, question 755, p. 33.

15 Evidence of S. O'Connor, *ibid.*, question 1104, p. 51.

16 Evidence of C.H. Nicolson, *ibid.*, question 16903, p. 634.

17 Robert Ramsay (1842–1882).

18 Evidence of C.H. Nicolson, Royal Commission, question 933, p. 42.

19 *Ibid.*, question 16903, p. 634.

20 XII – Mr Nicolson Resumes Charge of the Pursuit, 'Second Progress Report of the Royal Commission of Enquiry into the Circumstances of the Kelly Outbreak', p. xxi.

21 Evidence of C.H. Nicolson, Royal Commission, question 773, p. 34.

22 Appendix 3: Superintendent Hare's Report, Royal Commission, p. 685.

23 Item 5, Unit 2, VPRS 4967, Public Record Office Victoria.

24 O'Connor to Seymour, 2 June 1880, Royal Commission, p. 452.

25 Evidence of John Sherritt, *ibid.*, question 15115, p. 548.

26 Evidence of M.E. Ward, *ibid.*, questions 13860–13861, pp. 503–504.

27 'Mr William Canny', *Age*, 5 August 1935, p. 8.

28 Evidence of Alf Falkiner, Royal Commission, question 5484, p. 224.

29 *Ibid.*

30 Hare, *Last of the Bushrangers*, p. 235.

31 Evidence of Mrs Sherritt senior, Royal Commission, question 13182, p. 476.

32 *Victoria Police Gazette*, 30 June 1880, p. 171.

33 Evidence of Francis A. Hare, Royal Commission, question 1615, p. 99.

34 Evidence of S. O'Connor, *ibid.*, question 1111, p. 52–3.

35 O'Connor to Graham Berry, 7 September 1880, Royal Commission, p. 683.

36 Appendix 3: Superintendent Hare's Report, Royal Commission, p. 685.

37 Sadleir, *Recollections*, p. 222.

38 *Ibid.*

39 XV – Glenrowan, 'Second Progress Report of the Royal Commission of Enquiry into the Circumstances of the Kelly Outbreak'.

40 Ned Kelly, Euroa letter, Record 1, Item 3, Unit 1, Consignment P0, VPRS 4966, Public Record Office Victoria, p. 17.

41 *Ibid.*

42 'The last outbreak of the outlaws', *Ovens and Murray Advertiser*, 29 June 1880, p. 2. Other estimates put the weight of the powder at 45 pounds. *Argus* (Melbourne), 3 July 1880, p. 5.

43 *Australasian Sketcher with Pen and Pencil* (Melbourne), 17 July 1880, p. 166.

44 *Ibid.*

45 Kelly, 'The Jerilderie Letter', p. 24.

46 'Capture of the Kelly Gang', *Kilmore Free Press*, 1 July 1880, p. 2.

47 *Australian Pictorial Weekly*, 10 July 1880, p. 33.

48 'The tragedy at Sebastopol', *Age*, 1 July 1880, p. 3.

49 Evidence of Mrs Sherritt junior, Royal Commission, question 13290, p. 479.

50 William Duross (1852–1887).

51 Evidence of H. Armstrong, Royal Commission, question 12223, p. 438.

52 Anton Wick, born 1826, Germany; died 18 March 1893, Beechworth Hospital.

53 On 22 September 1873, Byrne was fined 20 shillings plus costs.

54 Kenneally, *Complete Inner History*, p. 191.

55 'The murder of Aaron Sherritt', *Age*, 1 July 1880, p. 3.

56 *Ibid.*

57 Evidence of William Duross, Royal Commission, question 3657, p. 180.

58   *Ibid.*, question 3679, p. 181.
59   'Another Kelly outrage: cold-blooded murder', *Argus* (Melbourne), 28 June 1880, p. 5.
60   'The murder of Aaron Sherritt', *Age*, 1 July 1880, p. 3.

Chapter 16
1   Evidence of James Reardon, Royal Commission, questions 7736–7740, p. 280.
2   *Ibid.*, questions 7770–7772, p. 281.
3   Ann Jones, née Kennedy, born 1830, Newport, County Tipperary, Ireland; died 7 October 1910; buried Wangaratta Cemetery.
4   John Sarsfield Stanistreet, born 1827, Cork, Ireland; died 30 November 1896, Bendigo.
5   Ned Kelly to Governor of Victoria, 5 November 1880, Condemned Cell Correspondence, Record 11, Item 4, Unit 2, Consignment P0, VPRS 4966, Public Record Office Victoria.
6   XV – Glenrowan, 'Second Progress Report of the Royal Commission of Enquiry into the Circumstances of the Kelly Outbreak'.
7   'The six little demons', *Bendigo Advertiser*, 3 July 1880, p. 2.
8   Ned Kelly to Governor of Victoria, 5 November 1880, Condemned Cell Correspondence, Record 11, Item 4, Unit 2, Consignment P0, VPRS 4966, Public Record Office Victoria.
9   *Ovens and Murray Advertiser*, 23 September 1879, p. 3.
10   Ann's maiden name was Kennedy and she might even have been a distant cousin.
11   *Herald*, 25 November 1880.
12   Mrs Jones compensation case, 18 November 1881, File 83/27754, Unit 3, VPRS 4966, Public Record Office Victoria.
13   Evidence of James Reardon, Royal Commission, question 7740, p. 280.
14   'Compensation to Mrs Jones, of Glenrowan', *Argus* (Melbourne), 5 December 1881, p. 10.
15   Mrs Jones compensation case, 18 November 1881, File 83/27754, Unit 3, VPRS 4966, Public Record Office Victoria.
16   'Destruction of the Kelly Gang', *Argus* (Melbourne), 29 June 1880, p. 5.
17   James Reardon, born 1833; died 1902, Glenrowan.
18   Evidence of James Reardon, Royal Commission, question 7607, p. 276.
19   'Australian bushranging', *Lithgow Mercury*, 5 January 1904, p. 4.
20   'The murder of Aaron Sherritt', *Age*, 1 July 1880, p. 3.
21   The 1881 Royal Commission on the Police Force of Victoria found that the four constables were guilty of 'disobedience of orders and gross cowardice' ('Second Progress Report of the Royal Commission of Enquiry into the Circumstances of the Kelly Outbreak', p. vi). One had already resigned and the commission recommended that the other three be dismissed.
22   XIV – Superintendent Hare Supersedes Mr Nicolson, 'Second Progress Report of the Royal Commission into the Circumstances of the Kelly Outbreak', p. xxiv.
23   Mrs Jones compensation case, 18 November 1881, File 83/27754, Unit 3, VPRS 4966, Public Record Office Victoria.
24   'Destruction of the Kelly Gang', *Argus* (Melbourne), 30 June 1880, p. 6.
25   Mrs Jones compensation case, 18 November 1881, File 83/27754, Unit 3, VPRS 4966, Public Record Office Victoria.
26   Greta Watch-house log book, 1870–1882, Victoria Police Museum.
27   Evidence of Francis A. Hare, Royal Commission, question 1477, p. 81.
28   Thomas Curnow (1855–1922).

29   Evidence of Thomas Curnow, Royal Commission, question 17597, p. 664.

30   *Ibid.*, question 17635, p. 667.

31   *Ibid.*, question 17597, p. 664.

32   Evidence of Francis A. Hare, Royal Commission, question 1501, p. 84.

33   Evidence of A.L.M. Steele, *ibid.*, question 8995, p. 326.

34   Evidence of Mrs M. Reardon, *ibid.*, question 10542, p. 378.

35   Fifteen-year-old Tom Cameron, to his brother, Mrs Jones compensation case,
      18 November 1881, File 83/27754, Unit 3, VPRS 4966, Public Record Office Victoria.

36   Evidence of Thomas Curnow, Royal Commission, question 17597, p. 664.

37   *Ibid.*

38   Evidence of Captain F.C. Standish, *ibid.*, question 77, p. 6.

39   Evidence of Thomas Curnow, *ibid.*, question 17597, p. 664.

40   *Ibid.*, p. 665.

41   *Ibid.*, p. 664.

42   *Ibid.*, p. 665.

43   Letter of Captain Standish to Sub-Inspector O'Connor, Royal Commission, p. 684.

44   Thomas Prout Webb (1845–1916).

45   Evidence of S. O'Connor, Royal Commission, question 1114, p. 53.

46   James Murdoch Arthur, born 26 March 1854, Port Fairy, Belfast; died 16 May 1924, Port
      Melbourne.

47   Mrs Jones compensation case, 18 November 1881, File 83/27754, Unit 3, VPRS 4966,
      Public Record Office Victoria.

48   Evidence of James Reardon, Royal Commission, question 7769, p. 280.

49   *Ibid.*, question 7764, p. 280.

50   Evidence of Thomas Curnow, Royal Commission, question 17597, p. 665.

51   *Ibid.*

52   *Ibid.*

53   *Daily Telegraph* (Melbourne), 29 June 1880.

54   'Destruction of the Kelly Gang', *Argus* (Melbourne), 21 July 1880, p. 6.

55   John McWhirter (Melbourne *Age*), George Allen (Melbourne *Daily Telegraph*), Joe
      Melvin (Melbourne *Argus*) and Thomas Carrington (Melbourne *Australasian Sketcher
      with Pen and Pencil*).

56   *Daily Telegraph* (Melbourne), 29 June 1880.

57   'Destruction of the Kelly Gang', *Argus* (Melbourne), 29 June 1880, p. 5.

58   Appendix 3: Superintendent Hare's Report, Royal Commission, p. 685.

59   Mrs Jones compensation case, 18 November 1881, File 83/27754, Unit 3, VPRS 4966,
      Public Record Office Victoria.

60   'Destruction of the Kelly Gang', *Argus* (Melbourne), 30 June 1880, p. 6.

61   'Trial of Mrs Ann Jones, of Glenrowan', *Ovens and Murray Advertiser*, 27 November 1880,
      p. 1.

62   Mrs Jones compensation case, 18 November 1881, File 83/27754, Unit 3, VPRS 4966,
      Public Record Office Victoria.

63   'Trial of Mrs Ann Jones, of Glenrowan', *Ovens and Murray Advertiser*, 27 November 1880,
      p. 1.

64   Evidence of James Reardon, Royal Commission, question 7615, p. 277.

65   'Destruction of the Kelly Gang', *Argus* (Melbourne), 30 June 1880, p. 6.

66   *Ibid.*

67   *Argus* (Melbourne), 1 July 1880, p. 6.

68   Evidence of James Reardon, Royal Commission, question 7761, p. 280.
69   *Daily Telegraph* (Melbourne), 29 June 1880.
70   Evidence of Mrs M. Reardon, Royal Commission, question 10551, p. 379.
71   'Catching the Kellys', *Argus* (Melbourne), 5 July 1880, p. 6.
72   'The Destruction Of The Kelly Gang', *Ovens and Murray Advertiser* (Beechworth), 24 July 1880, p. 6.

Chapter 17
1   Evidence of Charles Gascoigne, Royal Commission, question 9674, p. 349.
2   Evidence of Francis A. Hare, *ibid.*, question 16317, p. 595.
3   Evidence of Daniel Barry, *ibid.*, question 7380, p. 284.
4   Evidence of Francis A. Hare, *ibid.*, question 1506, p. 87.
5   Evidence of William Duross, *ibid.*, question 4145, p. 191.
6   Appendix 3: Superintendent Hare's Report, Royal Commission, p. 687.
7   Evidence of S. O'Connor, Royal Commission, question 1201, p. 58.
8   'Destruction of the Kelly Gang', *Argus* (Melbourne), 30 June 1880, p. 6.
9   'The fight at Glenrowan and annihilation of the gang', *Herald* (Fremantle), 24 July 1880, p. 1.
10 'Arrival of Ned Kelly in Melbourne', *Age*, 29 June 1880, p. 3.
11 Declaration of Constable Phillips, Royal Commission, p. 674.
12 Evidence of James Arthur, *ibid.*, question 11191, p. 399.
13 'Ned Kelly', Culture Victoria, cv.vic.gov.au.
14 McQuilton, *The Kelly Outbreak*, p. 166.
15 Evidence of Mrs M. Reardon, Royal Commission, question 10590, p. 379.
16 Evidence of Daniel Barry, *ibid.*, questions 7378–7379, p. 284.
17 *Ibid.*
18 Evidence of Charles Gascoigne, *ibid.*, question 9677, p. 350.
19 Evidence of James Reardon, *ibid.*, questions 7701–7702, p. 279.
20 'Inquest on young Jones', *Ovens and Murray Advertiser*, 1 July 1880, p. 2.
21 Appendix 3: Superintendent Hare's Report, Royal Commission.
22 Detective report, Eason to Sadleir, 26 July 1880, Kelly Papers, Public Record Office Victoria. There would be claims that Metcalf was accidentally shot by Ned Kelly before the battle began.
23 'Martin Cherry, the platelayer', *Sydney Mail and New South Wales Advertiser*, 3 July 1880, p. 22.
24 'Another Glenrowan victim', *Kerang Times and Swan Hill Gazette*, 22 October 1880, p. 4.
25 Francis Thomas Dean (Tom) Carrington, born 17 November 1843, London; died 9 October 1918, Toorak, Melbourne.
26 Evidence of Francis A. Hare, Royal Commission, question 1509, p. 87.
27 Declaration of Constable Phillips, *ibid.*, p. 674.
28 Evidence of A.L.M Steele, *ibid.*, question 8998, p. 326.
29 Evidence of John Kelly, *ibid.*, questions 8163–8174, p. 303.
30 Various estimates number his supporters outside Glenrowan anywhere from 30 to 150 men.
31 Evidence of Charles Gascoigne, Royal Commission, question 9678, p. 350.
32 Evidence of Mrs M. Reardon, Royal Commission, questions 10616–10636, pp. 380–381.
33 Evidence of James Arthur, *ibid.*, question 11126, p. 397.
34 Ibid.
35 Evidence of James Arthur, *ibid.*, question 11127, p. 397.

36   Evidence of Mrs M. Reardon, *ibid.*, question 10668, p. 381.

37   *Australasian Sketcher with Pen and Pencil* (Melbourne), 17 July 1880, p. 166.

38   Evidence of S. O'Connor, Royal Commission, question 1142, p. 55.

39   Evidence of James Dwyer, *ibid.*, questions 9483–9487, p. 343.

40   Evidence of James Reardon, *ibid.*, question 7673, p. 278.

41   'Catching the Kellys', *Argus* (Melbourne), 5 July 1880, p. 6.

42   *Ibid.*

43   Evidence of A.L.M. Steele, Royal Commission, question 9034, p. 327.

Chapter 18

1   Evidence of John Sadleir, *ibid.*, questions 7484–7485, p. 286.

2   Evidence of James Arthur, *ibid.*, question 11183, p. 399.

3   Evidence of John McWhirter, *ibid.*, question 10345, p. 372.

4   'The Kelly Gang', *Mercury* (Hobart), 9 July 1880, p. 3.

5   XV – Glenrowan, 'Second Progress Report of the Royal Commission of Enquiry into the Circumstances of the Kelly Outbreak', p. xxvii. Constable Kelly later said he was misquoted, and that he actually said, 'He's bulletproof, boys!'

6   Evidence of A.L.M. Steele, Royal Commission, question 9034, p. 327.

7   'Destruction of the Kelly Gang', *Argus* (Melbourne), 29 June 1880, p. 5.

8   Evidence of James Arthur, Royal Commission, question 11188, p. 399.

9   'Catching the Kellys', *Argus* (Melbourne), 5 July 1880, p. 6.

10   John Montiford, born 1847, Kilkenny, Ireland; died 1910, Melbourne. In later life he changed his name to Montiford-O'Brien.

11   Evidence of James Arthur, Royal Commission, question 11162, p. 398.

12   'Sergeant Steele, The story of my fight with Ned Kelly', *Euroa Advertiser*, 21 January 1910, p. 2.

13   *Ibid.*

14   'Destruction of the Kelly Gang', *Argus* (Melbourne), 2 July 1880, p. 7.

15   Report, Constable Phillips to Sadleir, 2 July 1880, Kelly Papers, Public Record Office Victoria.

16   Brian W. Cookson, 'The battle of Glenrowan', *Sunday Times* (Perth), 19 April 1914, p. 2.

17   'The capture of the Kelly Gang', *Ovens and Murray Advertiser*, 24 July 1880, p. 8. The gun was loaded with cartridges too large for it and they had been cut to fit with a knife.

18   Evidence of A.L.M. Steele, Royal Commission, question 9034, p. 328.

19   *Ibid.*, question 9261, p. 335.

20   'The Glenrowan tragedy', *Geelong Advertiser*, 1 July 1880, p. 3.

21   Evidence of A.L.M. Steele, Royal Commission, question 9261, p. 335.

22   *Ibid.*, question 9261, p. 335.

23   Brian W. Cookson, 'The battle of Glenrowan', *Sunday Times* (Perth), 19 April 1914, p. 2.

24   *Ibid.*

25   Dowsett report to the Traffic Manager, Benalla, 2 July 1880, Railways Archives. *La Trobe Journal*, No. 11, April 1973, p. 61.

26   Evidence of George V. Allen, Royal Commission, question 10762, p. 384.

27   Evidence of Jesse Dowsett, *ibid.*, question 10934, p. 390.

28   Evidence of George V. Allen, *ibid.*, question 10762, p. 384.

29   Dowsett report to the Traffic Manager, Benalla, 2 July 1880, Railways Archives. *La Trobe Journal*, No. 11, April 1973, p. 61.

30   James Dwyer (1847–1912).

31   Evidence of C.C. Rawlins, Royal Commission, question 11754, p. 416.

32   Evidence of James Dwyer, *ibid.*, question 9467, p. 342.

33   Evidence of George V. Allen, *ibid.*, question 10762, p. 384.

34   Ned said he only had two shots left. 'The Glenrowan tragedy', *Geelong Advertiser*, 30 June 1880, p. 3.

35   'Destruction of the Kelly Gang', *Argus* (Melbourne), 2 July 1880, p. 7.

36   *Herald*, 29 July 1880.

37   Evidence of James Dwyer, Royal Commission, question 9539, p. 345.

38   John McWhirter, born 1851, Scotland; died 1917, Sydney.

39   Evidence of John McWhirter, Royal Commission, question 10386, p. 374.

40   *Age*, 29 June 1880, p. 2.

41   'Destruction of the Kelly Gang', *Argus* (Melbourne), 2 July 1880, p. 7.

42   'Catching the Kellys', *Argus* (Melbourne), 5 July 1880, p. 6.

43   Sadleir, *Recollections*, p. 238.

44   Evidence of John Sadleir, Royal Commission, question 2808, p. 150.

45   'Catching the Kellys', *Argus* (Melbourne), 5 July 1880, p. 6.

46   *Ibid.*

47   Joseph Talgarno Melvin, born 15 August 1852, Banff, Scotland; died 26 June 1909, Surrey Hills, Melbourne.

48   Matthew Gibney, born November 1835, Killeshandra, Cavan, Ireland; died 22 June 1925, North Perth.

49   Sir John Kirwan, *My Life's Adventure*, Hayes Barton Press, 1936, p. 130.

50   *Ibid.*

51   'The Rev. Father Gibney's statement', *Sydney Mail and New South Wales Advertiser*, 3 July 1880, p. 22.

52   'The fight at Glenrowan and annihilation of the gang', *Herald* (Fremantle), 24 July 1880, p. 1.

53   Evidence of George V. Allen, Royal Commission, question 10841, p. 387.

54   Evidence of James Dwyer, *ibid.*, question 9539, p. 345.

55   Evidence of John McWhirter, *ibid.*, questions 10405–10406, p. 374.

56   Evidence of Rev. M. Gibney, *ibid.*, question 12301, p. 441.

57   *Herald* (Melbourne), 9 July 1880.

58   Sadleir, *Recollections*, p. 237.

59   Evidence of Rev. M. Gibney, Royal Commission, question 12314, p. 442.

60   Evidence of James Dwyer, *ibid.*, question 9539, p. 345. Claims would emerge years later that Dan Kelly and Steve Hart escaped the blaze and that the two dead men were actually unknown swagmen who happened to be in Glenrowan that night. The testimony of Dwyer and Gibney, though, seems conclusive.

61   'Martin Cherry, the platelayer', *Sydney Mail and New South Wales Advertiser*, 3 July 1880, p. 22.

62   *Australasian Sketcher with Pen and Pencil* (Melbourne), 17 July 1880, p. 166.

63   *Ibid.*

64   'Ned Kelly interviewed', *Evening News* (Sydney), 29 June 1880, p. 2.

65   'Circular notes', *Ovens and Murray Advertiser*, 10 July 1880, p. 1.

66   'Ned Kelly interviewed', *Evening News* (Sydney), 29 June 1880, p. 2.

Chapter 19

1   Carolyn Webb, 'Old letter reveals fresh insight on Ned Kelly's fabled capture', age.com.au, 9 October 2013.

2   Evidence of John Sadleir, Royal Commission, question 2875, p. 153.

3   'Funeral of Aaron Sherritt', *Ovens and Murray Advertiser*, 29 June 1880, p. 2.

4   *Daily Telegraph* (Melbourne), 2 July 1880.

5   'The Kelly Gang', *Argus* (Melbourne), 3 July 1880, p. 5.

6   Oswald Thomas Madeley, born 24 October 1831, Derby, England; died 21 January 1913, Corindhap, Victoria.

7   'Circular notes', *Ovens and Murray Advertiser*, 10 July 1880, p. 1.

8   Evidence of C.H. Nicolson, Royal Commission, questions 886–888, p. 40.

9   Evidence of Captain F.C. Standish, *ibid.*, question 79, p. 7.

10   'Destruction of the Kelly Gang', *Argus* (Melbourne), 30 June 1880, p. 6.

11   Charles Snodgrass Ryan, born 20 September 1853, Longwood, Victoria; died 23 October 1926, Melbourne.

12   Ryan was in Rome when the war broke out and saw an advertisement of the Ottoman Government seeking 20 military surgeons.

13   'Destruction of the Kelly Gang', *Argus* (Melbourne), 30 June 1880, p. 6.

14   *Ibid.*

15   *Burrowa News*, 2 July 1880, p. 3.

16   'The Fate of Byrne', *Herald*, 29 June 1880, p. 3.

17   'Inquest on Byrne', *Weekly Times* (Melbourne), 3 July 1880, p. 2.

18   *Burrowa News*, 2 July 1880, p. 3.

19   'Ned Kelly's condition', *Weekly Times*, 3 July 1880, p. 22.

20   Andrew Shields (1839–1909).

21   'Embracery', *Ovens and Murray Advertiser*, 23 November 1878, p. 4.

22   *Hamilton Spectator*, 14 August 1880, p. 4.

23   Item 46, Unit 1, VPRS 4965, Public Record Office Victoria.

24   Item 50, *ibid.*

25   Hare to Mrs Emily Josephine Smith, Francis Hare Papers (2012.0001), University of Melbourne Archives, digitised-collections.unimelb.edu.au/handle/11343/21318.

26   'Latest police telegrams', *Herald*, 30 June 1880, p. 3.

27   'Threats against Curnow and others', *Weekly Times*, 3 July 1880, p. 21.

28   The Kelly tragedies', *Gippsland Times*, 2 July 1880, p. 3.

29   'Unfounded rumours', *Herald*, 30 June 1880, p. 3.

30   *Ibid.*, 1 July 1880.

31   'Circular notes', *Ovens and Murray Advertiser*, 10 July 1880, p. 1.

32   Evidence of S. O'Connor, Royal Commission, question 11864, p. 421.

33   *Brisbane Courier*, 20 July 1880, p. 5.

34   *Ibid.*

35   'Removal of Kelly to Beechworth', *Argus* (Melbourne), 2 August 1880, p. 6.

36   *Ibid.*

37   *Ibid.*

38   'Ned Kelly at Beechworth', *Weekly Times*, 7 August 1880, p. 20.

39   Evidence of A.J. Faulkiner [sic], Royal Commission, question 5498, p. 225.

40   'The trial of Ned Kelly', *Express and Telegraph* (Adelaide), 7 August 1880, p. 2.

41   David Gaunson, born 19 January 1846, Sydney; died 2 January 1909, Camberwell, Melbourne.

42   James Macpherson Grant (1822–1885).

43   'Trial of Kelly at Beechworth', *Age*, 7 August 1880, p. 5.

44   *Ovens and Murray Advertiser*, 7 August 1880, p. 4.

45   William Henry Foster, born 1832, Manchester, England; died 1894, Ballarat, Victoria.

46   Charles Alexander Smyth, born 1828, County Longford, Ireland; died 16 June 1908, Melbourne; buried St Kilda Cemetery, Melbourne.

47   'Trial of Kelly at Beechworth', *Age*, 9 August 1880, p. 3.

48   'Ned Kelly's trial', *Herald*, 9 August 1880, p. 3.

49   'Trial of Edward Kelly', *Border Watch* (Mount Gambier), 14 August 1880, p. 4.

50   'Ned Kelly', *Herald*, 12 August 1880, p. 3.

51   *Argus* (Melbourne), 13 August 1880, p. 4.

52   'Ned Kelly's arrival', *Herald*, 13 August 1880.

53   *Camperdown Chronicle*, 13 August 1880, p. 2.

54   *Age*, 14 August 1880, p. 5.

55   'The flogging missionaries', *Herald*, 28 August 1880, p. 2.

56   *Gippsland Times*, 18 August 1880, p. 2.

57   Arthur Wolfe Chomley, born 4 May 1837, Wicklow, Ireland; died 25 November 1914; buried St Kilda Cemetery, Melbourne.

58   *Bacchus Marsh Express*, 16 October 1880, p. 2.

59   Hickman Molesworth, born 23 February 1842, Dublin; died aboard the RMS *Omrah* between Melbourne and Sydney, 18 July 1907.

60   Henry Howard Massy Bindon, born 23 December 1844, Ireland; died 27 September 1893, at his home, 40 Great Davis Street, South Yarra, Melbourne.

61   *Sydney Morning Herald*, 22 September 1880, p. 3.

62   'Melbourne follies', *Bulletin*, 30 October 1880, p. 9.

63   *Ibid.*

64   'Melbourne follies', *Bulletin*, 30 October 1880, p. 9.

65   'The trial of Edward Kelly', *Bendigo Advertiser*, 29 October 1880, p. 2.

66   *Ibid.*, *Herald*, 29 October 1880.

67   'Trial and conviction of Edward Kelly: sentence of death', *Argus* (Melbourne), 30 October 1880, p. 8.

68   *Ovens and Murray Advertiser*, 30 October 1880, p. 5.

69   *Ibid.*

70   'Trial and conviction of Edward Kelly: sentence of death', *Argus* (Melbourne), 30 October 1880, p. 8.

71   *Ibid.*

72   *Ibid.*

73   *Ibid.*

74   'Trial of Edward Kelly', *Geelong Advertiser*, 30 October 1880, p. 3.

75   'The conviction of Edward Kelly', *Ovens and Murray Advertiser*, 2 November 1880, p. 4.

76   *Ibid.*

77   'Execution of Ned Kelly', *Launceston Examiner*, 12 November 1880, p. 3.

78   *Daily Telegraph* (Melbourne), 11 November 1880.

79   'Execution of Kelly', *Weekly Times* (Melbourne), 13 November 1880, p. 19.

80   *Maryborough Chronicle, Wide Bay and Burnett Advertiser* (Queensland), 13 November 1880, p. 2.

81   'The execution', *Australian Town and Country Journal* (Sydney), 13 November 1880, p. 14.

82   'The Kelly Gang', *Portland Guardian*, 13 November 1880, p. 2.

83   James Middleton, born 1847; died 8 February 1914, at his home on Royal Parade, Melbourne.

84   'The execution of Edward Kelly', *Herald*, 11 November 1880. This was the expression Kelly was said to have uttered when prison governor John Buckley Castieau told him his last appeal had failed (*Ovens and Murray Advertiser*, 13 November 1880, p. 4).

85   *Daily Telegraph* (Melbourne), 12 November 1880.

86   'The phrenological character of Edward Kelly', *Herald*, 18 November 1880, p. 2.

87   Maximilian Ludwig Kreitmayer, born 31 December 1830, Munich, Germany; died
      1 June 1906, Collingwood, Melbourne.
88   Oliver Milman, 'Skull thought to be Ned Kelly's ruled out as belonging to the
      bushranger', theguardian.com, 3 October 2014.
89   *Argus* (Melbourne), 23 November 1880, p. 7.
90   'The Kelly sympathisers', *Ovens and Murray Advertiser*, 25 November 1880, p. 2.
91   'Death of Mr Justice Barry', *Herald*, 23 November 1880, p. 3.

Chapter 20

1   Kelly Reward Board, 1880–1881, p. v, parliament.vic.gov.au.
2   Sadleir, *Recollections*, p. 240.
3   Evidence of John Sadleir, Royal Commission, question 16716, p. 617.
4   James Abraham Howlin Graves, born 14 December 1827, Maryborough, Queen's
      County, Ireland; died 23 November 1910, South Yarra, Melbourne.
5   'Destruction of the Kelly Gang', *Argus* (Melbourne), 30 June 1880, p. 6.
6   'The police commission', *Argus* (Melbourne), 16 May 1881, p. 6.
7   *Ibid.*
8   'Second Progress Report of the Royal Commission of Enquiry into the Circumstances
      of the Kelly Outbreak', p. iv.
9   'The Kelly enquiry', *Ovens and Murray Advertiser*, 14 April 1881, p. 2.
10   *Ibid.*
11   Kelly Reward Board, 1880–1881, Minutes of Evidence, p. 2, parliament.vic.gov.au.
12   *Ibid.*
13   'Second Progress Report of the Royal Commission of Enquiry into the Circumstances
      of the Kelly Outbreak', p. iv.
14   'The capture of power', *Age*, 6 February 1892, p. 1.
15   'Death of Mr Nicolson p.m.', *Argus* (Melbourne), 1 August 1898, p. 7.
16   *Argus* (Melbourne), 14 March 1882, p. 5.
17   Evidence of John Kelly, Royal Commission, question 8365, p. 308.
18   'The Kelly Gang from within', *Sun* (Sydney), 14 September 1911, p. 9.
19   'Kennedy's watch recovered', *Australasian* (Melbourne), 29 April 1893, p. 25.
20   Nicholas Kittel, 'Sergeant Steele's sword', abc.net.au, 27 November 2008.
21   'Police Commission – Charges Against Members of the Police Force', Report to the
      Legislative Assembly, Victoria 1881, digitised-collections.unimelb.edu.au.
22   'The Steele Board Report', *Ovens and Murray Advertiser*, 1 Apr 1882, p. 1.
23   Corfield, *Ned Kelly Encyclopedia*, pp. 453–454.
24   'Death Of Sergeant Steele', *Wangaratta Chronicle*, 11 February 1914, p. 3.
25   VII – Inspector Brook[e] Smith in Pursuit, 'Second Progress Report of the Royal
      Commission of Enquiry into the Circumstances of the Kelly Outbreak', pp. xii–xiii.
26   'Second Progress Report of the Royal Commission of Enquiry into the Circumstances
      of the Kelly Outbreak', p. v.
27   *Argus* (Melbourne), 14 March 1882, p. 4.
28   'Second Progress Report of the Royal Commission of Enquiry into the Circumstances
      of the Kelly Outbreak', p. v.
29   Sadleir, *Recollections*, p. 240.
30   *Argus* (Melbourne), 22 September 1919, p. 8.
31   Evidence of S. O'Connor, Royal Commission, question 1066, p. 49.
32   'Mr O'Connor's denial', *Herald*, 22 June 1881, p. 3.
33   Marilyn Kenny, 'The Shuter Estate', timetravellers.pbworks.com.

34   'Stocks and shares', *Age*, 3 September 1908, p. 11.
35   Item 394, Unit 5, VPRS 4965, Public Record Office Victoria.
36   Kelly Reward Board, 1880–1881, p. iv, parliament.vic.gov.au.
37   'Christmas festivities by Queensland black troopers', *Evening News* (Sydney), 12 January 1881, p. 4.
38   'Famous tracker dead', *Cairns Post*, 28 May 1920, p. 5.
39   'Tracking down a just reward', smh.com.au, 30 March 2000.
40   Noble & McBride v State of Vic & State of Qld, Appeal No 9023 of 1997, Supreme Court of Queensland.
41   Malcolm D. Prentis, 'Life and death of Johnny Campbell', *Aboriginal History*, Vol. 15, 1991, pp. 138–152.
42   'The late Mr Thomas King', *Maryborough Chronicle, Wide Bay and Burnett Advertiser*, 30 January 1917, p. 5.
43   'Old tracker's death', *Maryborough Chronicle, Wide Bay and Burnett Advertiser*, 16 January 1935, p. 10.
44   Gary Presland, *For God's Sake Send the Trackers*, Victoria Press, 1998, p. 53.
45   'The evidence of Aboriginals', *Maitland Mercury and Hunter River General Advertiser*, 23 February 1884, p. 14.
46   File T1371, Bundle 2, Unit 372, VPRS 937, Public Record Office Victoria.
47   Their names were Monkey Brown, Peter Brown, Paddy Brown, Jim Crow and Billy Nut.
48   Evidence of T. Kirkham, Royal Commission, question 6944, p. 261.
49   'Death of two old Prahran citizens', *Malvern Standard*, 22 Jul 1911, p. 3.
50   State Library of Victoria, Accession no: H2001.242.
51   'The Australian turquoise', *Geelong Advertiser*, 9 December 1893, p. 1.
52   'Mining intelligence and stock and share market', *Argus* (Melbourne), 30 January 1891, p. 7.
53   *North Eastern Ensign* (Benalla), 3 October 1924, p. 2.
54   'Obituary', *ibid.*, 30 September 1927, p. 3.
55   'Mr William Canny', *Age*, 5 August 1935, p. 8.
56   Victoria Police Record of Conduct and Service, ancestry.com.au.
57   'Deserters of wives and children', *Victoria Police Gazette*, 16 March 1892, p. 78.
58   'Ex-Constable Daniel Barry', *Age*, 22 June 1939, p. 14.
59   'Family notices', *Herald*, 17 May 1924, p. 22.
60   'Struck by electric train', *Argus* (Melbourne), 13 February 1924, p. 15.
61   'Senior-Constable James Allwood', *Weekly Times* (Melbourne), 8 June 1901, p. 13.
62   'The late fatal accident at the showgrounds', *Age*, 31 August 1886, p. 6.
63   'Presentation to Mr. Alfred J. Falkiner', *South Bourke and Mornington Journal*, 28 January 1915, p. 3.
64   *Australasian* (Melbourne), 13 November 1880, p. 20.
65   *Ovens and Murray Advertiser*, 21 May 1881, p. 4.
66   'Compensation to Mrs Jones, of Glenrowan', *Argus* (Melbourne), 5 December 1881, p. 10.
67   *Ibid.*, *Ovens and Murray Advertiser*, 8 December 1881, p. 1.
68   *Argus* (Melbourne), 20 April 1882, p. 5.
69   'Second Progress Report of the Royal Commission of Enquiry into the Circumstances of the Kelly Outbreak', p. vi.
70   *Argus* (Melbourne), 22 November 1881, p. 4.
71   Thomas Patrick Lloyd, born 16 March 1908, Wangaratta; died 25 November 1993, Heidelberg, Victoria.
72   Item 30, Unit 1, VPRS 4969, PROV.
73   Evidence of A. Fitzpatrick, Royal Commission, question 12903, p. 466.

74 *Ibid.*, question 12913, p. 466.
75 VPRS 4969: unit 1, item 30, PROV.
76 Evidence of A. Fitzpatrick, Royal Commission, question 12910, 12924, p. 466-7.
77 *Ibid.*
78 *Argus* (Melbourne), 7 May 1924, p. 1.
79 'The destruction of the Kelly Gang', *Singleton Argus and Upper Hunter General Advocate*, 7 July 1880, p. 2.
80 IV – The Wombat Murders, 'Second Progress Report of the Royal Commission of Enquiry into the Circumstances of the Kelly Outbreak', p. xi.